The
Elephant Voyage

The

Elephant

Voyage

Joan Druett

Also by Joan Druett

New Zealand and sub-Antarctic Islands

THE ELEPHANT VOYAGE

AN OLD SALT PRESS BOOK, published by Old Salt Press,
a Limited Liability Company registered in New Jersey,
U.S.A..

For more information about our titles go to
www.oldsaltpress.com

First published in 2013

ISBN 978-0-9922588-4-9

Cover image © 2013 Ron Druett
Interior art © 2013 Ron Druett

Contents

Prologue

Off Cape Cod, North Atlantic, November 4, 1881

When the white squall struck, the whaling schooner *Delia Hodgkins* of New London, Connecticut, was heading home after a hard, unprofitable season in the Arctic.

The breezes had been light and fair, but overnight the wind had dropped to a calm, so most of the men were below, stripped to underclothes and sleeping off exhaustion in the warm fug cast by the stove. When dawn finally arrived, Captain Sanford S. Miner was one of the few men on deck. There was a heavy fog, so thick that he could scarcely see his hand in front of his face. Moisture dripped off the rigging and motionless sails with a death-watch sound, but Miner had absolutely no fore-warning of the storm that was building in the murk.

The first hard squall arrived from the west, striking the schooner right ahead. It was as if the *Delia Hodgkins* had hit an invisible wall. Spars and canvas slammed backward. Miner stumbled to the weather halliard and managed to release it, but could not get to the other rope that would allow the heavy mainsail to tumble down onto the boom. Impelled by his urgent shouting, the off-duty men piled up as they were—without boots, without jackets, without oilskins. Somehow, they managed to get the jib half-lowered, but another hard gust struck before they could finish. The schooner groaned, leaned further, and collapsed onto her side. Overboard went the captain and all hands, floundering about in the freezing sea, clinging desperately to floating rigging.

Miraculously, no one had been trapped below, but it was if fate had saved them from drowning in order to deal them a slower, more agonizing death from exposure. The cold water bit to the bone, but worse still was the shock of icy wind on wet skin as the men clawed their way out of the plunging waves and onto the capsized hull, to hang on until the squall had passed. Then, they took stock. Just one of the three boats was seaworthy. Even that one had been overturned, and was now jammed in the rigging.

Somehow, by working together, they managed to prize her out, right her, and patch the splintered planks with reindeer hide that floated up from the hold. Then, after they had baled it out, they all clambered inside — fifteen men and a boy, in a boat that had been built to hold six. Oars were shared out, and they pulled for Pollock Rip lightship. According to the charts, it was only four miles away, but the wind and turbulent sea were against them. They had a piece of canvas for a makeshift sail, but it was impossible to set it. They had no fresh water, and no provisions.

Night fell. Their hands were raw, frozen into a curled grip as they struggled with their heavy oars, but they had made no apparent headway. Some, their minds numbed with cold and hunger, muttered in delirium. About midnight, the first man silenced. After an uncomprehending moment they realized he was dead. He was a German from New York by the name of Edward Lux. With scarcely a word they stripped their dead shipmate, shared out his few clothes, and slid the naked blue-white corpse into the sea.

Icy waves constantly filled the boat. Those who were not rowing had to bail continuously, using boots and hats because there was no bucket. One of the men who baled was Loren B. Chapman, of East Haddam, Connecticut. During the hours of darkness, he abruptly stopped work. He, too, was dead. Another man who baled was Daniel Hudson. Hudson died while they were stripping Chapman's corpse. They gave his clothes to the cabin boy, Henry Miner, who was Captain Miner's son. The mate, Sanford H. Miner, was Captain Miner's nephew. He died just before dawn. His body was stripped and discarded, just like the rest.

At daylight the lightship was nowhere to be seen. Racked with thirst, numbed with cold, cramped with hunger, men began to rave as hypothermia led to delirium. Loudest and most disturbing was William Townley. At seven in the morning he abruptly silenced, dead.

About an hour after Townley's body was stripped and cast over the side, another man let out a hoarse shout. The rest flinched, but he was rational. He had glimpsed the sail of a schooner. Frantically, men hauled their oars. Others staggered to their feet and waved — to no avail. Slowly and relentlessly, the sail drew out of sight.

Another dusk descended. Grimly, Captain Miner considered their chances. Five of his crew were dead already — five in the first thirty-six hours. How many would be alive in twelve more — if any? At nine in the evening, when one of the men yelled out harshly again, Miner was slow to react. Then he saw what the seaman had glimpsed.

The distant flicker of Chatham Light, and the faint silhouettes of sails.

Fur seal and pup

1: *The Seal Rush*

Macquarie Island, two years later

Another dawn, with freezing snow that swirled in
from the west, whitening the air. In early November, on
this bleak and inhospitable island far to the south of
Australia and New Zealand, the sun rises as early as four-
thirty in the morning, but Captain Sanford Miner was
already on deck, peering into the icy murk. A stocky,
weatherworn man with a straggling brown beard and
strong, dark brows that tugged grimly over his squinting
eyes, he looked much older than his forty-eight years.

Born January 21, 1835, in the town of Ledyard, Sanford
Stoddard Miner was a minor scion of one of Connecticut's
oldest families. His father, John Woodward Miner, was a
farmer, while his mother, Emelia Avery Stoddard Miner,
was the daughter of a businessman, Sanford Stoddard, the
proprietor of Stoddard's Wharf. Sanford Stoddard Miner
was named after this influential grandfather.

Perhaps it was a childhood of hanging around the
wharf that decided his tragedy-ridden path in life. Too
restless by nature to settle down on his father's farm,
Sanford ran away to sea, but returned in September 1860, to
marry Georgianna Buddington, a local girl who was two

years younger than he was. In 1862 he enlisted as a private in a Connecticut infantry unit, and served for nine months in Louisiana before joining the crew of the ironclad gunboat *Galena*, which was on active duty blockading Southern ports. The career change was promising for a while. After being noted for his gallantry at the Battle of Mobile Bay in 1864, Miner was promoted to the rank of Acting Master of the hospital ship *Home*.

The end of the Civil War led to a plunge in his fortunes. The labor market was suddenly flooded with seamen. Presumably lacking any other choice, Miner went into the wretched Chinese coolie trade (called "this cruel and cowardly commerce" by the editor of the *New York Times*), transporting Chinese migrants to San Francisco, to serve as labor on the Union Pacific Railroad. He was a hard man in a hard business: on one voyage the Chinese cargo rose up in mutiny, and the revolt was put down with what was described in his hometown of Ledyard, Connecticut, as "appalling loss of life."

Retreating from this grim career in 1866, Miner turned to deep-sea whaling, signing onto the *George and Mary* of New London, Connecticut, as a boatsteerer. There is no evidence that he had been whaling before, and harpooning whales demanded nerve as well as great strength, but Sanford Miner, being muscular as well as dogged, coped well. Within five years he had risen to the rank of captain— and in April 1871 he was given command of the 66-year-old bark *Milwood* of New Bedford, for a whaling cruise in the unforgiving waters of the Arctic Ocean.

Still, his luck did not improve. On November 13, 1871, a gale blew up, and the *Milwood* was driven onto Black Lead Island in the far north of Davis Strait, opening up some planks in the hull. The men were cutting in a whale at the time, and the great corpse, as big as the ship, was secured alongside, battering the ship so that the gaps opened even wider. Miner ordered that the whale should be cut loose and the topmasts taken down, but no sooner was the ship lightened than the wind changed. The *Milwood* drifted into deep water, and began to sink. With consummate seamanship born of desperation Miner brought her about and sailed her right up onto the beach. The small amount of oil and whalebone they had taken was saved, and the lives of all on board were preserved, but the hull of the ship was beyond repair.

An obstinate man, Miner planned to live with his crew on the wreck, and somehow survive the harsh Arctic winter until Spring, when the northward whale migration would start. By using the deck of the beached hulk as a flensing platform, and sending out the four whaleboats to kill whales and tow them in for processing, he had found a way of retrieving the situation—or so he thought. It would be a new kind of shore-whaling. The other masters in the area foiled this, by holding a survey and condemning the ship. An opportunistic lot, they then bought the gear and timbers of the old *Milwood* for the grand sum of 51 dollars. Most of Miner's men left him, sailing to England on the whaling brig *Perseverance*, which was returning home with her casks full of oil. Their captain returned to New Bedford without a ship, and just 160 barrels of oil to report.

There were no replacement commands on offer. Whaling, like fishing, depended so much on good fortune that the superstitious shipowners shied away from a man with such an unlucky reputation. After a lot of asking around, Miner finally found a contract. On February 8, 1873, he set out on the tiny 70-ton Gloucester fishing schooner *William Sutton* for a difficult passage round Cape Horn, to deliver her to San Francisco. After his return to Connecticut, he looked for work in his home port of New London, and was given the command of several short whaling cruises on small vessels, beginning in 1876. The first was on the schooner *Florence,* the second (in 1877) on the *Era,* and then, in 1879, he shifted to the ill-fated *Delia Hodgkins,* losing her at the end of the fourth voyage.

Meantime, in 1880, he and his brother, Ebenezer Perkins Miner — a substantial man, who had been named after their paternal grandfather, and who was secretary of the Lawn Mower Company of Hartford, Connecticut — invested in a schooner called *Sarah W. Hunt.* Their father John had died in 1878, so the sale of the farm may have provided the necessary funds. A two-masted schooner, 88 feet long, and registered at 116 tons, the *Sarah W. Hunt* was designed for the fruit-and-sugar business, so had been built for warm water voyages to the West Indies. The two brothers had left her in that trade, keeping the same captain, James McFadden, but after the *Delia Hodgkins* disaster Sanford Miner took her over, apparently unfazed by the fact that he had never sailed in the Caribbean before. With a German first mate, Charles (Karl) Streichert, he made at least two voyages between Cuba and New York, carrying passengers on the outward leg, and bringing "pinappel" (as Streichert, the logkeeper, spelled it) back to the city.

The schooner was not in a very good shape, being so leaky the pumps had to be manned even when the vessel was in port, and with rigging that needed constant repairs. Yet, in July 1882, at the end of the current fruit-freighting season, the Miner brothers decided to convert her for the brutally demanding sealing trade. After getting back to New York from her final Caribbean venture in May 1883, Miner and Streichert sailed her to New Bedford to be fitted out for a voyage to the sub-Antarctic.

As a decision, it was quite bizarre. Neither Miner nor Streichert had ever been that far south before. Neither had ventured into the vicious weather that rules the sub-Antarctic ocean. And, while money had been made in the early days of sealing, the era where fortunes wre reaped from furs was well over.

The American seal rush dated from as far back as the country's victory in the War of Independence. Speculators in New York and Philadelphia were already aware from reports of Captain James Cook's last expedition that fine seal pelts found a good market in Canton, being much in demand by Chinese nobles for lining their winter robes, but the sea routes to China had been blocked off by the British and their East India Company, and so they had been prevented from taking advantage of this knowledge. Now, because of the new-found freedom of being independent, the passage to the East was open.

The pioneer was Simon Metcalfe, captain of the Hudson River brig *Eleanora*, who in December 1787 dropped anchor off Macao with 13,000 fur seal skins that had been collected at the Falkland Islands in the South Atlantic. It was a purely speculative venture. The furs had been bought as a job lot in New York for $6,500, or fifty cents each, and shipped to Calcutta. There, they had been put on Metcalfe's brig, to see what he could do with them.

After reporting at Macao, he freighted them up the Pearl River to Canton (Guangzhou) — and they sold for $65,000, or five dollars apiece. It meant a profit of $58,500, or 900%, not counting the costs of the voyage, which were relatively tiny.

News of this impressive return for very little outlay inspired dozen of shipowners to send their little brigs, sloops, and schooners to bleak outposts in the southern seas, with the aim of raiding seal breeding grounds — rookeries — on the rocky terraces of uninhabited islets that often had not even been named. Because the ventures were cheap to finance, sealing quickly became a specialty of the little ports of New England, where the shipowners had had trouble affording expensive whaling voyages. Soon, the port of New London, Connecticut, dominated the trade, while the nearby village of Stonington produced a remarkable number of sealing masters. It took a special kind of grit to endure the grim existence, and Connecticut men seemed to have the right kind of stamina.

Arriving off a rookery, the skipper would send a gang on shore, where the men would live in rough camps — or even under their upturned whaleboats — and spend their days clubbing thousands of seals to death, stripping off their skins, and pegging them out to dry after rubbing them with salt. Weeks or months later, the skipper would return to pick up the gang, take the stockpile of furs on board, and then he would either sail for New York or steer directly to Canton. The living conditions were appalling, but the return made the ordeal worthwhile.

But only for the first few years. Because of the single-minded enterprise of Yankee sealers, the market soon became flooded. The value of the furs dropped sharply, descending first to a dollar per pelt, and then to even less than that. The sealing skippers compensated by collecting larger cargoes, focusing on quantity rather than quality. Every seal in sight was attacked and killed, in a wholesale slaughter of bulls, cows, adolescents, and pups that held no thought for the future. Within a couple of seasons the seal population of an island or a rocky coast would be almost wiped out, but instead of giving up, the hunters merely moved on. Battling gales and intense cold, they quartered the southern ocean, in the hope that they would blunder over yet another bleak island or yet another rockbound coast where there were more seal colonies to slaughter to near extinction.

From the Falklands the sealers fanned out to snow-covered South Georgia and the cheerless rocks of the South Shetlands, and made incredible forays into the deep Antarctic Ocean, inspired by mentions of seal sightings made by great explorers such as Captain Cook. In 1820, a young Stonington sealing captain, Nathaniel Palmer, was probably the first to sight the continent of Antarctica, after sailing far south in his tiny 44-ton sloop *Hero*. Other skippers, hearing tales of vast seal herds that had been sighted from China-bound ships passing the islands off the coast of Chile, doubled Cape Horn against the prevailing winds, and hunted as far north as the Galápagos.

A particularly rich ground was Más Afuera, one of the Robinson Crusoe (Juan Fernandez) islands, which yielded three million skins in three years—or so Captain Edmund Fanning of Stonington claimed. Seven vessels arrived in 1798, and made a good profit in Canton from the skins they harvested, and from then on the rookeries were quarried mercilessly—in 1799 twelve men from the *Neptune* killed 2,500 seals in just one day. The consequences were as predictable as they were awful. In 1803, a sealer complained that there were more men than seals on the island, and when Captain Charles Barnard called there in 1815, he found just ruins of huts. There were no men at all, and no seals.

The Elephant Voyage

Skippers who sailed the Great Circle route through the southern Indian Ocean, on the way to skirting the bottom of Australia, found seal colonies on the Crozets (where the weather was so dreadful the skins had to be entirely cured with salt, as it was impossible to dry them), and on Kerguelen, called "Desolation Island" by the Americans, because it was glacier-riven, and constantly windswept.

Survival there was possible only because of a local "cabbage" that was eaten to fend off scurvy, and the abundant wild life that provided meat. Yet, incredibly, in the early 1850s several New London sealing captains carried their wives to that inhospitable place—Captain William Brown of the *Peruvian*, Captain Henry Williams of the *Corinthian*, and Captain Ebenezer "Rattler" Morgan of the *Julius Caesar* being three of them. Captain Brown took his children, too, keeping a piano in the cabin of the *Peruvian* so that his daughter, Mary, could practise music. On August 17, 1840, Mary Caroline, wife of Captain Franklin Smith (also of New London), gave birth to a daughter while the ship was laboring in icy seas on the way to Bluff, New Zealand, to sell the ship's tender, as the master had been drowned in the surf the day before, along with six men. In true maritime tradition, the little girl was named Chelsea, after the ship.

After its discovery in November 1853, Heard Island, 260 miles south of Kerguelen, became another goal for the seal hunters. Though Heard is even more desolate than Desolation Island, being a rain- and wind-lashed barren rock that is almost entirely covered with permanent ice, another sealer carried his wife and children there. This was an Australian, Captain James William Robinson, who later confessed that it was "a wrong thing perhaps to do," though his wife had begged to accompany him, "and brought home two boys and one girl instead of a boy and a girl." The boy who was born on that remarkably unpleasant voyage was known as "Kerguelen Jim." Many years later, ironically, he perished of thirst in the Australian desert.

Sealing in Australian waters can be said to have started in late February 1798, when some of the sailors belonging to the colonial schooner *Francis* bludgeoned a few seals to death for their skins. This was in the Furneaux group of islands, off the northeast promontory of Tasmania. The explorer with them, Matthew Flinders, felt sorry for the seals, describing pups who "huddled together in the holes of the rocks, and moaned piteously" while at the same time "some of the old males stood up in defence of their families, until the terror of the sailors' bludgeons became too strong to be resisted." He was glad when they "left the poor affrighted multitude to recover from the effect of our inauspicious visit."

Pity was not a characteristic of the sealers, however. Eight months later, the English brig *Nautilus* arrived, and set a gang on Cape Barren island in Bass Strait (between mainland Australia and Tasmania), headed by an American from Providence, Rhode Island, Samuel Rodman Chace. They took just 14,000 skins, but Chace opted to leave the ship and stay in the colony, to found the Bass Strait sealing industry, and pioneer the southern seal rush in the sub-Antarctic ocean.

By the year 1803 at least 100,000 skins had been taken from the rookeries of Bass Strait alone, a devastation from which the seal colonies would never recover. That same year, Chace reported falling in with Captain Isaac Pendleton of the sealing brig *Union* of New York, who had set gangs on shore at Kangaroo Island. After taking about 14,000 skins and cutting down Australian trees to build a tender, called

Independence, Pendleton steered for the Antipodes Islands, a bleak archipelago 500 miles to the southeast of New Zealand. A gang, left there, collected 60,000 particularly valuable furs, starting a three-year seal-rush that led to the harvesting of over 330,000 more pelts, and the utter extinction of one of the local seal species.

The rocky coasts of southern New Zealand provided seals for the harvest, too. Dusky Sound, in the southeast, was a natural target, because of a report made by Captain James Cook on his second visit to New Zealand in 1773:

> *Thursday 22nd [April]. In the PM I went with a party a Seal hunting, the surf was so high that we could only land in one place where we killed Ten, these animals serve us for three purposes, the skins we use for our rigging, the fatt makes oyle for our lamps and the flesh we eat, their harslets [heart and liver] are equal to that of a hog and the flesh of some of them eats little inferior to beef steakes, nay I believe we should think it superior could we get the better of prejudice.*

The first to follow this up was Captain William Raven of the British ship *Britannia*, who left a gang at Dusky Sound in 1792. As was common, the ship sailed off on other business, leaving the sealers with boats, a few provisions, and tools to build a rough hut (the first European building in New Zealand), and then get on with the job of killing seals and stockpiling pelts. Raven went to the Cape of Good Hope to fetch a consignment of goods, coming back eleven months later to find that his gang had taken just 4,500 skins. Instead of sealing, they had been busy setting up the frame of a little vessel and planking it with timber cut from the surrounding forest, because they did not trust their captain to return for them.

Other, more focused, gangs followed — in just one month, April 1803, 2,500 skins were collected. Great difficulties of access to the greatly indented southwest coastline, with water often too deep for anchorage, and treacherous onshore winds, meant that the southern islands of New Zealand were more attractive to the sealers, however. Gangs were landed on Stewart Island and the islets of Foveaux Strait (between Stewart Island and the southern coast of the South Island of New Zealand), which was charted for the first time by Owen Folger Smith, an American sealing master from Cape Cod. The Snares, a series of treacherous rocks to the south of Stewart Island, were visited by sealers soon after their discovery in 1791, and by 1810 the seals were almost completely wiped out.

Meantime, in late 1806, Captain Abraham Bristow of the London South Seas whaleship *Ocean* reported the discovery of the Auckland Islands, far to the south of New Zealand. Samuel Rodman Chace, the man who had pioneered the Bass Strait seal rush, was given the command of the 185-ton *King George*, the largest vessel ever built in the New South Wales colony, to freight men, tools, and provisions to this new sealing ground. By the start of the 1807 season three gangs had been set ashore, and within four months 48,000 pelts had been harvested. Then, in July 1810, just as the Auckland Islands became so bare of seals that it was not worth leaving a gang there, Frederick Hasselburg, captain of the sealing brig *Perseverance*, went even further south, to discover a bleak island-outpost of the sub-Antarctic that he named "Macquarie" after the current governor of New South Wales, Lachlan Macquarie.

As usual, the location of this new sealing destination was kept secret, to prevent rival sealers from landing gangs on the island and destroying the rookeries before the discoverers had taken what they considered their rightful bounty. Sealers, however, were crafty by nature. Hasselburg called into Sydney to advertise for more men and load provisions, along with 35 tons of salt, and, their suspicions aroused, Samuel Rodman Chace and Owen Folger Smith, in the New York brig *Aurora,* shadowed the *Perseverance* as she departed from New South Wales.

Hasselburg arrived at Macquarie at the beginning of October. After landing the salt and provisions, he sailed for yet another island he had discovered and kept secret. This was Campbell Island, which he had first sighted in January 1810, and named "Campbell" after the brig's owner. He had left a gang in the harbor he called "Perseverance" after his brig, and then, apparently, had forgotten them in the excitement of finding Macquarie. By the time he arrived back at Perseverance Harbour, on October 22, the men were living entirely on sea birds, their provisions having run out.

A few days later the *Aurora* arrived, with Owen Folger Smith and Samuel Rodman Chace on board. Just a day or so earlier Hasselburg had drowned when his boat had capsized while ferrying some of the stockpile of pelts from the shore to the brig. This left his sealing master, Robert Murray, in charge, which proved to be a bonus for the two interlopers. Back in Sydney, there had been attempts to bribe Hasselburg's crew for information about the location of Macquarie Island, but, as the sailors had been kept ignorant of the ship's position, all that had been learned was that "the place was dreadfully cold, and the seals were as numerous as flies in a grocer's shop." The two Americans had much better luck with Murray, who owed Chace a favor, as Chace had rescued him a few months earlier, after Murray and his gang had been stranded on Stewart Island for so long that they only survived because the local Maori fishermen were willing to share their catch. After a great deal of persuasion, he sold Chace an approximate location of Macquarie for two hundred pounds (which, incidentally, Samuel Rodman Chace never paid).

After returning to Port Jackson, Sydney, Chace picked up men, provisions, and tools. He found Macquarie with little trouble, and landed gangs, and then the usual slaughter commenced. It has been reliably estimated that 120,000 furs were quarried from Macquarie Island over the first eighteen months, and that within three years the population of furred seals was reduced to almost zero. By 1815 the original seal population of about 250,000 had been so drastically reduced that only 5,000 skins were taken over the whole of that season.

But still the hunters came, because another source of profit beckoned—"elephant" oil. Immense numbers of elephant seals still roosted on the rocky beaches, and wallowed in the stinking mud.

They had survived the rapacious sealing gangs because "elephanting" was so much more difficult than fur-sealing. Not only was the quarry huge and unwieldy, but the precipitous terrain made it hard to find a level platform to process the catch. Rafting the casks of oil out to the ships was yet another hurdle, as the rocky shores and high surf made it both difficult and dangerous. Accordingly, the elephant seal survival rate was high enough to attract sealing gangs until 1830, when about 70% of the elephant population had been destroyed. The number of vessels visiting the island diminished to a trickle—in 1851 and 1852 a couple of sealing parties arrived, but hunted with so little success that the effort was not repeated, and the elephants were left alone to breed.

Then, the situation changed. In 1875, two sets of New Zealand entrepreneurs, Nichol and Tucker, and Cormack, Elder and Company, revived the Macquarie Island elephant sealing business.

The sea elephant is much larger than the fur seal, a large bull being over twenty feet long and weighing over a ton. Unlike the furred seal, it has a long, drooping snout—the probable origin of its name, though "elephant" could also refer to its size. The elephant was different, too, in that it was never hunted for its skin, which was was only good for leather. What made elephant seals valuable was the thick layer of insulating blubber-like fat beneath the hide, which could be as much as eight inches thick on a big bull, and could be rendered down into a fine, colorless oil. Chace was probably the first to take advantage of this. While furs were the priority as long as the fur seal population lasted, elephant oil was good for filling out a cargo. When he arrived back in Sydney with his six-man gang on 19 May 1811, Samuel Rodman Chace had 60 tons of oil on board.

The blubber was cut off the elephant in long strips, very like processing a whale. The cut was made either from head to tail, or in a circular fashion around the great body, rather as whales were cut in at sea. The choice depended on the manpower available, as it took several brawny shoulders to keep the corpse of a one-ton bull revolving and make a spiral cut possible.

Whatever the method, the result was the same—a great pile of soggy strips of fat, with skin attached. These strips were then hauled to the rendering ground—a job that could be arduous in the extreme, as a journal kept over the 1877 season by one of the sealing masters, Donald Sinclair, makes plain. "After shooting the animals, the blubber is cut off and placed in bags which hold about one hundredweight," he wrote. "Sometimes the elephants are shot about eight miles away and the blubber, dripping with blood — which fills the boots and saturates the clothing — has to be carried that distance in the snow, the man picking his way over bogs, around precipices and among boulders as best he may."

When the heavy bags were finally heaved onto the rock shelf where the trypots were set up, the strips were rinsed and then cut up small with sharp knives or a mincing machine. These pieces were thrown into the cavernous iron pots, and slowly boiled into liquid oil. The scraps of fiber and gristle that floated to the top were taken out with a sieve on a long handle, shaken free of oil, then thrown into the fire beneath the pots, where they quickly caught alight, producing a lot of heat and a billow of black smoke studded with flaring sparks, which smelled like a charnel house on fire. The "thick nauseating smell of burning fat" the French explorer Dumont d'Urville described after encountering a whaleship trying out at sea was the same ghastly stench that polluted the shingle beaches of Macquarie.

This was not the only similarity of elephanting to the whaling trade that Sanford Miner knew so well. Elephant seals, like sperm whales, are carnivorous, feeding on large squid. Like whales, they are relatively enormous; and, as with whales, it took strength and nerve to attack and kill them. Cows, pups, and small males could be bludgeoned or lanced to death, but it could take several musket balls to finish off a large bull. The usual method was for the hunter to wait until the bull advanced on him, roaring, and then fire into the open mouth, upward into the brain — but it took a lot of grit to do it, as a Kerguelen sealer, Captain Joseph Fuller, related, saying "if you have no way of retreating you are gone up the spout, for if they once get you, or any part of your anatomy, between their powerful jaws nothing will save you."

So, had Miner brought the *Sarah W. Hunt* to Macquarie to hunt elephant seals, after hearing gossip that the elephant-oil business had revived there? Was this, in fact, an elephant voyage?

It certainly made more sense than sealing for furs, as while there were apparently elephants on Macquarie still, there were not enough fur seals left to be worth an expedition. Elephant oil was considered as good as the best whale oil, fetching an average of $22 per barrel, even after the advent of petroleum oil, as it burned with a bright, clear flame, and provided an excellent lubricant for machinery. Prior experience was yet another advantage. While Captain Sanford Miner was almost certainly new to sealing, his background in the whaling trade was a good preparation for flensing elephants, and turning their fat into oil. As a voyage, it made much more sense than one after furs.

"Gone to see the elephant" was a common saying in Miner's time, often applied to men who joined the various rushes after gold. It meant experiencing an exciting and often dangerous adventure—so it was a term that certainly applied to a sea elephant voyage. And, at least two of Miner's young foremast hands seem to have signed up for the voyage for a lark.

In their case, however, "seeing the elephant" was going to be an experience more dangerous than anything they could have possibly imagined.

2: The Crew

In the morning I sah the Land right a head, ouer first stopping place, went to lowart of the Island and was looking for a plas to Anchor
—Streichert's logbook, Sarah W. Hunt, *November 3, 1883*

As the day drew on, the *Sarah W. Hunt* worked closer to Macquarie Island.

Steep bluffs loomed into view, with snarling rocks at their feet where the surf foamed and tugged. Each time that the sea drew back, gathering force for another lunge at the narrow belt of shingle beach, the lookouts in the rigging could glimpse thick, fleshy kelp lashing back and forth in the foam.

On the map, Macquarie Island is a mere dot on parallel fifty-three south, midway between Tasmania and the Antarctic, distinguished by its utter remoteness. Just twenty miles long and less than four miles wide, and so primeval that it is composed of uplifted oceanic crust, it thrusts out of one of the coldest and wickedest seas in the world. At the time, the bleak, precipitous hills, rearing an average of one thousand feet into the cap of dark clouds, must have seemed uninviting in the extreme.

The Elephant Voyage

There were no trees to be seen, because the winds of latitude fifty south, whipped up to extreme violence during their unimpeded whirl about the globe, are too strong for tall trees to grow. Instead, the streaming, wind-scoured mountain sides were colored brown and dark green by some short, clinging growth, which was thickest where the cliffs were furrowed by cracks and precipitous gullies.

This was the exposed, westerly side—was the island as bleak on the lee? Miner told Streichert to order the men to tack ship, and the schooner was cautiously sailed northeast along the ironbound ramparts of the windward coast.

After some miles the island diminished to a stony isthmus, where tracts of shingle and swampy tussock swept down to the sea, and then culminated in a ridge-backed point and a line of surf-bound rocks. Miner gave orders to come about, and steer southeast by east-quarter-east, down the island's lee. The sheltered side of Macquarie, however, proved to be just as grim as the windward coast. The men in the rigging, who had orders to call out for anything that looked like a protected anchorage, were silent. Though the German first mate had noted, after raising Macquarie Island, that this was "ouer first stopping place" after leaving New Bedford, it was bleakly evident to every man on board that this was by no means a proper port of call.

They had struggled across the Atlantic and Indian Oceans for seventeen long and arduous weeks, only to find no likely harbor.

Miner was forced to drop anchor offshore, and send boats to the beach. The problem—or so his charts told him—was that until the schooner was dangerously close to the surf, the water was too deep for an anchor to find the bottom. Accordingly, as the *Sarah W. Hunt* approached the long curve of an embayment in the line of coastal cliffs, he ordered a leadsman into the forward chains to take soundings — to find out how many fathoms of water were beneath the hull.

Clumsy in wet oilskins, the sailor clambered over the bow and balanced precariously in the forward channels, holding on to the foremast chains with a crooked elbow, and averting his face from the splash of the waves. In his right hand, he gripped a long, curiously knotted rope, which he swung in increasing circles until it reached its fullest extent. Then he let it drop. Weighted with a plummet of lead, the line plunged to the bottom. A moment's pause as the schooner sailed up to it, and then the sailor hauled the rope up again, counting off bits of water-soaked leather and bunting as the knots ran through his fingers, and coiling the wet length about his left arm.

"By the deep, twenty-four!" he shouted. Twenty-four fathoms of water under the hull meant it was too deep for the schooner's anchor to reach the ground. The *Sarah W. Hunt* kept underway, inching closer to the arc of shingle beach, where the coarse dark gray sand and the restless shallows were piled with rock and washed-up kelp.

Rows of penguins stood along the edge of the sea, all facing toward the oncoming schooner, looking like soldiers on stumpy legs, lifting their flippers every now and then. Behind this army vertiginous hillsides rose up high, reddish green in the slowly lowering sun. Great flocks of seabirds swirled in the threatening sky, screaming in unison, and the leadsman had to shout to make himself heard as he cast the lead over and over again. Twenty-two fathoms … eighteen…

At the call for thirteen fathoms Miner spoke to his first mate, who hurried to the foredeck and ordered the men there to drop the anchor. With a muted splash it hit water, and disappeared. There was a moment of suspense as the schooner kept on moving forward, but the flukes held tight. They might not have found a safe harbor, but at least the schooner was safely tethered, though rolling and pitching in the outer limits of the breakers.

It was four in the afternoon. After ordering the sails furled, Miner headed below, and the steward served out the evening meal. "Souper" the German first mate called it in the log, and it could very well have been just soup, since the provisions were running low. Back in June, in New Bedford, the ship had been well victualed, with six casks of flour, seventeen casks of hard ship's bread, thirty barrels of salt beef, and twenty barrels of salt pork, but nothing had lasted as expected. The captain, quite correctly, was convinced that the foremast hands had been stealing food from the hold.

Hopefully, however, this particular problem was about to be solved. Macquarie Island might appear to be inhospitable in the extreme, but the wildlife was abundant. Hundreds of petrels swooped down upon the circle in the sea where the steward, George Duncan, had emptied his scrap bucket, while prions danced over the surface, and thousands more birds screeched from the cliffs. According to the charts, there were freshwater ponds on the plateau at the top of the cliffs. Once an elephant colony—or, even better, a fur seal rookery—was located, a camp could be set up on shore. The men would be supplied with just the scantiest of provisions to tide them over until they learned how to live off the land.

As Miner knew—not from experience, but from Connecticut lore—sealing gangs fended for themselves by killing birds, raiding their nests for eggs and chicks, and eating fried or stewed meat from the seals they killed. They considered the flippers of young seals a delicacy, and relished a stew made out of the snouts that gave sea elephants their name. On Macquarie, the roots and stalks of a local wild herb, *Stilbocarpa polaris*, could be scraped and sliced to make a healthful broth.

Admittedly, there would be no coffee, tea or sugar to civilize the diet of any men who were left on Macquarie Island, and, because no timber grew, they would have to burn dead penguins and blubber scraps for fuel. That this dank, miserable place was constantly overcast and the average daily temperature was only just above freezing would be something else to test their endurance. However, Miner was convinced that a sealing gang could manage to live and work here until the end of the southern summer — March — when the schooner would load their stockpile of oil and skins. By long tradition, that was the way it was done.

His problem was that this was not part of the tradition of the boys who made up the foremast crew of the *Sarah W. Hunt*. None of them had ever lived off the land while they learned to kill sea elephants and render their blubber into oil, or bludgeon seals for their furs.

Even getting the two whaleboats through the heavy surf to the shingle beach was going to be a hurdle. In the boats, just as on the deck and in the rigging, the boys were all amateurs. While Miner had put them down in the ship's papers as able seamen, in order to get round the regulations, the young men in his crew were all inexperienced sailors — what New Englanders called "greenhands."

Before they boarded the *Sarah W. Hunt*, not a single one of Miner's foremast hands had ever served under sail before.

The Elephant Voyage

The boys had joined the crew in response to a small advertisement, which had been placed in a New York daily newspaper, *The Sun*, at the end of the first week of July 1883:

> WANTED: For sealing and whaling voyage, 12 strong young men; also cook and steward. Apply at 186 West S
> — D. L. PEARL

Mr. Pearl, one of the many shipping agents who had offices near the waterfront, made his money out of recruiting seamen for ships, charging a fee of about $25 per head. Ebenezer Perkins Miner, in Connecticut, had retained him for this, evidently because it was easier to find willing (or gullible) seamen in New York than it was in New London.

Though Pearl advertised for several days, however, his luck with filling the crewlist for the *Sarah W. Hunt* was abysmal. He may as well have added "no experience necessary" to the wording of the newspaper notice, because no seasoned sailormen responded. Instead, the boys who arrived at his door were a motley lot, a collection that included a drover, a brass finisher, a clerk, an apothecary's assistant, a barman, a farm laborer, and at least two with no stated occupation at all. A significant number were not even American — like the first mate, Streichert, they were German. With one exception, they had been in the States for a relatively short time, and had trouble with the English language, particularly when trying to read it.

The exception was 30-year-old Alexander Henderson (who was German despite his English name), who had been in the country for ten years. Henderson was a brass finisher by trade, but that work had run out, so he had signed onto a steamer as a fireman, laboring as a stoker in the hot hell of a boiler room on passages between New York and Antwerp. Then that, too, had finished. Knowing nothing at all about the sealing and whaling trade, he had believed Pearl could give him a job as a fireman. When the agent told him that the voyage would be under sail, Henderson had tried to withdraw his application, protesting that he was not any kind of canvas sailor, but Pearl had persuaded him to ship as a greenhand, saying he could learn about sail handling on the job.

Two other Germans, Wilhelm Hertwig and Louis Scharffenorth, both twenty-two, had been in New York for just a short while. Hertwig was a barman, and had seen the advertisement in a German newspaper. When he asked Pearl about the job, he was told it was sealing, but for nine months only, and so, despite his utter lack of seagoing qualifications, he was also persuaded to sign on as a greenhand. Another who may have been German-born, though he described himself as a New Yorker, was 23-year-old Julius Jaeger. His occupation is unknown. Nothing much is known about him at all—because Julius Jaeger drowned on the passage to Macquarie Island.

Another German speaker was 28-year-old Emil Huber, who was Swiss, his birthplace being Berne. He had been America for just six months, working as a clerk, though it appears that his real profession was barbering. Emil Huber also emphasized to Pearl that he was not a sailor, and was not willing to go before the mast, but added that he would be happy to take a job as a cook or steward. Somehow, though, he was persuaded to ship as a greenhand, too. Like Hertwig, he was told the voyage would be for nine months.

Those who were German had come to America for jobs, but there seems to have been high unemployment in New

York in that month of July 1883. Alongside Pearl's post in the situations vacant column of *The Sun* there were just 47 other wanted notices, advertising positions that ranged from plumbers, cheroot-makers, and printing devils, to an enigmatic request for "strong young boys." Significantly, the construction of the Brooklyn Bridge, a project that had employed many hundreds of foreigners, had ended back in May, putting those many men out of work, along with those who supplied them with goods and services. But, if the young Germans had gone home, it would have meant conscription into Bismarck's army. Even embarking on an unknown voyage would have seemed preferable to that.

The motives of the other boys for shipping on a small schooner to go sealing on the other side of the world are harder to guess. Joseph M. Arthur, 24, who gave his home town as Washington, D.C., but who had been born in New York (to recently arrived Hungarian parents, who may have been refugees), was so keen to sail that he shipped under a false identity, his real name being Max Augenstein. His occupation, according to the 1880 census, was clerking.

James Alymer Samis, who had been born in Ontario, Canada, in 1860, was a laborer on a farm in Vermont before he joined the schooner. Thomas Ennis and Martin Tierney, both 22, were New York city boys, of no stated occupation. James Judson, 23, and Thomas Whittle, 25, hailed from Brooklyn, so should have been familiar with the docks. However, while Judson's previous trade is also unknown, Thomas Whittle was a teamster, accustomed to handling oxen, loading freight, and driving drays. Whittle was eager to go on voyage, turning up at Pearl's office three times to make sure he was shipped. However, he was shrewd enough to make sure it was as a greenhand, emphasizing that he was completely unfamiliar with life under sail.

There is a chance that these young men were looking for adventure. The whaling business had its own rousing literature, replete with popular yarns, and magazines were full of stories of excitement under sail. And there was the imaginary enticement of a fortune to be made, too. If any of the boys had been to coastal New England, and seen the fine houses built with fortunes made in the early days of sealing and whaling, it could have looked as if a sealing and whaling voyage was a good way of making money. If so, disillusionment was inevitable. Men on whalers and sealers (like fishermen) were not paid in wages, but in a "lay" — a share of the profits that was calculated by the ship-owners after all the expenses of the voyage had been deducted. For a greenhorn, the lay could be as small as just 180th of the final balance — which was precisely what the *Sarah W. Hunt* greenhands were offered.

This tiny share of the catch was further reduced by the seaman's expenses. First, Mr. Pearl's $25 fee was deducted. Then there was the outfit of seagoing clothes, which was supplied by a storekeeper, who was usually one of the agent's or captain's friends, and who sold the outfit to the sailor at a price that is very likely to have been inflated.

Additionally, there was the sailor's share of the cost of stocking the medical chest, which worked out at about $1.50, plus the value of any medicines he might have been given during the voyage. If he was sick, his "days off" were deducted, along with any money that might have been advanced to his family at home.

And on top of that there was the ubiquitous "slop chest" — the store of clothes, soap, tobacco, and other small necessaries that was put on board by the owners, and sold to the men as needed, again at extortionate rates.

Even in the old days, when the ships arrived home with their holds full of valuable furs or oil, it was not at all unusual for a man who had shipped as a greenhand to walk off the ship after a three-year voyage with just $25 in his pocket, or even be in debt to the ship.

And, in this year of 1883, rich cargoes were a legend from far back in the past.

Pearl had better luck with finding a steward who was willing to cook for the whole crew, as well as look after the captain and his cabin. This was George Duncan, a 34-year-old Englishman who named New York as his residence. According to his own account, he had been at sea "off and on" since shipping as a cabin boy at the age of thirteen. Since then, over the intervening twenty years, he had acquired book learning, an educated writing hand, and an insatiable thirst for liquor.

Perhaps because of the last, he was extremely sociable when he felt like it, and disagreeable when not. Duncan was also not afraid to stand his ground against those in authority. He demanded, and got, a lay of one sixty-fifth of the voyage, though it was usual for the cook and steward to be allotted just one ninetieth. When given the outfit that he would have to pay for, he flatly refused to accept it. Leander Brightman, the New Bedford storekeeper who had supplied the clothing, was forced to take the steward to his shop, to choose his own seagoing clothes according to his fancy.

The second mate, a lanky six-footer, was Irish. Apart from Streichert, he was the only member of the crew who had not been recruited by Mr. Pearl. Michael Crawford by name, he volunteered to sign onto the schooner in New Bedford at the very last moment, just one day before departure.

On the face of it, the Miner brothers were lucky to find him (especially as they must have been wondering by then if the schooner would have to sail without a second officer), because Crawford was an experienced whaleman. He had been working on American ships since 1844, when he had shipped as a greenhand on the whaling bark *Belle*, at the start of a voyage that lasted eight years. Then, after getting back to Massachusetts in September 1852, he had joined the *George & Susan* as a "mariner" under Captain Joseph Jenks, returning five years later.

With his next voyage, he managed at last to rise in the ranks. Michael Crawford was promoted to the post of boatsteerer (harpooner) on the bark *A. R. Tucker*, where the captain's wife, Annie Ricketson, recorded in her journal in April 1872 that he was terribly ill—"Did not know if he would live till morning so Husband went down in the steerage and see him. Found him in great distress. Gave him some medsine but did not seem to do him any good as he grew worse." Crawford recovered only because Captain Daniel Ricketson "worked on him several hours" through the night, evidently trying out different potions.

Persistent bad health was one of Crawford's drawbacks. Another was that he was not an experienced leader, this being the first position as an officer that he had ever been offered. And while, like all whalemen, he might have killed the occasional seal, he had never been on a sealing voyage before. Nothing in his past existence had prepared him for taking charge of a sealing gang on a distant, desolate island.

The greatest disadvantage of all, though, was his age. Michael Crawford was sixty-four years old, far too old for the grueling existence of a whaleman, let alone for the unpleasant job of blowing out the brains of a sea elephant before stripping the corpse of its blubber. He must have been really desperate to even think of courting exposure on some bleak rock, while trying to lead inexperienced boys in the grim business of bludgeoning seals to death, and stripping and curing their skins.

To compound the problem, his right shoulder was out of joint. It had been dislocated when he was knocked over by a sudden heavy pitch of the vessel, while the *Sarah W. Hunt* was crossing the Indian Ocean—"Second mate got hurted on deck and is lay op now," wrote Streichert in the log on 11 October.

When Captain Miner and the steward had tried to put the dislocated shoulder back into place, the pain had been so terrible that Crawford had begged them to stop, and he had been crippled ever since.

3: *Macquarie Island*

After tacken about 4 or 5 times we went in 13 F. of water to Anchor at 4 PM. After the Sail was furl, and St.B Anchor put on the Bow took Souper and den Kpt Miner me and boats Crew went a shore
— Streichert's logbook, Sarah W. Hunt, *4 November 1883, in latitude 54°37' South, longitude 158°54' East*

Getting to the nearest beach was a much harder proposition than Karl Streichert's matter-of-fact log entry hinted, current maritime guides like the *Oriental Navigator* carrying dire warnings that landing a boat at Macquarie Island was hazardous in the extreme.

It had begun to earn this grim reputation as far back as July 1811, when a blizzard had blown up as the London brig *Concord* had tried to take off a sealing gang. For six long weeks it had been too dangerous to land boats, while the frostbitten sealers had slowly starved. On the *Concord's* next visit to the island, one of the boats had overturned just twenty yards from shore, and all six of the boat's crew had drowned.

This grim past history was daunting enough. What made getting to shore particularly nerve-wracking for Miner and Streichert was that their oarsmen were so unsure of their job. Sealers were supposed to be the most daring and expert small boatmen in the world, but the small boat skills of the foremast hands were rudimentary. A couple of times during the early part of the voyage, the boats had been lowered, so the boys could practice pulling the long, heavy oars — "set 1 Boat out and Kp. Miner went with his crew to learning how to handle a Boat," wrote Streichert on July 27, and again, on August 28, "at 4 PM set my boat out and we went for practis till Souper time." But only twice had any of the boys gone down in the boats for serious work.

The first time had been on August 27, when, luckily, the weather had been just as calm as it was during the practice sessions. In the early morning, the off-duty watch had come on deck to find their shipmates up in the rigging, squinting about at the sea. While washing down the decks, Louis Scharffenorth had accidentally dropped a wooden bucket overboard, and Captain Miner was determined to get it back. Both boats were lowered, and the men pulled back and forth for more than two hours — in vain. Miner simply refused to accept the self-evident truth that the bucket had filled and sunk.

After that the weather became rough, and the boats were turned bottom-up on deck and lashed into place. This proved very unfortunate. At a few minutes past eight in the morning of 3 October, Louis Scharffenorth, who was at the wheel, screamed, "Man overboard!" Julius Jaeger, who had been sent aloft to fix the weathervane, had lost his footing, and fallen from the mainmast crosstrees.

Orders were shouted to clear away one of the boats, but when the steward grabbed a carving knife to slash the lashings, the first mate stopped him. They had to be untied in the regular way, Streichert said, as the ropes were too important to be cut. So the men had worked frantically to release the knots, wasting many precious minutes — twenty-five, according to some — before the search could even begin. In the meantime, Jaeger was being dragged astern by the relentless current. By the time the boat got away, with just three men to row and the first mate at the steering oar, he was nowhere to be seen. Like the bucket, he had sunk and gone.

So today, while the boys labored at their oars to inch the boat through the breakers to the rocky beach, it would not be surprising if the silence was grim.

The first mate, Streichert, was standing at the steering oar, in the stern. Thrusting the twenty-foot blade deeply into the water to steady the boat and keep the bow pointing forward, he stared over the heads of the oarsmen as he searched for a passage through the surf-lashed rocks. He could not afford to make even an instant's mistake. There was a white cairn at one end of the long, shallow bay, and as the boat crept closer, Streichert could see it was a great pile of bones — elephant bones, as it turned out — but it could have just as easily been the bonelike remains of lost ships and boats.

Petrels squalled, spiraling in the murk above. Thick beds of kelp lashed back and forth in the foam. The bitter wind, which had been westerly, was veering to the south, gusting up from Antarctic ice. Leaving the schooner was a crazy thing to do. The scent of snow was in the air, and the weather threatened to squall up again as the wind shifted further around the compass. But in these latitudes it would not be dark for another three hours, so Captain Miner, perched in the stern sheets, urged the crew on.

Somehow, after a mighty struggle, the oarsmen caught a wave that rushed them up onto the beach. The bottom of the boat grated on shingle, and the crew hastily jumped out and hauled it higher. Mountainsides, matted with short, wet tussock, soared up into the murk. High above, narrow cliff terraces and zigzag cracks were packed with lines of birds, and the noise was tremendous.

The multiplicity of bird life was overwhelming. Sent out to search the beach for traces of seals, the boys had to battle their way through lines of penguins. The unafraid birds flapped their stubby wings and leaned forward to deliver vicious pecks at defenseless legs. Mud wallows, turbid with rotting reeds, fouled the beach where the cracks and gullies drained, and puddles slimed with guano surrounded the stones where the rowdy penguins perched. The fetid stench was so strong it snatched away the breath.

Clouds scudded fast in the blackening sky as the gale pushed closer to the island. Harried by Captain Miner and Streichert, the boys fanned out, stumbling over lichen-crusted rocks and wading through heaps of rotting kelp, while all the time the rows of penguins watched. As they made their way up the bluish stone of the beach, they encountered more and more great clumps of tussock. Trying to skirt around these involved stumbling into hidden mud wallows, so the boys were forced to jump from one clump to another. And so they slowly progressed.

At the crown of the beach, where there was a reasonably level terrace that was partly sheltered from the freezing wind by an outcrop in the abrupt cliff face, the growth was higher and thicker. When they got there, it was to make the ghoulish discovery that it was littered with half-buried bones—elephant bones, ribs and vertebrae and gaping skulls lying helter-skelter in the dense, high tussock, and jutting out of the puddles. It was possible to see the trail where many more of these bones had been dragged up the beach to make the cairn of bones that marked the end of the bay. Old rusting trypots lay amongst the tussock clumps, too. Obviously, the growth here was thick because the ground had been well manured with rotting elephant flesh, the detritus left after stripping off the blubber.

Then, at the back of the terrace, directly below a creek that dribbled down the hill, the boys found a hut — the place where past sealing gangs had lived. And it was made of timber, which was a surprise on this island without trees.

In the old days, sealing gangs had been forced to build their shelter out of flotsam and rubbish they had fossicked from the beach. When the Russian explorer, Thaddeus von Bellingshausen, visited Macquarie in 1820, he described a hut measuring twenty feet by ten that was made of sod on a rough frame of stone and timbers from shipwrecks. The exterior was covered with clumps of tussock and the interior was lined with second-grade skins. Apart from smoky elephant-oil lamps, the only illumination came from small windows paned with stretched and dried elephant bladders.

The hut the boys found, however, was made of lumber that had evidently been freighted to the island. Though they did not know it, this shack had been the living quarters of the gangs that had worked here in the late 1870s. Inside, every surface was covered with cold, greasy soot from the fat that had been burned as fuel for cooking and heating the room, and a reek of old smoke clung to the walls.

Perhaps a dozen men had lived in this rough shelter, but now it was empty — as empty of men as the beach was of elephants. "Found a little House and plenty of Birds," wrote Karl Streichert after he had got back on board the *Sarah W. Hunt*, "but no Seals."

Captain Miner must have looked about with a sense of puzzlement that bordered on desperation. The seal breeding season normally began toward the end of August, when the big bulls hauled out to fight for territory while they waited for the females, who slithered up onto the terrace in September and October. The cows avoided these battle-hardened warriors, hurrying instead to join companionable clusters of other females, but nevertheless their arrival triggered a mayhem of testosterone-driven posturing and fighting as the big bulls competed for the right to claim the females for their harems.

The cows, still taking little or no notice of this male aggression and bluster, huddled together, nudging and rolling against each other as they waited to give birth, which happened about a week after hauling out. A period of intensive suckling followed, but when the pups were about a month old, they were abruptly abandoned. Losing interest in their young, as they went into estrus, their mothers undulated off to solicit the attentions of their bulls.

Once they had succeeding in mating, the cows returned to the sea, to be followed by the bulls once the complete harem was impregnated. When they were gone, the pups, marooned on the rookery, practised their swimming skills over the next month or so, until they were expert enough to head through the surf toward their first meal of fish and squid.

And not until then was the rookery empty.

This was just the first week of November. The beach should have been an arena of alpha bulls—"pod masters"—servicing one cow after another. And there should have been other males, too, opportunistic peripheral bulls who hovered about the fringes, hoping to ambush the females as they headed for the sea. And young sea elephants should have been there too — newly weaned pups who nervously watched their parents' antics from the stinking wallows. But there was not a single elephant, large or small, to be seen. And not a single fur seal, either.

"And dat ended this day," wrote Streichert.

At midnight, a blizzard blasted up from the south.

All hands were called up to the heaving deck. The boys cursed as they skidded and fell on the icy planks, grabbing for handholds as the schooner pitched and tossed. Above, the moon glimmered intermittently in a cloud-torn sky, while the turbulent surface of the sea showed up in vivid, vicious flickers, scudded with foam.

Then the storm-front closed overhead, and the night became pitch dark. The surf roared, crashing onto rocks that loomed perilously close on their lee. Bellowed orders were lost in the whine of wind through rigging, while the men worked desperately to keep the schooner up to her anchor, and away from the threatening shore.

Dawn revealed a boiling mass of purple-black clouds, which covered the flat summit of the island and hung down over the cliffs, while sheets of snow slanted down, and hissed onto the surface of the sea. The *Sarah W. Hunt* had crabbed sternward — the breakers and the rocks were beckoning. The anchor was losing its grip on the stony mud, thirteen fathoms below, giving way to the pressure of the gale on the hull.

Their situation was hazardous in the extreme.

Macquarie was notorious for the tremendous gales that tossed ships onto the rocks. The very first seal hunters on Macquarie had found the wreckage of a large vessel when they arrived, so old and so scattered that it was impossible to guess its name. The full-rigged sealer *Campbell Macquarie* had been lost on June 11, 1812, when the anchor dragged. The men, after struggling ashore, built a shelter from canvas and timber salvaged from the wreck, and killed seals and processed skins while waiting for rescue. Four died before the *Perseverance* arrived in October.

In March 1825 the American sealer *Caroline* ran onto the rocks when her cables parted while her men were loading elephant oil; the crew built a boat from the wreckage to save themselves, and a party rowed all the way to Hobart, in Tasmania, to summon rescue. On December 2, 1851, the guano bark *Countess of Minto* was blown onto the rocks and lost, and in 1875 the *Eagle* suffered the same fate. There were nine men and one woman on board the *Eagle*, who endured two long years on this barren beach, living in an open cave; the woman died the day they were rescued.

To avoid the same fate, Captain Miner had to work the *Sarah W. Hunt* away from the threatening rocks, and find a good offing, well out to sea. Eight men gathered about the windlass on the foredeck, buffeted with the gusts and the snow as their numb fists heaved down on the handles to haul round the chain and bring up the anchor. It was slow, brutal work, while the clanking of chain and thump of the windlass brakes made a harsh accompaniment to the storm.

Other boys tore at ropes and fought with canvas, heaving to get the huge sails aloft, while two more struggled with the helm to keep the schooner's bow to the wind. Then Captain Miner shouted out to Streichert to wear ship, and with more hard work they brought round her stern, so that the force of the wind came from directly aft. Canvas slatted madly and then snapped full, and after a sickening series of lurches the *Sarah W. Hunt* flew off like a bird, leaving the island of Macquarie behind.

Even taking to the open sea was no guarantee of safety. Back in August 1815, in exactly the same circumstances, the

Sydney sealer *Betsey* had been swept out so far that it had been impossible to sail back. Instead, she had been forced to limp all the way to New Zealand, while her crew expired one after another of starvation and scurvy.

Now, in November 1883, it seemed as if the *Sarah W. Hunt* might meet a similar fate. For three days she was blown out to sea, in conditions so rough that first mate Karl Streichert did not have a chance to keep up his logbook. When he did pick up his pen again, at noon on November 7, it was to record that a particularly furious gust had burst the flying jib to pieces.

But then the gale moderated and hauled to its old quarter, the west, and so they were able to mend their sails and retrace their course to Macquarie, which was raised in the late afternoon. In an eerie repetition of the events of the previous week, the *Sarah W. Hunt* steered north along the barren crags of the western, windward side of the island. Then she tacked about North Head to their old anchoring place. Again, Streichert took his boat and his boat's crew "to look for Seals" and again, there were none to be found.

But, by climbing one of the precipitous gullies, he did see rabbits, and shot five, the progeny of rabbits released by the sealers during the elephant revival of the 1870s. The rabbit stew was the last hot meal the crew of the *Sarah W. Hunt* had for a while, because that night the wind turned back to the south, and blew up into another gale. Miner did not hesitate nearly so long before giving the order to head out to sea, but this time there was a hitch. When they hauled up the starboard chain, there was no anchor at the end. There was no time to dredge for it. Instead, they set sail, and fled from the island again.

Though this latest storm was as violent as the last one, it moderated much more quickly. Within twenty-four hours they were back at their old anchoring place, where the search for seals and elephants was abandoned so the men could "fish" for the lost anchor, a back-breaking business that went on as long as daylight lasted—eighteen hours in these latitudes, unless the weather closed in.

It was a reminder of the time the captain had made the men row back and forth in a fruitless, tedious, highly exasperating hunt for the bucket that had fallen overboard, but with a difference. Where Miner had made the men row for two hours in the hunt for the lost bucket, now he forced them to labor for a *week* in the search for the sunken anchor.

For seven days the men trawled up and down the area where the anchor had been lost, with a long length of chain roped between the two boats, which were rowed along in tandem. The dangling loop of chain was dragged along the bottom, Miner's theory being that it was bound to snag on the anchor if they tried long and hard enough. Instead, it snagged on rocks and crags and bits of sunken wreckage. At times it caught on jagged outcrops, so that the oarsmen hauled away at solid reef until the chain slipped off again. Then it would be back to sweeping the area, while all the time tempers flared, in the captain's case becoming violent.

On November 11 the hard work was interrupted so that Captain Miner and George Duncan, the cook and steward, could replenish the pantry. "Kaptain and Stuart went ashore shooted Rabits and fetched 14 on board," wrote Streichert. Otherwise the only relief from fishing for the anchor was when the wind blew up and Miner was forced to order the men to set sail and take to the open sea again.

Inevitably though, the schooner returned, and the men were set back to work—"This day strong breeze from the S, got back to ouer plas drop Anchor, and started again to fish for ouer Anchor," wrote Streichert on 16 November.

Unlikely as it seemed all that long, endless week, however, there was a limit to Miner's grim determination. At dawn next day the men turned out on deck, to hear welcome new orders — to make sail, and steer northeast for Campbell Island. Not only had Captain Miner given up the search for the missing anchor, but he had given up hope of finding elephants on Macquarie, too.

The Elephant Voyage

4: *Campbell Island*

The first part of the day strong gale with cloudy weather from S. sah Campbells Island at 4 P.M. on ouer Stboard bow 20' of at 9 P.M. Anchort in a little Bay on the West side of the Island mad ouer Sails furl and kept Anchor watch
— *Streichert's logbook,* Sarah W. Hunt, *November 20, 1883.*

At four in the afternoon the lookout in the rigging of the *Sarah W. Hunt* raised sharply pointed peaks in the distance, rising from the sea off the starboard bow. An icy gale was blowing from the south, and as they came closer the schooner pitched and slewed sickeningly.

Again, they were approaching their objective from the west. Ahead, tall rock pillars rose like sentinels from the sea, twisted and eroded by wind and waves into strange angry shapes, their bare crowns surrounded by screaming flocks of frigate birds, and surf snarling at their feet. Cautiously, Captain Miner navigated a path around and between them.

This side of the island was dominated by black igneous rock that thrust dramatically out of the sea, in spectacular stacks of convoluted stone. Thousand-foot cliffs reared into the sky, their sides shining with constantly running water that was whitened with spray where the sea pounds savagely on the reefs at their feet. Just as on Macquarie Island, Miner and his men were deafened by the constant screaming of the birds that packed the narrow fissures in the cliffs. Occasionally great flocks of them rose as one, to wheel like clouds in the sky. As on Macquarie, too, the vegetation was low, dun in color, and sparse, cowed into submission by the constant freezing wind.

This day, the bitter wind came from the south—which was a rare piece of good fortune for Miner, as the really dangerous wind came from the west, when it arrived in vicious gusts, interrupted by light, baffling, contrary winds. In October 1828, the brig *Perseverance* had succumbed to one of these violent gusts. Driven onto the rocks, she had been swiftly reduced to floating wreckage.

Favored by this unusually kind wind, Captain Miner steered along the western coast. Just as the light was failing, a lookout called out that he had glimpsed a bay that was set into a hook of land that was dominated by a mountain peak—Mt. Paris, according to Miner's chart. Like many of the island's features, it had been named by the French expedition that had come here in 1874 to observe the transit of Venus.

A cautious approach was made, with a man with a leadline constantly sounding, and at nine in the evening the anchor was dropped. "Mad ouer Sails furl," wrote Streichert in the logbook. Once that was done, an anchor watch was set, and most of the crew turned in.

At daylight they were roused—"at 4 A.M. set one Boat out and Kaptain went on shore." Streichert himself stayed on board to work on the foresail, which was fraying from the stress of the storm-wracked flights from Macquarie. Within a couple of hours, however, he was interrupted by the return of the captain, who conveyed the terse and hurried message that they were to weigh anchor, set sail, and get round to the eastern side of the island as fast as possible.

Frustratingly, Miner had just had his first sight of their prey — a single large bull seal on the beach. However, there was a gale blowing up — from the dangerous quarter, the west. It was impossible to stay where they were.

To get around the cape, they had to beat into the teeth of the gathering storm. With constant adjustments of the sails they worked around the southern side of the island, where the vista was even more intimidating than the view from the west. Precipitous, contorted cliffs led the eye inland to six great peaks. Twisted rock pillars stood out of the sea.

On Captain Miner's chart, the roughly semi-circular shape of the island, thirty miles in circumference, was fractured and tortured in appearance, the primeval rock torn and dissected by glaciers. Of these, the most prominent fissure was Perseverance Harbour, a long, narrow inlet that penetrated in great curves right to the centre of the island. About three-quarters of a mile across at the mouth, this crack in the landscape widened a little further up, then ran in an east-west direction for about three miles before it turned to the southwest for another mile and a half.

For some time the westerly gale made it impossible to even think of sailing up this long fissure, to find a safe anchorage in the interior. Then the wind relented, moderating a little. Captain Miner called for tacks and sheets, and the *Sarah W. Hunt* beat slowly into the mouth of the channel.

Sheer cliffs, rising abruptly from the water's edge, towered hundreds of feet high on either side. This was the place where Campbell Island's discoverer, with two others, had been drowned by the upsetting of a boat; the same place where Robert Murray had taken over the quarterdeck of the *Perseverance* after Hasselburg's death; this was the same long harbor that Samuel Rodman Chace and Owen Folger Smith, on the New York brig *Aurora*, had navigated in stealthy pursuit of the *Perseverance*; and where Chace had bribed Murray for the location of Macquarie.

It was abruptly much quieter as the *Sarah W. Hunt* left the thundering coastal surf behind. The long fissure led west-north-west, winding so that it was impossible to see where it ended. The steep slopes on either side became more rounded, dun-colored with tussock and drifted with snow, glistening in the dull light.

Casting a lead confirmed that the water was too deep to drop an anchor, which was unsettling information, because the channel formed a natural funnel for gusts coming out of the mountainous interior. Right at that moment, one such violent gust hit them hard, squalling down the inlet with such astounding force that the *Sarah W. Hunt* was brought aback, lurching to a sudden standstill—just the way the *Delia Hodgkins* had been capsized and wrecked.

Urgent orders were hollered, and the schooner was hove to, keeping her in the same position by setting her sails so they pulled against each other. Then everyone nervously watched the water as the schooner pitched and rolled.

The sailors did not have too long to wait, however, as in the afternoon the wind lightened again, just enough to resume their cautious progress. With a man casting the lead constantly, the *Sarah W. Hunt* beat slowly forward, taking four arduous hours to work up the outer arm.

At the great bend that led to the inner harbor, the lookout on the foredeck signaled shoal water, marked by a bed of restless kelp. The schooner tacked west-south-west to avoid the hazard. Then, at last, four miles from the entrance, they found soundings. At five-thirty in the afternoon the man in the chains called out, "By the deep . . . five fathoms" and Captain Miner gave the order to drop one anchor.

The wind had dropped, and a unexpectedly flat, glimmering landscape lay before them. The head of the harbor was divided into a number of shallow bays, with mudflats that gleamed in the lowering light. A tall spar, evidently part of the wreckage of some large ship, had been erected on a point as a kind of beacon, and stood out starkly against the pale background. Slippery grass- and scrub-covered slopes, sprinkled with snow and studded with outcrops of white-streaked stone, undulated upward to blend with rising mountains.

In the distance, to the west, a single pyramid-shaped peak was sharply silhouetted against the lowering sun. A lone wandering albatross circled the clouds.

On the *Sarah W. Hunt* the sails were stowed and supper was served. As soon as it was eaten, Streichert selected sailors from the port watch — the half of the crew that was on duty — for a boat's crew. The schooner had not replenished her store of fresh water since leaving New England in mid-July, and so Captain Miner had ordered him to go on shore in search of a readily accessible stream.

They pulled toward the beckoning flagstaff, and after they arrived on the beach they dragged the boat up onto the mud. Leaving Emil Huber and another man to keep an eye on the grounded boat, the rest investigated the tall signal post. There was a strong-box at its foot, which the first mate broke open.

The seamen heard the lock snap and the lid crack, and watched as he took out three coats, an ax, blankets, some pannikins for cooking, and a kettle. The temperature was close to freezing, so the coats and blankets, despite their damp condition and age, looked enticing. Then they were interrupted by a distant shout from the schooner. Captain Miner had been watching through his spyglass, and wanted them back at the schooner at once.

The mate, Karl Streichert, did not go with them. Instead, he stayed at the flagpole with his plunder while the sailors pulled back to the *Sarah W. Hunt*, where Captain Miner was impatiently waiting.

Curtly ordering them to take him to Mr. Streichert, he clambered into the boat, and back they rowed again.

The instant the boat touched the mud Miner jumped out. Obviously, he was in one of his sudden bad tempers, but for the moment he said nothing. He strode toward the beacon, stopping once to pick up a bottle he had glimpsed. It was corked, and there were rolled-up papers inside. They needed drying out before they could be read properly, being too damp to unfurl, but the official insignia on the outside one was ominously evident.

Coming back, Miner saw that the strong-box had been forced. Jerking round to face Streichert, he asked him what the hell he thought he was doing. Then he was distracted by a glimpse of a notice board, about a hundred yards away from the flagstaff.

Again, he tramped through the tussock, this time to see what was on it. Coming back with tightened lips, he found that the seamen had shared out the clothing, and were putting the coats and other things inside the boat. He said little, however, merely grunting that finding water was the priority. So, once the boat had delivered him back to the schooner, along with the contents of the strong-box, he sent them off in search again.

This time the men went to the south side of the bay, where they found a stream. Beside it was a little hut, built of overlapping deal boards with a steeply pitched roof made of thatch. There were no windows, and just one narrow door. When they went inside they found it held another cache — twelve cans of preserved mutton, two boxes of sea biscuits, a bottle of salt, and six boxes of matches, along with a sheet of instructions from the marine department of the New Zealand government.

It was then that they realized that this place was a castaway depot — a refuge for shipwrecked sailors. In that remote, desolate, uninhabited place, so subject to sudden, wild storms, the discovery was a bad omen.

The story of the castaway huts in the sub-Antarctic islands of New Zealand and Australia began with two highly publicized shipwrecks on Auckland Island, both of which happened at almost the same time.

One was of the Australian sealing schooner *Grafton*, and the other was of the Aberdeen windjammer *Invercauld*. The story of the *Invercauld*, which crashed into the cliffs at the northwest end of the island on the night of May 10, 1864, was particularly horrifying. Not only was there terrible loss of life from starvation and exposure, but there was evidence of poor leadership and complete loss of morale, even cannibalism. Almost exactly twelve months after the wreck, three survivors of the appalling ordeal were rescued by a passing ship. No effort was made to search the island for any other castaways.

By contrast, the events that followed the wreck of the sealer *Grafton* were so uplifting and inspiring that the published accounts of them have been popular reading ever since.

The Elephant Voyage

At midnight on January 3, 1864, four months before the wreck of the *Invercauld,* the schooner's anchors dragged, and the *Grafton* was thrown onto the rocks at the southern end of Auckland Island. All five men on board survived, to struggle ashore. Over the next nineteen months they built a substantial cabin, hunted sea lions for food and clothing, found edible herbs, and established an efficient daily routine, at the same time eking out a civilized existence in the most challenging circumstances possible. And, all the while, they were completely unaware that there was another shipwreck in the north of the island.

By the end of the first year they were forced to face the fact that rescue was not coming. Instead of giving up, they built a forge and burned a mountain of charcoal, so they could make the tools to fashion a small boat from timbers salvaged from the wreck. It was a huge task, involving the manufacture of many thousands of nails, as well as such necessities as tongs, chisels, bolts, and hammer-heads. And so it was not until July 1865 that the captain, Thomas Musgrave, with two of his men, sailed the makeshift craft through appalling seas to Stewart Island, New Zealand.

After returning to fetch the two seamen who had been left behind, Musgrave discovered the skeletonized corpse of one of the victims of the *Invercauld,* and commenced a campaign to search for other castaways. Because of his lobbying, the Australian colonial steam-sloop *Victoria* was sent out to check all the sub-Antarctic islands for marooned sailors, with Captain Musgrave invited to go along as pilot.

On October 28, 1865, following a search of Auckland Island and leaving caches of provisions, the *Victoria* arrived at Perseverance Harbour. After liberating a boar and two sows, some guinea-fowl, and three geese, they erected a signboard, listing the animals, and requesting visitors not to shoot them, as it was hoped that they would breed, providing a food stock for castaways. They also secured a bottle to it, which contained a letter that gave a brief account of the *Victoria*'s mission.

A second expedition to the southern islands was triggered by another well-publicized wreck. This was of the American-built *General Grant,* which was driven onto the rocks at the northwestern end of Auckland Island just the following year, in May 1866. Only fourteen men and one woman (the stewardess) survived, to face severe hardships over the next eighteen months.

In January 1867 the first officer, Bart Brown, with three other men, set off for New Zealand in one of the open boats, but was never seen or heard from again. In September, one of the ten men remaining on the island died. On November 21, 1867, the colonial brig *Amherst* called by. Captain Paddy Gilroy, a famous southern New Zealand whaleman, sighted their signals, and carried them to New Zealand.

News of this latest disaster led to a decision by the government of New Zealand to establish castaway depots on Auckland and Campbell Islands. The brig *Amherst* was contracted to go to the islands on this mission, with Paddy Gilroy in command, and a Justice of the Peace, Henry Armstrong, on board.

They first sailed to the north of Auckland Island, where they strengthened one of the huts built by the *General Grant* castaways, and left a strong-box with supplies. On the lid of this Armstrong wrote, "The curse of the widow and fatherless light upon the man who breaks open this box whilst he has a ship at his back." They then went south, and tidied up and reinforced the hut that the five *Grafton* castaways had been built from the wreckage of their schooner.

After releasing a pair of *weka* — New Zealand wood-hens — in the hope they would breed, the *Amherst* steered for Perseverance Harbour with a large spar in tow. Captain Gilroy was determined to hoist a flagstaff on tree-less Campbell Island, so that those in need could fly a signal of distress.

They arrived at the mouth of Perseverance Harbour on February 14, 1868, but for some days the wind blew so forcefully from the interior that it was impossible to enter. It was not until the twenty-fourth that they were able to drop anchor and check the situation.

There were no traces at all of the animals that the *Victoria* had landed, so they released five pigs (two boars and three sows) and five goats (three nannies and two billies), in the hope that they would do better. Then they erected the spar a hundred yards from the notice board that had been left by the *Victoria,* and put a strong-box and a spade at its foot — the same flagpost that drew the attention of Streichert's boat's crew, and the same strong-box that Streichert broke open.

The party from the *Amherst* then stumbled across the grim sight of six graves and, alongside them, the skeleton of a man. Further impelled by this ghoulish discovery, the *Amherst* sailors fixed up a hut they found nearby, which had presumably been built by these unknown castaways, or maybe by long-past sealers. It was about ten feet long and eight feet wide, with overlapping deal boards and a pitched roof made of thatch, which they repaired.

Then, after placing a chest of provisions inside, Gilroy and Armstrong sailed away, their mission in sub-Antarctic seas accomplished.

This was the same hut that first mate Karl Streichert and his boat's crew discovered.

After inspecting it and taking note of the contents of the cache, they returned to their boat and rowed to the schooner, arriving after nightfall to face a most unexpected quarrel. The steward confronted Streichert as the crew clambered on board, to tell him that he had had no right to take the goods out of the chest at the foot of the beacon.

George Duncan said he had already complained to Captain Miner, who had ordered one of the seamen, Martin Tierney, to take the stuff from the seamen and stow it in the lazarette—a small hold beneath the captain's cabin—until the first mate returned. Now, the steward wanted the first mate to take the goods on shore and put them back into the strong-box—now, right away. Streichert flatly refused, and an argument commenced.

Captain Miner came up on deck to see what the fuss was about. Impatiently, he told Streichert to return the appropriated goods in the morning. Then he asked if a source of fresh water had been found. Streichert replied that he had, but "hard to get at," and then informed the captain about the castaway hut, and its contents.

When he went on to describe the sheet of instructions that had been found in the cache of provisions, Miner became agitated. While the boat had been away, the steward had been helping him to dry and decipher the papers that had been in the bottle, which had evidently become a kind of mailbox over the intervening years, as captains added letters to the original document left by the *Victoria*. Two of these were reports from HMS *Blanche* and HMS *Cossack* (dated 1874 and 1873, respectively), which strongly implied that the depot had been inspected at least twice by the British navy. And now that Miner had learned about the official instructions in the depot, too, it was evident that the hut was also regularly checked by a vessel from the New Zealand government.

So he immediately wanted to know if they had removed anything from the box of provisions. Streichert swore that they had not. Reassured on that score, Captain Miner reminded him that the other things were to be returned to the chest at the foot of the flagpole at first light. Then he went back into his cabin, to carry on with the difficult task of trying to copy a report from the American whaling bark *Tamerlane* of New Bedford, dated 1875, which had also been in the bottle.

Next morning, Streichert summoned a boat's crew, and went on shore with the goods they had purloined the day before. After they had put them back in the chest, they spent the rest of the day collecting fresh water from the stream. It was a tedious job that involved towing a line of empty casks behind the boat, then holding them under the water with the bung-holes open until they filled, and then dragging the barrels back to the schooner, where they were hoisted on board with the windlass. However, the work went well, so in the afternoon the crew was allowed time off for the luxury of washing their clothes. It was their first chance to clean up in over four months.

On the next day, Friday, November 23, the rest of the water casks were filled — only just in time, because another gale struck.

Terrifyingly, the schooner began to drag, but before she came up onto the beach they managed to drop another anchor. The following day, the storm veered round the compass to the southwest, so they had to let out more chain. Finally, however, the weather moderated.

"This day light wind from the N.," wrote Streichert on Monday, 26 November:

> *In the morning set boats out, and schrub the Vessel round, after dat hoisted Fore and Mainsail and Topsails to dry in the afternoon Kaptain me and second Mate was menden sails sah a Seal longseide the Vessel, in the evning, I went with my boat to look for him, sah him and shoot him, but sunk lik a stone after waiten till 9 PM went on board, hoisted boat in and dat ended this day. Pumps attended to.*

That Streichert had shot the seal in the water bode badly for the success of the voyage. Any experienced sealer knew that a seal had to be taken on the beach, because it invariably sank if killed in the water. As it happened, however, the first mate's ignorance proved to be of no significance, for this is the last entry in Streichert's hand.

The heading for the next day's record — "Tuersday 27 of Novbr." — is there, but the rest of the page is blank.

The Elephant Voyage

5: The Lost Boats

At or about 6 AM on the morning of the above date while lying at anchor, the Port and Starboard boats left the vessel with orders to search in shore for seals … leaving the Steward on board and Captain in charge of vessel
— George Duncan, log of the Sarah W. Hunt, *November 27, 1883.*

Another dawn, calm but icy.

Both of the boats belonging to the *Sarah W. Hunt* were in the water, being readied for a reconnaissance of the south-eastern coast of Campbell Island. Twelve young men looked up as Duncan handed down sealing clubs, skinning knives, and sharpening steels. Two wooden buckets of fresh water followed.

On impulse, Emil Huber scrambled back onto deck and filled a bag with hard biscuit from the barrel of ship's bread that stood at the foot of the foremast. After he had dropped back onto the thwart that served as his seat, the two boats pulled off with the first mate's boat in the lead. Captain Miner's last words to them was a shouted promise that the first man to capture a seal would get a bounty of a silver dollar. Then they were out of earshot.

After thirty minutes of pulling, they were around the curve into the lower arm of the harbor, and the schooner was out of sight. The two boats floated in a stark, lifeless, snow-drifted expanse of steep tussock-covered slopes, the only sounds the ripple of dark water and the thrust and drip of oars. The going was easy, the current carrying them toward the open sea, helped by a light northwest wind blowing at the steersman's back.

That wind was bitter, despite being slight, and Emil Huber, hauling his heavy oar back, up, round, and forward in rhythm with the other four oarsmen, was glad of his oilskins, even though they cramped his movements. Like the others, he worked with his back to the bow, and was watching the second mate, who stood facing forward as he hauled at the twenty-foot steering oar, and was the only man who could see where they were headed. Michael Crawford's stance was hunched and uncomfortable. It was obvious that he trying to spare his dislocated shoulder.

Just as the steep, water-drenched cliffs of the entrance of the harbor rose on either side, Huber saw storm clouds gathering in the island's interior. Flocks of birds lifted and squalled in the gloom above. The sound of surf grew and thundered as the second mate gestured at the oarsmen to hurry their pace. Evidently first mate Karl Streichert, at the steering oar of the other boat, had indicated that he wanted them to catch up for a conference.

Huber and his fellow oarsmen obediently pulled harder, while Crawford leaned on his steering oar to bring them round to the side of the first mate's boat. Streichert was in charge of both boats, and the one to give orders. As they neared, Huber could hear him shouting two words. A few more hauls at the heavy fifteen-foot oar, and the two words became plain—"Hoist sail!"

The breeze was beginning to gust hard from the interior of the island, funneling down the inlet toward the sea. The boat suddenly rocked, and the bucket of fresh water tipped over, spilling its contents into the bottom. So there went their only supply of drinking water. Huber wondered if it was wise to raise the sail, considering the direction of the wind. Nevertheless, he and his fellows obediently lifted up the mast, stepped the foot of it into the proper niche in the bottom of the boat, fixed it in place by hammering in a fid, and then set the canvas. Ahead of them, the first mate's whaleboat was scudding off, heading northeast to get about the tall cliffs of a dimly seen cape. Huber felt the lift as their own canvas took the wind, and then they were bouncing along in Streichert's wake.

Abruptly the gale blasted down, and the sea became very rough. The other boat's sail kept on disappearing in the troughs of the increasingly heavy waves, but they followed in its general direction, steering east to keep ahead of the storm but getting a dangerously long distance from the land. Michael Crawford evidently felt apprehensive too, because he urged his crew to row harder, to get within shouting range of the other boat, but though he yelled his hardest, they could hear no reply. The other boat sailed on into the waves, which were starting to crest, so that it regularly disappeared from sight in the troughs.

Then, just as night fell, Huber realized with a lurch that not only had he not glimpsed the first mate's sail for quite a long time, but Campbell Island was lost to sight as well.

That evening, because the logbook was locked away in Streichert's sea chest, Captain Miner gave a sheet of writing paper to the steward, George Duncan, and instructed him to note down the day's events.

"*Schr. Sarah W. Hunt,*" the steward neatly headed the page, and then added the location, the date, and the details of the departure of the two boats, "the Port boat being in charge of the first Mate and 5 Seamen and the Starboard boat of the second Mate and 5 Seamen. Taking no provisions," he elaborated. This was terrible lack of foresight, considering what they had already learned about the sudden wild gales in these high southern latitudes. Yet Captain Miner was surprisingly relaxed. He had expected the boats to come back in time for the evening meal, if not earlier, but even when the afternoon turned into twilight, he remained unworried. "During the day no anxiety or fear was felt for their safety," wrote Duncan on the piece of paper, "although the weather became more squally towards afternoon and a succession of heavy squalls came down during the night but abated between 2 & 3 AM."

As midnight passed, and a succession of stronger gusts whistled shrilly from the rocky heights and spurted down the anchorage toward the open sea, Captain Miner did begin to feel a little apprehensive. But his two mates would know how to last out the storm, he reassured himself—as the steward went on to note, there were "plenty of creeks & inlets around the island," so it was easy to imagine that Crawford and Streichert "had put into one of them to wait till morning." Once beached, the boats could be overturned for shelter. By long sealing tradition, gangs were routinely left to live off the land in cold and inhospitable places like this—Samuel Rodman Chace would have taken it for granted.

Perhaps the two boats' crews had even found a rookery. By noon this second day, November 28, Captain Miner would surely see the boats coming up the harbor, storm-battered but otherwise unharmed, and perhaps with good news.

When light grayed the eastern horizon, Michael Crawford was standing at the steering oar, with no idea how far they were from the island. All night the boat had drifted at the mercy of the currents.

While the oarsmen had slumped in an uneasy doze, one or another wakening at intervals to bale, the second mate had remained at the oar to prevent the boat falling broadside of the waves. His legs, braced against the surge and lift of the boat, must have felt as numb and heavy as stone, while his back would have ached unbearably. His eyes were slitted, the lashes stuck together, and his face would have felt raw with wind and salt water; undoubtedly his chapped lips gaped open, and there was frozen phlegm in his beard.

When he glimpsed a shape on the horizon, he shouted out, startling the others awake. Bleary-eyed, they sat up straight to follow his pointing arm—and there was the craggy silhouette of Campbell Island. Energized, they picked up their oars and hauled with a will.

It was too rough to make much headway, so Crawford decided to set the sail. Laboriously and slowly, the mast was hoisted upright, stepped and fidded. No sooner was the canvas unfurled than he glimpsed the silhouette of a boat that was also under sail—"The first mate!" he shouted.

By painful degrees, by both rowing and sailing, they got within a half-mile of the other boat, and waved and yelled to get Streichert's attention. Inexplicably, however, they got no response. To their horror and disbelief, they watched the other sail veer away.

The Elephant Voyage

It was a disaster. None of the men in Crawford's boat had any experience of sailing small craft, except for the second mate himself, and Crawford was utterly exhausted.

Very little was said right then. Instead of talking it over, the crew heaved doggedly at their oars, aiming for the distant land. Morsels from the bag of ship's bread Huber had collected were rationed out, but the crumbs were damp with salt water, and everyone was very thirsty. The tops of the waves kept flicking up with the gusts, so that icy water penetrated their oilskins and drenched their clothes. Despite their sea-boots, their feet were frozen, soaked in the ice-cold water that pooled in the bottom of the boat.

The day wore on, and the silhouette of Campbell Island was not getting any closer.

And then the second night loomed.

As the sun's watery rays lengthened and still the men had not come back, Sanford Miner was forced to face the grim possibility that the boats had been blown away from the land. If so, the crews were going through the same ordeal he had endured after the wreck of the *Delia Hodgkins*, dying one by one as they waited for rescue—with the difference that these boats were stranded in an ocean with no lightships, no other vessels, and no hope. These were unfrequented waters. Miner was the only one who knew that his men were in trouble, so somehow he had to get the *Sarah W. Hunt* under sail.

He talked it over with the steward, George Duncan, who was in a state of obvious misgiving as he resumed his entry on the page that was serving as an interim logbook. "Not having returned by noon of the second day great anxiety was felt for their safety, and preparation was made to go in search of them," he wrote, adding, "but being only two men on board it was difficult and exceedingly dangerous to undertake anything, the vessel at anchor with both anchors down with 38 fathoms of cable on one and 20 on the other and laying in 10 fathoms of water with the wind dead on a lee shore."

Any seaman would have understood his trepidation. The schooner might be small in comparison with great ships and barks, but she displaced more than a hundred tons. And yet Miner planned to raise the two heavy anchors, set the massive sails, and steer down the long harbor with just George Duncan to help. Then, once this seemingly impossible feat had been accomplished, he proposed to search the heaving sea, with himself at the helm and the steward to tend the ropes.

Duncan had been at sea for nearly three decades, but never as a seaman, only as a cabin boy, cook and steward, and he was acutely aware that he was not at all prepared for the enormity of this task. But Miner was convinced that he had no choice. It was his responsibility to search for the lost men, because there was no one else to do it.

So he ordered the steward to help him reef the foresail as it lay along the boom, with the aim of reducing the area that would be exposed to the force of the wind when it was raised. It took a long time, because they had to fight the recalcitrant canvas with frozen fingers. Finally, however, it lay in stiff folds on the spar, and by the time night fell everything was ready "to start at the break of day."

The second mate, standing at the steering oar in the full bite of the wind, was gray-faced with exhaustion and pain.

Just as dark descended, he gave a hoarse, agonized cry, and dropped his oar. The boat had pitched, wrenching his dislocated shoulder. There was a thump, and then a splash.

The Elephant Voyage

Michael Crawford fell overboard, and sank at once in the sea.

For two long heartbeats the oarsmen merely stared, unable to take in what had happened. Then Huber saw the second mate's fingers clawing desperately at the side of the boat. He let out a shout and dropped his oar to grab the drowning man's arm.

It was a terrible struggle to get Crawford back, while the Irishman screamed every time they pulled at his injured arm. The other two oarsmen were nervously balanced on the other gunwale to keep the boat on an even keel—all of them were terrified that the boat was going to tip and capsize.

Somehow, they got Crawford over the edge, and then, with a crash, he was in the bottom of the boat. He lay there, soaked in icy salt water, gasping and groaning, but at least he was alive—for the moment. If nothing was done, he would be dead by dawn.

"Give him the bow oar," said Huber. It was the shortest, lightest oar, and the foremost oarsman had the most sheltered place, because he sat within the tight curve of the bow. Crawford did not want to move, but Huber persuaded him that the exercise would help him get warm.

Then Emil Huber took over the steering oar. It was the first time the Swiss clerk had ever done so, but he was an intelligent man who had observed the steering process closely. The oar, a twenty-foot length of ash, had a peg-like grip projecting about a foot from the head. He gripped this with his left hand, turned the oar so that the shaft led backward through the crook of his left elbow, and laid his forearm along it. When he leaned on this arm, the blade dug about in their wake. After some experimentation he found out how to keep the boat head-on to the waves.

And so the night drew on.

"Very anxious all night about the crew no tidings yet," wrote George Duncan.

"At 2 AM this morning thick fog with rain and later blowing very strong breeze with thick fog & rain," he went on. At daybreak the winds were gale force, but failed to disperse the mist. Instead, the murk became mixed with freezing sleet and rain — "making it impossible to attempt to get under weigh with any chance of safety and have only to remain in suspense and wait."

The fabric of the schooner groaned constantly, lines thrumming and blocks squealing, while the wind whined through the rigging. The rocky shore was on their lee. Miner put the time to good use, climbing the ladder-like shrouds to the top of the foremast, where he spent the wet and freezing day adapting the rigging to make it easier for just two men to work the ship — "The Captain went aloft and fitted new sheaves into the peak foresail halliard blocks and had everything in readiness to get under weigh as soon as it moderates."

At five in the afternoon Miner was finished. The storm had moderated a little, and so he and Duncan weighed the starboard anchor, heaving and grunting at the windlass as the cable crept up the hawse pipe, inch by laborious inch. No sooner was it out of the water and secured, however, than yet another storm arrived — "Commenced to breeze up again, and by 9 PM blowing a gale, with tremendous and very heavy sudden squalls until about 12 midnight."

At three in the morning the storm moderated, but again there was "a very thick fog with rain." Still there was no sign of the men, and it was very hard not to give up hope.

"Can do nothing more," wrote Duncan, "than wait a chance to get under weigh to look for signs of them."

Just two hours later, the weather made a miraculous change for the better — "Very moderate with a light breeze from the westward," noted the steward. He and Captain Miner set to work at the windlass — "Hove short, and got our anchor." The schooner was now at the mercy of the current, so they had to work fast to get a sail up, bringing the schooner under some sort of way, so that the rudder would respond to the helm.

Hoisting and setting the great sail was a heavy job that was normally carried out by four men, two at each of the two halliards, one at each end of the big spar called the "gaff" to which the top of the sail was tied, working in unison to keep that gaff parallel with the deck as it rose, to avoid the gear jamming. Duncan and Miner managed it only because of the tackle that Captain Miner had rigged, which allowed the work to be alternated between the two ropes as the sail inched upward, first one end, then the other, back and forth until it was set.

In contrast to the painfully slow and brutal job of bringing the huge foresail up the mast, the lighter sails — the forestaysail and the jib — were easily set, and at long last the schooner was well underway, with Captain Miner's expert hand at the helm. As the wind and current were both in their favor, coasting down the harbor was easy, and by nine in the morning the *Sarah W. Hunt* was clear of the harbor.

There, however, they hit a hitch. The schooner did not have enough canvas spread to heave her out of the troughs of the big waves in the open sea. Captain Miner and the steward had to set to work again, double-reefing the great mainsail as it lay on the boom and then heaving it aloft with tackles, like the foresail. Then at last, with the decks cleared up, they were able to commence the search.

The schooner cast back and forth, but to no avail. "Calm during the remainder of the day. Course N by W," wrote Duncan. At midnight the wind fell completely away, and the schooner wallowed in the blackness of the sea. Day dawned at last, still without sight of either of the boats. At noon on December 1, Duncan completed his log entry, writing, "Have not seen no sign of boats or men, given up all hope of ever hearing of them—"

It was a pivotal moment. Inevitably, Miner was haunted throughout that fruitless thirty-hour search with memories of the terrible aftermath of the sinking of the *Delia Hodgkins.* He surely remembered how the cold salt spray had bit into wet, exposed flesh, and the shock of the icy wind. It would have been impossible not to relive the awful experience of stripping the marble-like bodies of men as they died, and slipping the blue-white, naked corpses over the side of the boat into the sea.

Four had expired in just one night, and another soon after dawn. Without the buoyancy of air trapped in clothing, the bodies had sunk—but not far, not far enough. Because they had not been weighted, they bobbed back and forth just below the surface, looking at the desperately laboring oarsmen with wide-open eyes, nudging the boat with their frozen limbs. It would have taken a long time to leave them behind. One of them had been Captain Miner's nephew.

It did not take him long to make up his mind. That noon, instead of searching further, Captain Miner charted a northward course for the south of New Zealand. The wind was fair. By morning, Campbell Island was out of sight.

The Elephant Voyage

6: *Battle for Survival*

A grand set of men, the reader will say, to put a schooner about in a squall, or navigate a whaleboat back to an island in the teeth of a South Pacific storm!"
— Otago Daily Times, *26 January 1884*

Martin Tierney calculated that their boat had been blown sixty miles every time it was swept away from Campbell Island, so that they must have rowed and sailed hundreds of miles in their dogged attempts to get back.

Sometimes, after hours of pulling, they were rewarded by the sight of peaks on the horizon, but most of the time they could make no headway at all. For all they knew, they were going backward. And, even if they did glimpse Campbell Island, the evening would bring another gale, so that by nightfall the dark silhouette had dropped beyond the horizon, and again they were alone in the heaving sea.

Such frustration was so debilitating for weak and exhausted men that it posed yet another threat to their survival. To drive away despair and keep themselves sane, the six men began to tell each other stories, delving into memories of their widely different pasts. It was a tacit but mutual recognition that they were an odd assortment, representing not just a mixture of nationalities—American,

German, Swiss, and Irish—but of trades, as well, and turning this to their advantage. Between them, they had strength, intelligence, and stamina—and many tales to tell, which not just distracted them from their troubles in the most difficult circumstances possible, but kept them attentive and reasonably alert, instead of descending into a mindless fog.

Historically, groups have survived incredible privation because of the leadership of one strong man, but there was no particular leader in this boat. The second mate was too sick and pain-wracked to take charge, and no one stood out from the rest. It was because of their remarkable solidarity and willingness to keep each others' spirits up that this assortment of men had survived so long—that not a single one had died, not even Michael Crawford, who must have been suffering badly from hypothermia after his plunge into the icy sea. When the last of the bread ran out, though, it was very hard not to despair.

Starved and spent, the last crumbs of ship's bread nothing but a memory, the men let the boat drift each night to get what little rest they could. With dawn, they spurred themselves and each other into hauling at their oars again, in yet another struggle to get closer to the unseen land by forcing their way against the prevailing westerly. After a hundred hours of sitting on hard thwarts with their boots planted in icy salt water, their legs, feet, and ankles were black and swollen, and their thighs and buttocks were patched with angry, weeping sores.

But still they talked, though their mouths were parched and their tongues swollen, one boy's anecdote triggering a story from another. Emil Huber's fists, curled about his sixteen-foot oar, were red, numb, swollen, and raw, but the exercise brought a vestige of warmth, and he remembered later, too, that it distracted his mind to listen.

On the morning of December 1—the same morning that Captain Miner gave up the search for his lost boys—the watery sun rose to reveal the distant peaks of Campbell Island. Massive clouds gathered directly above the drifting whaleboat, but the grim, timeworn silhouette of the island stood out clearly against the pale dawn sky, its cliffs and slopes flushed a gentle pink.

The one man who was awake could easily have kept silent. His first thought must have been that it was pointless and cruel to rouse his shipmates from whatever rest they had found. A cry of "Land-ho!" would simply lead to yet another horrible, arduous, fruitless struggle to reach the shore. Too, while the prevailing westerly gale had died, now it was a dead calm, with not a single puff of wind to fill the sail. But, because he was acutely aware that if he kept silent he would be rebuked by the rest of this astonishingly resilient group, he called out.

His hoarse hail was accompanied by a piece of luck. A sea breeze sprang up, bringing a brief shower of rain, which they caught on a spread oilskin, and shared out. There was crusted salt on the coat, so the water tasted brackish, but it was a lot better than the seawater some had sipped, and the urine others had used to rinse their mouths and wet their lips. At that critical moment, it gave them strength.

It took twelve hours of heaving and hauling at the cold, heavy oars, while the wet salty wood bit into their raw palms. But constant croaked encouragement kept themselves and each other going. And at last they were getting somewhere—the shape of Campbell Island took on detail, and was visibly getting closer. Then the cliffs loomed over them. Just as the sun dropped behind the mountains, and night descended, they felt and heard the bottom of the boat grating on unseen mud and shingle.

The overwhelming need was for water to drink. They could hear the trickle of a spring nearby, and smell its cold freshness. Desperate to get to it, they all tried to stagger to their feet, but four collapsed. These were Crawford, Huber, Hertwig, and Henderson. Their blackened, swollen legs and feet were too painful to take their weight. The two Americans, Thomas Whittle and Martin Tierney, were the only ones capable of dragging themselves out onto the beach.

Whittle and Tierney floundered to the spring, fell to the ground, and then from their cupped hands drank until they could hold no more. After that, they fetched the bucket, rinsed it, filled it, and fed water to the others. The spring water was bitterly cold, on the verge of freezing, but the men gulped it thirstily. Then they huddled together in the bottom of the beached boat.

All six desperately needed to rest, but they were shivering uncontrollably, their teeth chattering. Several doubled up every now and then, seized with agonizing cramps. Crawford's arm was a bar of agony, and all of them were tormented by the pain of the seeping, ulcerated sores on their buttocks, feet, and legs.

A gray pre-dawn light revealed cliffs, shingle, and water lapping on mud. Stranded kelp rotted in piles, crawling with tiny insects. Hundreds of birds were lifting into the sky, filling the air with their noise. The wet, green smell of land was intoxicating, but there was nothing to eat, and the men had little idea of their whereabouts. They recognized nothing — all the cliffs and narrow shingle beaches looked the same, and nothing seemed familiar.

After some discussion they decided that this could not be the mouth of Perseverance Harbour, because none of them felt as if the schooner had sailed past this part of the coast. They had landed too far north, they thought, so Whittle and Tierney shoved the boat out into the rising tide, and with a concerted effort, they lifted and fidded the mast and set the sail.

The wind was getting up. They watched the sky nervously, afraid that they would be blown out to sea again. Painfully heaving the heavy oars up, down, back, and forward, the five boys worked to keep the boat as close to the shore as they could, while Crawford tended the sail. After about five miles they saw another inlet, and approached it just as another westerly gale stormed out of the heart of the island. They did not recognize this as the entrance to Perseverance Harbour, either, but they did not dare put out to sea again.

Whittle and Tierney hauled the boat up onto the beach, and somehow managed to roll the four crippled men to one side. They cut bundles of grass and piled them into the bottom of the boat, before rolling their shipmates back onto the makeshift beds. Once the crippled men were as comfortable as possible, the two Americans limped along the beach, looking for food.

To their surprise, they blundered over an old bull seal. Summoning the strength of extreme hunger, they rushed at him, but he simply studied them with the utmost disdain, then turned and floundered into the water. Finding two dozen mussels growing on a rock was poor compensation for the meal of raw, warm, steaming meat they had envisaged, but it was better than nothing. They took the shellfish to their companions, and after that there was little else to do but grimly hold on until the wind abated.

The storm lasted forty-eight hours. While the men dozed, drank water, and talked, they came to the conclusion that their first landing had been the right one—that it had been the entrance to the fissure that led to Perseverance Harbour. If they had not made that stupid decision to look further, they would be safely on board the *Sarah W. Hunt* by now, or so they thought. It was a desperately disheartening realization. At long last, however, at dawn on the fourth day after reaching the island, the wind dropped.

It was snowing heavily. Summoning their last reserves of strength, Whittle and Tierney shoved the boat back into the water. Then, after setting the sail and taking up their oars, the boys laboriously retraced their course to the mouth of the long ravine. Then they turned into it.

The current was against them, and though the wind was in their favor it was light, so it took hours to get to the great bend, and then still more time to navigate the hazards of half-seen rocks and beds of kelp, pulling with the oars all the time. Finally, the tall spar and the mudflats loomed ahead, glistening in the last light of the day—"& at last found Perseverance Harbour," Emil Huber recounted later.

"But," he added grimly, "the *Sarah W. Hunt* was gone."

It was providential that Emil Huber was one of the party. On the schooner he had been in the port watch, which was headed by the first mate, and so by rights he should have been in Streichert's boat. For some reason he had exchanged places with some less fortunate soul, and joined the starboard watch (nominally the captain's watch, but headed by the second mate), and so was in Michael Crawford's boat for the disastrous seal hunt. Not only had it saved his life, but it helped save the lives of his companions, because of the bag of bread he had fetched at the last moment, before leaving the schooner. Having been in Streichert's group during the search for a freshwater stream, he also knew the location of the castaway hut.

The hut was a mile away, however—a mile-long crawl through mud, snow, and slimy, slippery shingle. It was providential, again, that Whittle and Tierney had the strength to half-carry, half-drag their crippled companions through the thick clumps of sharp-leaved tussock. As a passenger on the *Amherst* had observed fifteen years earlier, the soil was very wet, soggy, and peaty, and the footing was slippery and treacherous, with hidden holes that could be as much as two feet deep.

Twenty-five-year-old Thomas Whittle was a short and husky man who had been a teamster back home, used to heaving heavy boxes and sacks onto drays, but still it must have taxed his remaining strength to the limit. Tierney had more resilience than the others, because he had been better fed during the weeks before the ordeal—he was the one who had been sneaking into the hold to steal provisions. Also, he had been relatively well rested. On August 30, he had been knocked down by the boom when the schooner was caught aback, and had been off duty for two weeks (presumably with concussion, because no wound was mentioned in the log). It was a combination that gave him the strength to lift Emil Huber over his shoulder, and carry him to the shelter of the castaway hut.

The relief when the last man was wedged into place in the shack must have been enormous. They were forced to lie close together, but proximity meant warmth. On the other hand, while there were matches and a small amount of salt, there was no means of procuring more food—no fishing lines, no rifle with ammunition—and no medicines. But at that moment, canned mutton and pilot bread looked like a banquet. And, though it was very difficult to find firewood on this tree-less island, where only scrub and dried tussock could be used, having matches to light a fire was a blessing.

In the beginning it looked as if twelve two-pound tins of preserved mutton and two boxes of sea biscuits—each holding three dozen of the thick, rock-hard crackers—would be plenty to tide them over, because there was an unlimited supply of fresh water from the stream. Also, after more discussion, the boys had decided that Streichert's boat must have made it to Perseverance Harbour some days earlier, meaning there was enough crew to raise the anchors and set sail. Undoubtedly, they thought, the schooner was at sea, searching for their boat. Soon, having failed to find them, Captain Miner would come back. They pictured Captain Miner's surprise and pleasure when he found his lost boys waiting for him in the hut.

Three days later, they finally realized that they had been stupidly over-optimistic. At last they understood that the *Sarah W. Hunt* was not going to return.

Crawford was the most charitable, speculating that Streichert would have told such terrible stories about the struggle to get back to Perseverance Harbour that Captain Miner must have been convinced that everyone in the second boat was dead. The others disagreed. Though equally certain that Streichert must have made it back to Perseverance Harbour—being convinced that Captain Miner and the steward could not possibly have got the schooner under sail and underway by themselves—they remembered how quickly Captain Miner had given up after Julius Jaeger fell from aloft and was washed away astern.

He might be dogged about retrieving dropped buckets and lost anchors, but he was much less determined when it came to lost men.

The priority, however, was the conservation of their scant resources. The tinned meat and bread that had saved their lives was now rationed to one meal a day, but even then the stock, which though it had been scant in the first place, had been eaten without forethought while they held hopes of rescue, so had diminished frighteningly fast. The blankets, coats, and ax had been retrieved from the strong-box under the signal post, and had been put to good use. They had also appropriated the pannikins and cooking pot, but these were of no value to them unless they could find something to cook.

They weren't totally without resources. While, like the rest, Whittle and Tierney had ulcers all over their legs and buttocks, and were suffering the stomach cramps and shooting bowel pains of severe constipation, they could still get around, using sealing clubs as walking sticks. Crawford was very ill, with his injured arm turning gangrenous, but Huber, Hertwig and Henderson, though they still couldn't stand on their swollen and blistered feet, were capable of tending the fire while the two Americans foraged for food and fuel.

Finding something substantial to cook over that fire was an unconquerable hurdle, however. When the weather allowed it Whittle and Tierney limped out to search the beach for mussels, and usually managed to gather a few, but anything more than that was impossible. They could not fish, because there were no hooks or lines. There were clubs and skinning knives in the boat, but the pigs and goats released by the *Amherst*, like the stock released by the *Victoria*, had vanished into oblivion, and there was not a seal to be seen. There were thousands of birds, but no gun to shoot them, and the slippery cliffs were too great a hurdle to raid nests for eggs.

It rained almost every day, a cold rain that trickled freely through the thatch, so that their bedding and clothes were constantly sodden. The occasional howling storms, when the shrill wind whistled through the cracks in the boards, were almost unbearable, but somehow, the calms were even worse. The empty, dun-colored, snow-sprinkled landscape stretched around them, rising up to inaccessible peaks without even a ripple in the tussock. Birds screamed in the distance, but their cries only served to punctuate the overwhelming silence of an uninhabited land.

The nights were particularly harrowing. To conserve their scant fuel, the castaways let the fire burn down after they had huddled into their accustomed sleeping places, and once the crackle of flames died away, and one by one they had stopped trying to make conversation, it was very dark and cold. If the wind blew, it was harrowing, but if it died down the long night was oppressively quiet, with not even the distant thump of surf or the cry of a gull to mark the slowly passing hours.

By the fifth cold, watery dawn, even the most doggedly sunny-spirited of the boys was forced to face the fact that the chance of being rescued before they used up the last of the cached food was remote in the extreme. And, once the tinned meat and biscuit ran out, a slow, horrible death from starvation was inevitable.

7: Hailed as Heroes

ARRIVED LYTTELTON. Dec. 8 – Sarah W. Hunt, *schooner, 110 tons, Miner, from Campbell Island (on a sealing cruise, put in in distress)*
– The Star, *Christchurch, 10 December 1883.*

Captain Miner's passage to New Zealand was a constant battle against northwest storms and a heavy head sea, while the schooner beat north through the roaring forties. "This day begins with a strong gale from the Westward, continuing during the day with terrific squalls," wrote George Duncan on Thursday, 6 December. The schooner was in latitude 46° 16′ South—"at 3 pm this day hauled down Jib, there being a very heavy sea running, 5 pm moderating a little, 12 midnight wearing ship."

Bringing the schooner's stern around was a nightmare in a sleet-wracked tempest, with one man at the helm and just one to the lines of the hundred-ton vessel. Both worked desperately to prevent the schooner falling off and getting broadside to the huge waves that marched in from the depths of the night. At three in the morning they had to wear ship again, but at long last, "at 4 am sighted land right ahead."

The Elephant Voyage

The landfall was Cape Saunders, the gateway to the port of Dunedin, in the south of the South Island of New Zealand. Frustratingly, the hard gale hauled southwest, effectively barring the grossly undermanned vessel from entering. They hove to, hoping for a change, but at ten in the morning gave up, and squared their sails: "Steering NNE for a Harbour and continued fine during the remainder of the day & night," wrote Duncan.

At last both wind and weather were with them. By late the next afternoon the golden hills of Canterbury lay directly ahead. Captain Miner and his steward could see the boat coming out from the pilot station, and beyond, the curving mole that sheltered the harbor. And there was the port of Lyttelton, with its wharves, its busy waterfront strand, and its scatter of wooden houses on the slopes above.

"Arrival of a Schooner in Distress," ran the headline on the front page of the *Star* of Christchurch: "The *Sarah W. Hunt,* a shapely American-built fore-and-aft schooner, of 115 tons gross register, whose great spars and immense spread of canvas denote a vessel of fine specs, arrived quite unexpectedly on Saturday night, at half-past seven o'clock."

Astonishingly, the schooner had come all the way from Campbell Island, though crewed by just the captain and the cook. "Campbell Island, high and rocky, is some hundred miles or so south of New Zealand. Here she lost 13 of her hands, and for a vessel of her size, only to be navigated by two men some hundreds of miles in about 11 days, shows signs of no little pluck, seamanship, and endurance."

"On Saturday afternoon last a large fore-and aft schooner, flying the American flag, was seen from the pilot-station at the Heads, making towards the port," reported the

Weekly Press of Christchurch. "Pilot Galbraith and a boat's crew put off to the stranger, and on boarding her found her to be the *Sarah W. Hunt*, a smart looking vessel of 110 tons register. The only persons on board were the captain and the steward."

After giving a transcription of George Duncan's log, along with the names of the lost crew, the report continued, "The supposition of both the master and his worthy steward, Mr. Geo. Duncan, is that the boats were struck while under sail by one of the heavy gusts of wind, and capsized, drowning the poor fellows who were in them. Either that, or, what is much more fearful to contemplate, that the two boats got too far off shore, and were blown off by the gales that prevailed after they left he schooner, the crews perishing by starvation."

Naturally, Captain Sanford Miner was anxious to emphasize that these were the likely scenarios, as they both justified his decision to give up and sail away. And, as well as that, he was quick to place the blame for the disaster on Karl Streichert. "Captain Miner, in a conversation with a reporter of this paper, said that when the boats left the mate remarked that he thought he would be able to get right round the island that day, " the reporter went on; "and Captain Miner particularly said to him, 'Well, use your best judgment, but keep as close (the boats) together as you can, for if an accident in landing happened to one boat the other might be ready to render assistance;' also 'to be sure and not get far off shore, as nothing could be seen by doing so'." He had told Streichert to steer to windward, Miner went on, as that would make it easier for him to sail back, when he would be downwind.

"The mate was, however, an experienced sealer, and the second mate an old whaler, facts which tend to strengthen the belief of the captain that the boats were capsized in a squall." After all, according to both *Brett's* and the *South Pacific Pilot*, "sudden and violent rushes of wind is a characteristic phenomenon of the place."

If the journalist had remembered a dramatic story that had appeared in New Zealand newspapers just two years earlier, which was called "Terrible Sufferings of a Whaler's Crew" and described the tragedy that had followed Captain Miner's loss of the *Delia Hodgkins,* he may have wondered about this man's history of bad luck, and asked more questions. Instead, however, he returned to marveling about the extraordinary feat in sailing the big schooner with its huge spread of canvas from Campbell Island to New Zealand. "The captain measuring the track he made that he and the steward had brought the schooner close upon 680 miles through some severe gales and storms, with but poor hearts for enduring them. What they have achieved in bringing the vessel in safety so speedily on to this port is certainly deserving of notice."

It was very pleasant for Captain Miner and George Duncan to be lauded so generously for their remarkable feat of seamanship. The steward made the most of it, telling his tales while he was being plied with congratulatory liquor in the taverns of Lyttelton. Captain Miner, by contrast, briskly returned to business. First, he broke open Streichert's sea chest to retrieve the logbook, and recommenced the record by noting in his small, crabbed script that they had arrived off Godley Head at four in the afternoon, and had dropped anchor at Lyttelton at seven. Then he moved on to his next priority, which was to compose a letter to his partners in Connecticut, telling them what had happened — "Wrote to my owners and mailed it at 8:30 P.M," he recorded in the log.

Next morning, he attended to the badly needed restocking of the ship's pantry — something that was easily done, because of the chandleries and stores that lined Norwich Quay, the busy waterfront strand. "Engaged a Butcher and got some fresh Provisions," he wrote on return from the big butcher's shop, Garforth & Lee.

That organized, Miner set out to notify the local United States consular agent that he had lost twelve men and needed him to find him a whole new crew. He had not a notion who the official American representative might be, so asked the advice of the man who had piloted him into the harbor. This was Mr. Galbraith, who told him to go to "Capt. D. McIntyre formerly Consular Agent at Wellington NZ." And Captain Miner followed up this advice at once, expecting nothing less than practical understanding from McIntyre, particularly since the agent had been a ship's master, too.

Born in Glasgow, Scotland, in 1827, Daniel McIntyre had made quite a name for himself as the captain of emigrant ships, including the famous *Chrysolite*. Deciding that New Zealand was the right place to be, he had set himself up as a chandler in Wellington, selling ships' stores from his warehouse on the waterfront.

As a mark of his success, on June 11, 1868, the U.S. consul at Melbourne, James MacGuire, nominated him to the post of consul in Wellington. However, as MacGuire had no authority in New Zealand, the appointment was never formalized by either the U.S. State Department or the colonial government, so Daniel McIntyre had no official standing. Instead, when the Scotsman had tried to establish his position, it had led to a mortifying row with the U.S. consular agent in Dunedin. For some weeks, their fight for recognition as the prime American representative in New

Zealand was a prominent feature in the newspapers, as well as in State Department despatches.

And, even more embarrassingly, the Dunedin man won. Accordingly, as Daniel McIntyre still harbored resentment about the public embarrassment, Captain Miner found a perfunctory reception. After tersely informing his visitor that he was the Marine Assessor for the Port of Lyttelton, and had nothing to do with United States consulate affairs any more, McIntyre ordered Miner to attend a meeting at the Custom House at Christchurch at ten o'clock the next morning. And, he added, Captain Miner was to make sure that the steward was there, too.

And that, as far as he was concerned, was the end of the interview. Captain Miner, however, did not leave. Alarmed at this stiff formality, he asked how he could find the U.S. Consul's office. Not anywhere near here, McIntyre informed him — the consul was a fellow from Kentucky by the name of Gilderoy Wells Griffin, and his office was in Auckland, in the north of the North Island. While there was a consular agent in Christchurch, an American timber-merchant and speculator by the name of Charles B. Taylor, he was not in the country, and could be as far off as Boston.

However, undoubtedly to Miner's relief, the marine assessor unbent enough to suggest that Taylor's deputy, a shipping agent by the name of Joseph Frederick Ward, might be able to help. And Ward, contacted by telegraph, responded at once, to say he would be in Lyttelton within the hour.

True to his word, he arrived on board the schooner that same afternoon, accompanied by a man who was to play a pivotal part in the unfolding drama. This was 49-year-old James Drummond Macpherson, a Scot from Greenock who had arrived in New Zealand some time before 1859, when he had built a chandlery store on the Lyttelton beachfront. Originally a commercial agent for the British China trade firm of Jardine & Matheson, he had invested widely on his own account in farmland, coal, ships, and businesses. In Lyttelton, he had taken over a marine supplies and insurance agency, Cookson, Bowler & Co. (which had failed, owing Jardine & Matheson £50,000); and he had also set up premises in Cashel Street, Christchurch. Macpherson was an important man in local politics, too. As a past member of the Provincial Council for Christchurch (from 1865 to 1866) and the Town of Lyttelton (1869 and 1870), he had powerful contacts in the capital, Wellingon.

His official reason for coming with Ward was that he was the local agent for Lloyds Shipping and Insurance. Most significant of all, however, was that he was also the president of the Christchurch Chamber of Commerce.

Next morning, December 10, Mr. Ward collected Captain Miner and the steward, and after walking to the station they caught the train to Christchurch. As they came through the other end of the tunnel that linked the port and the city, the skies opened, and the heavy rain continued throughout the day. It was mild, however, with a noon temperature of 56 degrees, a distinct contrast to the weather Captain Miner had left behind in the sub-Antarctic.

James Macpherson and Captain McIntyre were waiting at the Custom House, where the crowd also included journalists from three local papers — *The Press, The Lyttelton Times*, and *The Star*. The inquiry was a formal one, presided over by the Collector of Customs, Alexander Rose. He conducted the cross-examination, while Captain McIntyre, as Marine Assessor, took notes and collected documentary evidence.

Captain Miner was called up first. When asked for his full name, he said, "Sanford Stoddard Miner" and then deposed, "I am master of the American schooner *Sarah W. Hunt*, of Middletown, Connecticut, official number 115432, signal letter J.N.R.H., register No. 1, 1882, of Middletown, U.S.A., register tonnage 109 87-100th tons." He had the ship's papers to authenticate this, and presented them.

"On July 10 last I cleared my vessel at New Bedford, bound on a sealing voyage in the South Seas," he went on, taking his cues from Streichert's entries in the logbook, which he had also carried along. Nothing particular had happened on voyage, he said, until "a seaman named Julius C. Jaeger" fell overboard, "and by the time we had got the boat out he had sunk. He was seen again, but before the boat could get to the spot he had disappeared, there being a heavy sea on."

The arrival at Macquarie, the loss of the anchor, the arrival at Campbell Island, and the discovery of "a small hut and a small quantity of stores for castaway sailors" were briefly described, and then Miner turned to the sheet of paper that had been covered on both sides by the steward's much more fluent script.

"On the 27th, whilst still at Perseverance Harbour, Campbell Island, about 6 a.m., the port and starboard boats left the vessel with orders to search in shore for seals, a light breeze blowing from N.W.," he began, and then read out the rest of the sad story, up to the arrival at Lyttelton. All of this, as the reporter from *The Lyttelton Times* remarked, was "a repetition of what has already been published."

The Collector of Customs then asked the question that would ultimately decide the court's opinion of whether Miner had acted properly or not: Did Captain Miner think that it was at all possible that the boats had made it back to the island?

Captain Miner reiterated that it was highly unlikely. As Mr. Rose cross-examined him in detail, his reasons were explained. "Had the crew reached the island they could have made a fire to signal to the ship, as there were matches in the list of stores in the hut," he said:

> *The stores appeared to be in good condition when I saw them. The island is said to be thirty miles in circumference, and the rocks precipitous. If the boats had got into inlets where the cliffs are precipitous they must have been destroyed, but in others they could have got ashore and crossed the island in any direction. The distance across the island from the Eastern to Western Harbour seemed about three miles. The crew all knew that there was a store house with provisions on the island.*
>
> *We were lying about three miles up Perseverance Harbour. The entrance of the harbour was not visible. I therefore cannot say which way the boats proceeded on getting outside. The wind continued on the 27th and 28th from the north-west. If the boats were blown off the island it would be almost impossible for them to get back, as the seas were very high and the prevailing winds are either south-west or north-west. In that case there is no probability of the boats reaching land, and they had no provisions excepting water.*
>
> *If the boats were blown off shore they would be too far south to be in the ordinary course of vessels going from Australia around Cape Horn. The first mate had a pocket compass. The boats were new 28ft whaleboats and in good condition.*

Changing tack, Alexander Rose asked, "Did you know that on November 1, 1881, the sealing season closed, and that it will not reopen until June next year?"

"I was not aware of that," said Miner warily. "I told the men not to kill seals, but to search the island for the kind I wanted, which were clapmatches and two-year-old dogs, which are allowed to be killed in the U.S.A., Alaska sealing islands."

The court, it seems, knew that "clapmatches" were female seals, because there is no record of Miner being asked to explain. Instead, evidently in response to yet another question, he concluded, "I have reported myself to the Acting Consular Agent at Christchurch." Then he was dismissed, and George Duncan was called to the stand.

"I am a British subject and steward on board the American schooner *Sarah W. Hunt,*" Duncan confirmed. In reply to queries, he went on, "I have heard the evidence given by the captain. It's true in all particulars. I have been at sea about 20 years off and on. We could have done nothing more in aid of the missing crew, and I do not think that any steps would be successful in searching from them."

Then he reiterated, "I do not believe there is any chance of the crew being on the island." And that could have been that—a virtual sentence of death for the castaways. As of this date, they had existed at the hut for five long, freezing days, getting weaker by the hour, their weeping sores worsening. Only three or four cans of preserved mutton remained, and the first box of biscuits was almost emptied.

In less than a week those supplies would run out, and if no rescue mission arrived, they were doomed.

8: *Questions*

Whether the crew are lost or are still on the island is at present unknown, but no doubt efforts will be made to discover their fate and to rescue them if still alive
— Evening Star, *Auckland, December 10, 1883*

James Drummond Macpherson left the Customs House feeling far from satisfied by Captain Miner's glib and gloomy assurance that all the men were dead. And, being a strong-minded man, he was determined to do something about it.

Going straight to the post office, he sent an urgent wire to William Rolleston, the Minister of Lands, Immigration, and Education, who was running the country while the Premier, Major Harry Atkinson, was in Sydney. The telegram read:

Feeling here very strongly in favour of Government despatching steamer Campbell Island search for twelve missing seamen of schooner Sarah W. Hunt. Urge compliance if at all possible. Kindly reply.
J.D. MACPHERSON, President Chamber Commerce

Rolleston would have already known about this strong feeling in Christchurch and Lyttelton, because as he was the Member of Parliament for Avon, one of the constituencies of

Christchurch, he regularly read the local papers. And, three days before, on 10 December, the shipping reporter of *The Star* had commented that "some efforts should be made to ascertain whether any of the unfortunate men have survived," while the newspaper's editor had declared in the same issue that while anyone reading the strange story must feel "mingled sensations of admiration and sympathy," of these two sensations the stronger would be sympathy for the missing men. "What has been the fate of the sealing party?" he demanded. How could anyone be sure that they were dead? "They may all have perished in some way, but on the other hand it is not improbable that by some accident to the boats they may have been imprisoned on the rocky island." Altogether, it was a clear case for "*prompt* action" by the government.

Additionally, one of Rolleston's fellow politicians, the Member of Parliament for Lyttelton, Mr. Harry Allright, had sent a telegram to the Secretary of the Marine Department, William Seed, suggesting that the colonial government steamer *Stella* should be sent out. As he said, she was the obvious candidate for searching the rugged coast of Campbell Island for any survivors, having been designed for the rough work of establishing and maintaining light-houses and patrolling New Zealand's tortuous coasts. Not necessary, Secretary Seed had replied. The government schooner *Kekeno* would be checking the stores at Campbell Island very soon — "She will be probably back in a few days at the Bluff to report. If nothing is then heard of the missing men she might return and search."

And, being aware of all this, William Rolleston treated Macpherson's telegram with caution.

A handsome older man, unfashionably clean-shaven, with a square, hard jaw, a deeply wrinkled forehead, and carefully groomed brown hair, William Rolleston was a diligent and eloquent politician, capable of producing an electrifying speech, but loyal enough to keep to the party line. Critically, though he was liberal-minded, he was also famous for his prudence and his hatred of extravagance. It was not in his nature to send out government steamers on expensive search and rescue missions at a time when money was scarce, and government revenues were falling.

Accordingly, his first move was to check the facts of the case. An urgent telegram was sent to Alexander Rose, asking for full details. The Collector of Customs responded at once, sending the text of Captain Miner's deposition. A decision, based on this, was quickly made, and telegraphed to Macpherson the same day.

"Have wired Collector of Customs for full information about boats of *Sarah W. Hunt*" — it began:

> *Present information very imperfect. If boats went to sea from Campbell Island there would seem to be no hope of finding them. If men on Campbell or Auckland Islands food and clothing will be found at the depots. If any prospect of saving life Government would take action, but sending Stella would delay work at Waipapa, important in interest of navigation generally, and so far as information now goes would not be likely to be of any good. On receipt of full information will decide whether anything can be done. Meantime it would appear that Captain of schooner should re-man her, and return in search of the missing men – W. ROLLESTON*

In view of the "strong feeling," William Rolleston also took the precaution of issuing a press release, in which he said much the same—that "the *Stella* cannot be spared, as it would seriously delay the work in connection with the lighthouse at Waipapa Point, which is to be ready by the 1st of January." There were castaway huts on both Campbell and Auckland Islands, which would be the salvation of the crew if they reached either shore. "If the crew did not reach either of these islands, a search would be perfectly useless. There is no land to which they might be blown, and the chances of finding them alive would be small indeed." Captain Miner should re-man his vessel and go in search of the men himself, but in the meantime the public was assured that a full report from Christchurch was pending, "and it is probable that on the return of the schooner *Kekeno* from Auckland Island she may be ordered to make a strict search.

"It is alleged that the men were sealing," the release concluded on a sterner note. "It is quite illegal, as the present is a close season."

James Macpherson was disappointed and angry. Granted, the building of the lighthouse at Waipapa Point (on the wreck-ridden south coast of the South Island) was in response to one of New Zealand's most awful maritime tragedies—the loss of the steamship *Tararua* with a death toll of 131 men, women, and children, just two years earlier. Undoubtedly, the building of this lighthouse would save many lives in the future—but this crisis was immediate.

Understanding that to have any chance of forcing Rolleston to change his mind he needed a public outcry, Macpherson released the telegrams to the press.

"Is Our Civilisation A Failure?" demanded an editorial in *The Star* the very next day, Tuesday, 11 December. The government had been telegraphed the "obvious suggestion" that the *Stella* should be sent "on a possible life-saving expedition"—and a reply had been received "that fills us with astonishment and indignation. That reply is to this effect—The *Stella* can't be spared; there are stores somewhere on Campbell Island, and the Government schooner *Kekeno* is supposed to be somewhere in that region; these men—common seamen—must take their chance. This is official flippancy with a vengeance! It is possible that these thirteen [sic] men are alive; it is possible that they are lying on those inhospitable rocks, where only the albatross and the seal find a congenial resting place, lingering out that awful 'death-in-life,' which even to think of makes one's blood run cold. It is opposed to all ideas of civilisation, of Christianity, of common humanity, and we emphatically denounce it."

Having seized attention, Macpherson's next move was to hold a special meeting of the Christchurch Chamber of Commerce, which he managed to convene as early as Thursday, 13 December. Among those invited to attend were journalists from the local press, and the presence of Captain Miner was also requested.

Outside, it was a congenial day with variable breezes, mild temperatures, and occasional showers. Inside, the atmosphere was fiery. Because New Zealand and the sub-Antarctic islands lie across a belt of prevailing westerly winds that can turn into savage gales, the newspapers often carried sad reports of ships lost and seamen stranded on rocky coasts and islands—indeed, the *Sarah W. Hunt* tragedy had been just one of three shipwreck accounts in the December 15 edition of *The Weekly Press.*

But, according to public opinion, the *Sarah W. Hunt* story was different, because of the behavior of the ship's master. Not only had he given up hope for his men too quickly and easily, but by now it had become obvious that his only intention was to re-provision his schooner and find a new crew, so that he could return to the seal hunt. He had expressed no desire whatsoever to go back to the island and search again for the twelve mariners he had lost. Obviously, Mr. Rolleston's opinion of what he should do had made not a shred of difference to Miner, because he was convinced they were dead.

Every other man in the chamber, by contrast, was acutely aware of the possibility that at least some of the men were hanging on to life while they waited for rescue. All of them had read or heard tales of terrible privation that had been told by people who had survived shipwreck and come home to talk about it. Castaway stories had a particular fascination for the public as a whole, and books like *Robinson Crusoe* had a loyal and enduring audience. The English translation of the memoir written by one of the *Grafton* castaways—*Wrecked on a Reef*, by François Raynal—was a current bestseller. Not only was its account of remarkable survival in the face of extreme hardships on Auckland Island exciting to read, but the message it carried of the triumph of the human spirit was an inspiration to all.

Because of the popularity of these castaway accounts, Macpherson's audience thought they knew exactly what kind of ordeal any survivors from the *Sarah W. Hunt* disaster were going through, if they had indeed made it back to Campbell Island—the formidable cliffs and storm-swept slopes, the clinging mud and slippery snow, the constant wet, and the occasional terrific gusts of wind.

Even if the chance that the men had made it back to the island was as remote as Captain Miner reckoned, how could a decent captain abandon his crew to this kind of fate?

Macpherson opened by apologizing for the short notice, saying that the meeting had been very hurriedly convened, then went on to state that there was no doubt that they, as a community, should do their best to rescue the unfortunate fellow-creatures who had been left in such a miserable plight. Either they were beyond all human hope, or they were anxiously looking for relief. Therefore, he thought something should be done for them at once—that action should be immediate.

Then he read out the telegrams exchanged between himself and Mr. Rolleston, in Wellington. Believing that the response was inadequate, he had sent another telegram, he said, again urging action. The sister ship of the *Stella,* the government steamer *Hinemoa,* could take up the *Stella*'s work at Waipapa Point, releasing the *Stella* for a mercy trip to Campbell Island, which should take only about thirty hours. Or so, he said, he had suggested.

No sooner had Macpherson finished reading this out, than he was interrupted by a heated query, which was duly reported by the papers. Mr. Rolleston was right, the interlocutor exclaimed—the responsibility was the captain's. So why had the *Sarah W. Hunt* not been re-provisioned and re-manned at once, so she could be sailed back to the island?

This interruption was closely followed by another, from a member who wanted to know why the captain had left his safe anchorage in Perseverance Harbour in the first place. He could have stayed there for a month, waiting for the boats' return—indeed, it was his *duty* to remain, to be ready to succor the poor men if they returned. Instead, Captain Miner had made that injudiciously swift voyage to New Zealand. Another member then demanded to know "why was not the schooner under weigh with a crew of volunteers or paid men within twelve hours of his arrival?" As he pointed out, a fair wind had been blowing during the past six days.

The Elephant Voyage

James Macpherson, after he had managed to restore quiet, pointed out that as the actions of Captain Miner had been called into question, it was only fair that he should have a chance to counter the charges. As the reporter from *The Star* phrased it, "The President suggested that the captain should be allowed to explain his position, especially as he had suffered great hardships and anxiety."

The men present all looked at Miner, who stared back mutely. How could he possibly use this moment to describe the foundering of the *Delia Hodgkins*? How could he tell these businessmen how his shipmates had died so quickly and easily during the thirty-six-hours in the boat? How could he persuade them that it was because of that terrible experience that he was so deeply certain none of the men had survived?

Instead of speaking he kept his silence—a silence that dragged on. Macpherson then suggested that perhaps Mr. Ward would speak up for the captain. When Sanford Miner nodded, Joseph Ward stood up. Conscious of his role as the only American representative present, he was unwavering in his support of Miner's position. After testifying that he had read the evidence, he said that he "considered the captain had acted judiciously in saving his ship."

Another silence followed, broken by yet another member of the chamber. This man, sensible of the passing of the hours, pointed out that criticizing the captain's actions was a waste of time, when it was so crucially important to get a search and rescue mission underway as quickly as possible. The plain fact of the matter, as he went on to say, was that the government had two steamers, and one should be made available. If it was a question of money, then that money should be raised.

And with that, undoubtedly to James Macpherson's relief, the meeting got down to business.

A motion was called:

> *That this meeting expresses the deepest regret and indignation that the Minister acting in Wellington hesitated to despatch a search party to look for the missing seamen of the schooner Sarah W. Hunt, and would urge prompt action upon the Government. Failing such action on their part, a steamer should be chartered and despatched, and the expense should be defrayed by public subscription.*

This was seconded, but a great deal of debate about the wording followed. Some members were of the opinion that the resolution was too strong, while others declared that it was not strong enough — "that the delay of the Government had degraded New Zealand in the eyes of the world." As a member heatedly argued, the inaction "was a reflection on the British flag, as the men were subjects of a friendly nation which had no means of rescuing these men, except through the British Government."

This led to a very lively argument, and a further waste of time. Several members pointed out that because Captain Miner's reasons for abandoning his men were so plausible, the government could not be blamed for its reluctance to send a steamer that could be of so much use elsewhere, while others reiterated that "the Government were behaving meanly, shabbily, and almost inhumanly."

Time passed, but finally a truce was called. A motion was put, "That immediate steps should be taken to despatch a steamer to the island to see whether the missing seamen are still alive, and that a Committee undertake to be responsible for the expense, and to collect the amount from the Government or the public," was posted and passed.

After that, progress was swift. Miner "expressed his willingness to go with any steamer which might be sent for the relief of the seamen," and the "sum of £630 was guaranteed in the room by those present towards the expense of sending a steamer." And Macpherson wired the resolution to Wellington.

Six hundred and thirty pounds sterling was a significant sum, and these were very influential men. Among those who signed the resolution were the Mayor of Lyttelton, two members of the harbor board, a founding director of the New Zealand Shipping Company, the head of a stevedoring firm, a prominent Christchurch city merchant, and two Members of Parliament.

This, for William Rolleston, was a most unwelcome development. He already had enemies in Canterbury, and surely did not need any more. A democratic man, he hated the growing gap between the rich and the poor, and for years had fought a steady battle against the powerful Canterbury land-barons, who were steadily amassing huge acreages, and creating land monopolies. Just recently, too, his ministry had raised the rates for freighting grain by railroad, an extremely unpopular move in the grain-growing Canterbury region.

So personal reservations were set aside. With no further argument, the *Stella* was made available, with all costs paid by the government, and a telegram was sent to Macpherson.

> *I can expedite sailing of Stella, now on slip, so as to leave Wellington on Saturday. Hinemoa is loaded up with deck cargo for North, which would have to be discharged,*

and would not be more than a day sooner. Captain of schooner should join Stella here, and for that purpose leave tonight, otherwise Stella will have to go out of way to call at Lyttelton. Will you let me know if this meets your views. If you think any arrangement can be made more expeditious by sending steamer from Lyttelton or Dunedin, Government will contribute. — W. ROLLESTON

The suggestion that Captain Miner should join the *Stella* was eminently sensible, because he would be able to pilot the steamer to Campbell Island and up to the anchorage at Perseverance Harbour. Macpherson telegraphed Rolleston at once, assuring him that Miner would comply.

But then a problem became embarrassingly evident. Miner had to sail on the Lyttelton-Wellington steam ferry *Takapuna* that very night, or he would be too late to join the *Stella* before she left Wellington—and when James Macpherson looked around, the Connecticut shipmaster was nowhere to be found.

Deciding that Miner had returned to Lyttelton early, Macpherson sent him an urgent telegram, but to his alarm he received no response. Neither was Miner on board the ferry when the *Takapuna* departed. Reported *The Star*, "The captain of the *Sarah W. Hunt*, who was to have gone to Wellington to join the Government steamer, was for some unexplained reason not on board or on the wharf when the steamer left for Wellington, although he was supposed to have arrived in Lyttelton at 8.50 by the Christchurch train."

"Captain did not go to *Takapuna* last night," James Macpherson telegraphed to Wellington, adding tersely, "Do not think it necessary to delay *Stella* for him."

All Friday, December 14, the day following the meeting, telegrams flashed back and forth between Macpherson and Rolleston, as the arrangements for sending the steamer *Stella* were firmed up, despite Miner's strange behavior.

"Should it be finally arranged *Stella* to go to Lyttelton Harbor tug could take Captain of *Sarah Hunt* out to meet her, to save time," wired Macpherson. Rolleston, having decided that the captain of the *Sarah W. Hunt* could not be considered reliable, replied, "*Stella* will call at Godley Heads, but I do not think that Captain Miner need go. He might meet *Stella* at Godley Head and give Captain Gray all information."

In the end, it was decided that the steamer should not call at Lyttelton at all, because of the delay it would cause, and that a Wellington customs officer who knew the island should go in Miner's stead. "Committee urge sending *Stella* straight to Campbell Island without calling for captain," Macpherson telegraphed. "Too late to negotiate anything else now."

And that is exactly what happened. "Dec. 15 – *Stella*, ss, 156 tons, Gray, for Campbell islands," ran the departure notice in the shipping column of the Wellington *Evening Post*.

Obviously, Miner's absence had given James Macpherson much frustration, but if the master of the *Sarah W. Hunt* was consulted during this exchange of telegrams, his replies are not in the record. Later, he admitted that the telegram had indeed been received on board the *Sarah W. Hunt*, and that the watchman had told him about it when he had arrived back from Christchurch.

"I immediately returned to the steamer wharf," he claimed, "but arrived there just as the steamer cast her lines off," but whether he was telling the truth is debatable. It is unlikely that a canny and responsible shipmaster would easily contemplate leaving his schooner unguarded in a foreign port, and Miner was in a particularly difficult position. George Duncan, who had worked so hard during the treacherous passage from Perseverance Harbour, and had been such a staunch supporter of Captain Miner's testimony, now turned up on board the schooner only when he felt like it, and refused to do any work at all.

Miner's log for Wednesday, December 12, ran, "Pleasant weather steward refused to do any duty came off and used abusive language to me, saying he was going on shore again. So Ends," while the entire entry for the next day — the day Miner attended the meeting but missed the *Takapuna* — runs, "Fine weather steward doing no duty came on board during the night. So Ends."

On December 15, the same day the *Stella* set sail from Wellington on her long passage to Campbell Island, Miner recorded, "Steward still off duty coming on board and going ashore without leave." When the watchman tried to reason with the truant, he was abused and threatened. On 24 December, after Duncan had brought some drinking cronies on board, the watchman resigned, "refusing to remain with steward bringing strangers at night."

Miner reported George Duncan to the consular agent, but Mr. Ward could do nothing, apart from making a fruitless attempt to reason with the man. So he reported him to the police, but all they could do was collect the steward from the Lyttelton Hotel, bring him back on board, and advise Miner to lock him in his cabin until he sobered up.

On Christmas Day George Duncan appealed to Miner's Christian nature, begging not to be confined, and giving his word that he would do his duty. When Captain Miner relented and freed him, however, Duncan claimed he was too sick to work. "Fine weather Steward on board saying he could do no work and was sick and wanted to go ashore for an hour to get some medicine and would return and relieve me," Miner wrote, concluding wearily, "Did not return this day So Ends."

After the captain had turned into his bunk for the night, George Duncan sneaked on board to retrieve the rest of his clothes, and then sneaked away again. When Miner got up next morning, the deck boards echoed emptily. This time, the steward had gone for good. "Pleasant weather. Steward deserted" is the whole of Captain Miner's entry for that day.

It was December 27, 1883, exactly one month since the two boats had pulled down Perseverance Harbour toward the waiting sea, and Sanford Miner had lost his last man.

9: Rescue

The stores, with one meal a day of biscuit and preserved mutton, would just have lasted till Christmas Day. What an anniversary would that have been to the one or two survivors of the castaway crew!
—The Lyttelton Times, *January 25, 1884*

In surprisingly calm weather, considering the vicious southeast gale that had churned up the sea the day before and prevented any landing on Campbell Island, a tiny 31-ton schooner tacked into the entrance of Perseverance Harbour. Then, after straightening her course, she glided up the smooth waters of inlet, with the man popularly known as "the King of Stewart Island" at the tiller, and five sworn constables working the ropes.

The "King," Scotsman Captain James Greig, had led a full and busy life ever since his arrival in New Zealand in 1862. During the Otago gold rush he had carried goods and passengers in his own coasting schooner. Then he had held the job of harbormaster for the southern ports of Invercargill and Bluff. In the early 1870s he moved to Stewart Island, south of Bluff and Invercargill, where he had taken on a bewildering variety of posts. Not only was he the resident magistrate (and his own clerk of court), but he was also the registrar of births, deaths, and marriages, the vaccination inspector, the coroner, the fisheries inspector; the property assessor, the inspector of distilleries, the census collector, and the keeper of the immigration barracks. Most importantly, he was also a "coastwaiter" (smuggler-hunter) for the Customs Department—which was not easy on a thickly bush-clad, deeply embayed island, where the American whaleship captains made a habit of anchoring in remote coves to land tobacco, spirits, and gunpowder, and the locals considered smuggling a sport.

In short, Captain Greig was the agent of law, order, and government in the far-flung south of New Zealand, an important man who would not have enjoyed retirement. But in 1882, just as he passed his sixtieth year, he had been invited by the Marine Department to patrol the south-western coasts and sub-Antarctic islands of New Zealand, and enforce the Seals Fisheries Protection Act.

The early 1870s had seen a revival of whaling about the south of New Zealand, by both Americans and colonials, and as the whales became harder to find it had proved more and more tempting to top up the catch with seal oil and seal skins. Revenue from skins was also improving. With the fashion for tophats, pelts that had been worth about $1.70 each were fetching up to five dollars in the New York market. In 1873, for instance, the colonial whaler Paddy Gilroy had gone to Campbell Island in command of the brigantine *Sarah Pile,* and, because of foul weather, had taken just four whales, so sixty seals were killed to help the cruise make a profit.

The seal populations had made some comeback since the seal rush had ended in the 1820s, but not enough to sustain this kind of activity for very long. In 1878 the New Zealand government passed the Seals Fisheries Protection

Act, which banned sealing from October to June each year, with the option of extending the closed season if necessary. As any Connecticut sealer could have told them, however, October to June was the breeding season, the time when the seals were most accessible, and so it was inevitable that the sealers would flout the law. In March 1881, disturbing rumors having reached Wellington, the Marine Department sent the government steamer *Stella* to the west coast and the Auckland Islands, to count seals and look for poachers.

Her commander, Captain William Grey, returned with a very grim report. He had interviewed quite a number of suspicious characters in known sealing places, and, while he had not found enough evidence to make any arrests, it was obvious to him that the rookeries were being savagely pillaged. Beaches of the west coast that had seen scattered seal life were now quite empty, and he had not seen a single seal in the Auckland Islands. His officially stated opinion was that unless the slaughter was completely stopped for at least two years, the seals species of New Zealand and the sub-Antarctic would soon become extinct.

Alarmed, the government amended the 1878 Act by an Order in Council, banning sealing from November 1, 1881, to June 1, 1884. Then the Marine Department looked around for some way of enforcing it, which was not very easy. The British Navy agreed to ask their captains to keep an eye out for illegal activity, but their ships were not very often in sub-Antarctic waters, and the colonial government's two steamers, *Hinemoa* and *Stella*, were fully committed to the lighthouse branch.

It was evident that a dedicated seals protection vessel was needed, plus an officer of the law to command her. Then, just as the search for a suitable vessel got underway, a small but seaworthy schooner named *Kohimarama* became available. She was almost new, having been built in 1879 as a school ship for delinquent boys—a scheme that had not worked out, as none of the boys had been reformed by the experience. Giving up on the idea, the school closed down, making the schooner redundant. The Marine Department took her over, renamed her *Kekeno* (the Maori word for "fur seal"), and put her in the hands of Greig, who, as an officer of the law with a long history of navigating the southern coasts, was the perfect candidate for the job. Five seamen were sworn in as special constables, provisions and firearms were taken on board, and in April 1882 the little 31-ton *Kekeno* set off on the first of her two-month-long patrols of one of the bleakest, most inclement seas in the world.

While Captain Greig's brief was to apprehend poachers, he was also instructed "to inspect, and if necessary repair and replenish, the stores of provisions" that had been left "for the relief of shipwrecked mariners." As the Marine Department grandly phrased it, the "mission of the *Kekeno*" was to be in the interest of "humanity as well as commerce."

This was also a result of Captain Grey's damning report. The Royal Navy ships *Blanche, Cossack, Nymphe, Sapphire,* and *Emerald* had inspected the castaway depots in the course of infrequent visits to the sub-Antarctic in the 1870s, and had all reported the huts in good order. Since then, however, the sealers had done a great deal of damage. During his 1881 tour of inspection, Grey had found the depots ransacked and vandalized. He had replaced the stores and repaired the huts, but had informed the Marine Department that he was quite convinced that the huts and castaway stores were very likely to be interfered with again.

Captain James Greig would have made inspection of the castaway depots a priority, anyway, as the sad plight of shipwrecked mariners was close to his heart. He had been the captain of the steam-schooner *Southland*, which had gone to the Auckland Islands in 1865, to search for survivors from the American-built clipper ship *Fiery Star*, which had been abandoned off the Chatham Islands on April 23, 1865, after catching fire. Seventy-eight passengers and crew, including the captain, had left the floating furnace in the only two seaworthy lifeboats, leaving the first mate and seventeen volunteer seamen on board. With remarkable doggedness and courage this remnant of the crew had kept on battling the flames, at the same time doing their utmost to work the ship toward land. Just moments before the *Fiery Star* foundered, these brave men were picked up by the ship *Dauntless*, which had glimpsed their rocket of distress. The people in the lifeboats, however, were never seen or heard from again. So Greig's rescue mission to the Auckland Islands had been a failure, something that stayed with him the rest of his life.

On the first *Kekeno* cruise, he had found more than enough damage to the castaway stores and huts to justify regular inspections. The hut at Erebus Cove on Auckland Island had been completely ransacked by sealers, who had used it as a place to boil out seal oil, and had left it in a filthy, stinking state. Greig and his men cleaned it up, repaired the hut, secured the door—which had been left open to the weather—and pasted notices of warning that the season for killing seals was closed.

The depot at Perseverance Harbour had been in a similarly wretched condition. The wooden box at the foot of the beacon was upside down, and when Greig turned it over the contents—an iron pot, a sheath knife, tools, and pans, all rusty, and clothes, all rotten—tumbled out. Greig fixed it up, filled it again, and nailed a notice to the flagstaff—"against killing seals, putting under it an intimation that stores for persons in distress had been placed in a small house about a quarter of a mile farther up the harbour on its west side." The hut, however, had also been vandalized. The provisions "had been consumed or stolen, so that had any shipwrecked persons reached the islands, the humane object for which these depots had been established would have been frustrated" — as Captain Greig reported, concluding with the grim prophesy, "whoever may have been the perpetrators of this outrage, it is certain that their conduct will be universally reprobated."

Now, he was coming to Campbell Island to check the beacon and the hut again, and to replace the stores, if necessary.

"Friday, 14th December, 1883," he noted in his log. "Reached the entrance to Perseverance Harbour at 4 p.m. and anchored at its extreme head at 6 o'clock. Found on the beach there a whaleboat."

This stranded whaleboat was an enlivening discovery. This cruise of inspection was Greig's fifth, and he would have been particularly pleased to catch a few poachers, because the *Kekeno*'s mission was beginning to be clouded by debate. Waters had been charted, but there had been little else to show for the £1300 a year that the enterprise was costing the taxpayers. Not only had there been no arrests, but there had been no highly publicized rescue missions. And so, when the lookout cried out that he had spied a whaleboat drawn up on the mud at the end of Perseverance Harbour, it caused a great deal of excitement.

Captain Greig landed, and inspected the boat, which was sound, though old, and the kind normally used by sealers. Then the constables drew his attention to two men who were hobbling as fast as they could through the tussock toward them, crying out hoarsely as they came. They leaned on sticks that looked a lot like sealers' clubs, so Greig jumped to the conclusion that they were poachers.

This led to an ironically comic incident, as a journalist in *The Lyttelton Times* described. Having taken the two strangers for a couple of lookouts, James Greig decided that they were staging a diversion while the rest of the sealing party was busily hiding their stockpile of skins in the bushes. Accordingly, he organized his troops for capture and arrest. Then Captain Greig saw the terrible condition of the two men, and realized his mistake.

Tierney and Whittle had been on a foraging excursion when to their disbelief and joy they had sighted the little *Kekeno*. After hastily describing their plight, they led Captain Greig to the castaway hut, where Crawford, Huber, Henderson, and Hertwig were lying on beds of grass that had been piled onto the squelching mud floor, and covered with rotten blankets. The four men, far too weak and ill to stand, had been lying in these grim conditions for ten days. Their legs and feet were swollen and black, and covered with boils, while their bodies and faces were emaciated and gaunt. Without the ministrations of Whittle and Tierney, who were themselves in a very bad way, these four wretched souls would most surely have died. As it was, the hut stank of the corruption of Crawford's gangrenous arm.

That all the men were so very ill posed a problem for Greig, because the *Kekeno* was far too small to accommodate six invalids. At the stern there was a tiny after cabin for the captain, while the crew bunked in a larger cabin forward, which had berths along the sides. The two rooms were separated by a minute saloon, which was furnished with a stove and pantry, and had a table built about the foot of the mainmast. There was no hold, the cabin floors being built right on top of the ballast of cast iron, as all she needed to carry was provisions for the two-month cruise, firewood, water, and firearms. So there was not even any space below the floor to put in extra berths.

But, if Greig sailed to New Zealand to get assistance, the four helpless invalids would be left in the care of Whittle and Tierney again, which was impossible to contemplate. All Greig could do was hope that the contents of his medical chest, like his provisions and firewood, would hold out until the *Sarah W. Hunt* returned to pick up her stranded men.

"Made the castaways comfortable for the night," he wrote in his log. Next day, he continued:

> *Blowing strong from N.W. Castaways in greater pain today than they were in yesterday. Lined their hut with sails. Gave them tea, sugar, fresh butter and potatoes, barley soup for dinner with as much apple tart as they could eat. Provided them with clean water, washing soap, oatmeal for poultices, salad oil, ointments, an ample supply of clean woollen and cotton rags, together with lint and wadding from the Medicine Chest, laxative medicines &c. Those for the body and to produce hilarity of spirits I gave them the vessel's "riding light" to burn in the tent after dark. My sailors cut up wood to afford them the cheerful influence of a fire throughout the night and I gave them a year's numbers of "The Young Ladies Journal," which I had brought with me in the vessel for my sailors to read.*

The date of that log entry was Saturday, December 15, 1883. In New Zealand, six hundred miles away, the steamship *Stella* was only just setting out from Wellington. Over the past ten days the castaways had eaten all the canned meat; all that was left was a little hard bread.

Thoughtfully, Captain Greig observed, "the *Kekeno* turned up for them just in the nick of time." As *The Lyttelton Times* solemnly phrased it later, "Had he cast anchor there a few days later he would have helped at a grave-digging."

Adopting the mantle of resident magistrate, Captain Greig took down the formal deposition "of the Second Mate, one of the castaways." Not only would it save time later, but it was a wise precaution. Michael Crawford was the worst off of the six—his dislocated shoulder was very swollen, and the arm below the crippled shoulder so black that Captain Greig thought it would probably have to come off. Crawford was an old sailor, who had suffered from frostbite and exposure as well as the agony of his injury, and his chances did not look good.

The cross-examination was a long process, with Captain Greig formulating patient questions, and Crawford pausing often to summon the strength to whisper his replies.

"Michael Crawford, having been duly sworn deposeth on his oath as follows," wrote Greig:

> *My name is Michael Crawford. I am on the articles of the Schooner "Sarah W. Hunt" of Middleton, Con. U.S.A. 109 tons Miner Master with 15 of a crew all told, as Second Mate ...*
>
> *We sailed from New Bedford, U.S., on the 15th July calling in nowhere until we arrived Macquarrie Island which took place on the first day of November last. The Master and part of the crew landed several times but brought off nothing save a few rabbits. We remained at anchor for ten days at that place and lost one anchor there. Sailed from Macquarrie Island on the 10th day of November and proceeded direct to Campbell Island. Anchored in*

Perseverance Harbour on the 16th day of November. Lay at anchor there from the 16th Nov till the 27th Nov., employed getting a supply of fresh water and searching for seals but killed none. On the 26th Nov. I saw Captain Miner chase a Seal to kill it but it got away. At the time I left New Bedford I was not aware that killing seals was prohibited within the New Zealand boundary. I know it now because I saw a printed notice to that effect a few days ago. I do not know whether Captain Miner knew of this prohibition or not.

On the 27th Nov. Captain Miner ordered me to go in a boat with five men (those now present) and to proceed along the Coast outside of Perseverance Harbour for the purpose of searching for seals. At the time I left the vessel as mentioned, the Mate left with another boat and crew, which took all hands out of the vessel but the Master and Steward. (One man fell overboard and was drowned on the 3rd of October.) Both the Mate and myself were instructed to keep company with each other and to keep close to the land. We departed from the vessel at 5 a.m. on 27th Nov., both boats proceeding down the Harbour and along the Shore Northwards.

All went well until 7 a.m., at which time we were off North East Bay, when the Wind got so strong from about W.S.W. that we were unable to pull to the land. Saw the Mate's boat about sunset, pulling inshore likewise. At length we got wearied out and had to let the boat drift out to sea. Next morning the 28th Nov (Wednesday) we found ourselves to be about ten miles from the land and not far distant from us was the Mate's boat with a sail set. We had a small sail likewise set, both to steady the boat and to keep her to windward. Lost sight of the Mate's boat about 9 a.m. and did not see her again.

Throughout all this day, also Thursday the 29th, Friday the 30th, and part of Saturday, we kept drifting about sometimes losing sight of the land; but in the afternoon of

Saturday the 1st Dec, it moderated sufficiently to enable us to reach North East Harbour. We landed there but found nothing to eat, and not having tasted food since Tuesday, we determined to pull round to Perseverance Harbour, at which place we supposed the vessel would still be. But we mistook the land in the dark, and passed Perseverance Harbour without seeing it, getting into a bay southward of it, which we reached at about 2 a.m. on the Sunday morning. We found nothing to eat at that place but a few shellfish. The wind again freshened up and kept us in that bay until Tuesday the 4th instant, when the weather became moderate and we were able to reach Perseverance Harbour by sailing part of the way and pulling the other, but to our dismay found on our arrival that the vessel had gone.

Captain Greig then asked Crawford what he thought might have been Captain Miner's reasons for not waiting for them to return. The second mate repeated his theory that Streichert's boat and crew had arrived back at the schooner with tales that were so grim that "Captain Miner, judging from the Mate's account and by the violence of the weather together with our non-appearance, had concluded that we never reached land, but had drifted off and perished."

Keeping his thoughts to himself, Greig wrote, "Sworn to and signed before me in a hut near Tucker Cove, in Perseverance Harbour, Campbell island, this 15th day of December 1883," got Michael Crawford to sign it, signed it himself, and then gave it to the other castaways to read. After making sure that they all understood it, he wrote, "We the undersigned Castaways do hereby make oath and say that we have read over the deposition of Michael Crawford, numbered from 1 to 4 [pages] inclusively, and that the particulars therein mentioned are true and correct, and to which we subscribe our names as follows:

    "Will Hertwig
    "Thomas Whittle
    "Alex Hinderson
    "Emil Huber
    "Martin Tierney."

When they had all signed it, Greig signed it again — "J.B. Greig, Resident Magistrate" — and took up a fresh piece of paper. "Wrote a letter addressed to Captain Miner of the American Sealer *Sarah W. Hunt*," he noted in the log that night; "and had it conspicuously and safely placed in the hut (Depôt)." It was only a precaution, as hopefully the *Sarah W. Hunt* would make her appearance very soon, solving Greig's problem of what to do with the castaways.

"Fresh breeze from N.W. Castaways much better to day, and the woebegone look in their faces has given place to one of cheerfulness," Greig recorded on 16 December. His constables were filling in the time usefully — "painted outside of vessel" he wrote on 17 December. "Castaways improving fast; two of them able to walk a little. They finished the last of the bread left in the Depôt today." It was a confirmation of how fortunate the marooned men had been that the *Kekeno* had arrived to check the hut.

On 18 December, "Blowing a strong gale from N.N.W. with continuous rain and thick fog." Greig's men were forced to work below decks, but on the bright side, "Castaways still improving and apparently in high spirits. Three of them able to walk today." The following day, it was still gusting hard, with fog and rain, but "a fourth man can walk a little today."

The next morning, December 20, dawned with fine weather. Perseverance Harbour was calm and serene again. It was possible to imagine the *Sarah W. Hunt* coming into sight around the nearest bend.

Instead, the *Stella* came steaming up the channel.

The Elephant Voyage

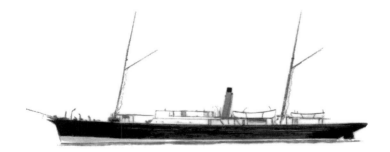

Colonial Government Steamer *Stella*

10: *Public Outrage*

ARRIVALS. December 26, Stella, C G s 136 tons, Gray, from Campbell Island. Passengers — Mr. M Crawford (2nd officer), M Tierney, T Whittle, A Henderson, W Hertwig, E Huber (boat's crew Sarah W Hunt)
— Otago Daily Times, *Shipping Intelligence, December 27, 1883*

Yorkshireman William John Grey, the 38-year-old captain of the *Stella*, was as thoroughgoing a seaman as the Scottish master of the *Kekeno*. Like Greig, he thought little of sailing his ship through turbulent seas to dangerous, rockbound islands and coasts.

The master of the steamship *Stella* was also as punctilious as James Greig in carrying out the paperwork involved. "S. S. *Stella*, 25 December 1883," he wrote, heading up his report to William Seed, Secretary of the Marine Department in Wellington:

> Sir,
> *According to instructions I sailed for Campbell Islands at 1 p.m. on the 15th, to search for the missing crew of the Sarah W. Hunt. Arrived off Campbell Island at 10 p.m. on the 20th after a rough passage and hove to for the night. At daylight of the 21st stood in shore and cruised round the*

Island. Called at North West Bay but could not land, sea too heavy. Stood on to North East Bay and anchored, but could not see anything about so stood on again. Put into Perseverance Harbour and there found one of the boats' crews in the store house, the Second Mate and five men, all very ill, only two able to walk.

I took them on board the Stella and did all we could for them. The Schooner Kekeno was there, and the men tell me that they could not have lived till we got there, only for the arrival of the Schooner. Captain Greig sends you full statements of the boat's crew.

From what I learned from the men, the wind must have shifted sharp to S.E., and drove them back to the Island, so that I determined to push on to the Auckland Islands, in case the First Mate and his crew were driven there. He had a compass in the boat, also two guns and some biscuits, so that there might be a chance for them. Arrived at the Auckland Islands on the 23rd, and searched all through Carnley Harbour, Camp Cove, also the Storehouse, but could not find any traces of them. Stood on for Tardy Inlet, and found the storehouse open and all the things gone, but no trace of anyone about. Called at Enderby Island, and found the storehouse broken open and all the things gone except one case of biscuits; no traces of anyone about. Also found the storehouse at Port Ross broken open and all the things gone except twelve tins of Meat. Here we found traces of people which we took to be about three weeks or a month old. We also found a stove pot in the house, which we remember putting in the store house at Tardy Inlet on the Stella's last trip to the Islands.

After searching about gave up all hopes of the missing crew and sailed for New Zealand on the 24th at noon. I may also state that before leaving Campbell Island I put one case of tinned Meats and some fishing lines &c in the Storehouse.

Captain Greig also put what things he had in tins, also two tins of biscuit into the store. I also gave him all the stores I could spare before leaving. Trusting this will afford all the information required.

 I have &c

 W. J. Grey

Though the six castaways were hurriedly admitted into Dunedin Hospital, they were soon pursued by the press, the news of their arrival having raced about the town. Interviews were permitted, leading to a story that appeared on the editorial page of the *Otago Daily Times* the very next day, December 27, 1883, and was copied by papers throughout the colony.

Headlined, "THE CAMPBELL ISLAND CASTAWAYS—RESCUE OF PART OF THE CREW OF THE *SARAH W. HUNT*," it announced: "The Colonial Government steamer *Stella* arrived at Port Chalmers yesterday morning from Campbell Island" with "Mr. Michael Crawford" and five boat's crew:

Although the men bear visible marks of the sufferings they have undergone, they are a very respectable and intelligent lot of young fellows, who, despite the treatment they seem to have met at the hands of the master of the schooner, speak with great moderation, and evidently strive to make matters appear as bright as possible, and bear their sufferings in a manly spirit.

This speaks volumes for them, particularly when we consider that for a week they were entirely without water, and only had a pound and a half of biscuit in the boat when they left the Sarah W. Hunt with orders to search 'inshore for seals'; while their supply of water was about a gallon, put into a bucket, which capsized shortly after they left the vessel, and it was painful in the extreme to hear the poor fellows describe their sufferings from thirst, and the methods they adopted to quench their craving for water; indeed, some of them tried to drink sea water, but found after taking a little of it they became partially delirious, and were compelled to refrain.

Yet still more painful is it to state that at last they were compelled to moisten their lips with urine, its use being apparently less injurious to them than the salt water. Their feet and legs have also been greatly injured by swellings and excoriations, and it will be some time before they are fit for duty again. They speak in grateful terms of the kindness shown them by Captain Greig, of the Government schooner Kekeno, and Captain Grey, of the Stella, who, with their officers and crews, did all in their power to assist them.

Captain Grey's description of the arrival of the *Stella* at Campbell Island, and the discovery of the castaways followed—"All of them were very ill, and only two out of the six men were able to stand, the whole of the poor fellows being covered with sores on the feet and legs. They were at once taken on board the *Stella*, where everything that could alleviate their sufferings was done, the *Stella*'s crew supplying them with what clothes they could spare."

Grey's attempts to find the other boat were recounted—"After making a further search at all the places that she could, no further hopes were entertained of finding the missing boat's crew, and the *Stella* left for New Zealand at noon on the 24th inst., had a very rough trip, with strong gales and thick weather, and arrived at Port Chalmers early yesterday morning."

The item then continued, "We subjoin the following statements made by the boat's crew."

An interview with Michael Crawford followed. While his account of the voyage and their ordeal closely echoed his deposition to Captain Greig, he no longer made any excuses for Captain Miner. Indeed, his bitter anger at finding out the true situation showed, as he stressed that Miner's mission in coming to New Zealand territorial waters was to hunt for seals. His orders as his boat had left the schooner, he said, were "to search both creeks and bays for seals" and the crews of both boats had been "provided with clubs, skinning-knives, and steels, for the purpose of killing and removing the skins from the seals."

The next to be interviewed was Wilhelm Hertwig, who made the same claim. Their orders had been to "catch seals," he said. "We had clubs and knives for that purpose with us."

With eloquence, the young German went on to describe their ordeal in the boats and the struggle to get to Perseverance Harbour, up to the heart-breaking discovery that the schooner had gone. "We landed, and went to the shelter-shed, where we found two boxes of biscuit, 12 cans boiled mutton, a bottle of salt, some matches, three coats, and four rotten blankets; and very thankful we were to find them.

"After taking a little food, the two men who could walk procured mussels and firewood; and upon the mussels, with the provisions we found in the hut, we lived until the Government schooner *Kekeno* arrived on December 15," he concluded. "The captain behaved very kindly to us, giving us food and clothes, as well as ointment and dressings for our feet, of which we were much in need. In addition to this he lent us some sails to keep the hut warm, for which we were very grateful."

The story reached Christchurch within hours, via a Press Association telegram, and was published the same day, 27 December, under the tiered headlines, "THE MISSING SEAMEN. Rescue of Six Survivors. Terrible Suffering." Undoubtedly, it was read by James Macpherson with a gratifying sense of justification. While it had to be recognized that the six men had survived because of the fortuitous arrival of the *Kekeno,* the fact they had been there at all justified the pressure he had put on the government.

The editor of *The Star* certainly thought so, remarking in the same issue that he hoped that it would teach the government a lesson: "Although the men, after several days' delay, succeeded in reaching the depôt of provisions, yet it is evident that if the schooner *Kekeno* had not arrived and supplied them with additional food, they might have perished. They might have perished also before the Government would have sent a search party for them, unless driven to it by the strong expression of outraged public opinion. The delay in despatching the *Stella* was most discreditable and reprehensible."

In other centers, the attack on the government in general and Rolleston in particular was even more savage, the editor of the *Otago Daily Times* writing on 28 December, "Had the *Kekeno* not chanced to come across them, the *Stella* would have been too late, thanks to Mr. ROLLESTON.

"When we remember that the *Sarah W. Hunt* arrived in Lyttelton on the 9th, and that it was not till the 15th that the *Kekeno* discovered the crew, we are able to estimate the carelessness and want of judgment which Mr. ROLLESTON displayed in the matter."

As the editor went on to point out, the Minister of Lands had been wrong in all his prejudgments — that a boat, once blown away, would never get back to the island; that there were sufficient stores in the castaway huts; that the castaways could easily cross the island on foot. "Had a steamer been despatched from Port Chalmers on the 10th or 11th much suffering might have been spared to the men who have been rescued, and possibly the other boat's crew might have been picked up at sea." The only redeeming factor was that Rolleston "was only *locum tenens* during Major ATKINSON'S absence, so there is something to be said in excuse of the lamentable dilatoriness he displayed."

The editor of *The Timaru Herald* condemned William Rolleston without mercy. The rescue of the six castaways "proves that Mr. Rolleston was entirely wrong in his conclusion that it was not worthwhile to send a steamer, and that the public were quite right in their determination that a steamer should be sent," he lectured in the issue for Saturday, 29 December. It was obvious to him that the Member for Avon "shared the belief avowed by the captain of the *Sarah W. Hunt,* namely, that the men had been blown away and lost at sea, and that, therefore, there was no occasion to take any further trouble about them." Instead, the poor fellows "were cast ashore half dead with exposure and fatigue, and barely able to crawl."

Granted, the *Kekeno* did find them, "as Mr. Rolleston calculated she would; but not until they were at the very point of death." If the government had been doing its proper job, "these unfortunate creatures would have been spared a week of frightful suffering," and there would have been a good chance of saving the men in the first mate's boat, too. "A very grave responsibility," the editor declared, "rests upon the Government for the consequences of their inaction."

"The six rescued sailors of the *Sarah W. Hunt* had a most providential escape from a horrible death," wrote the editor of the *West Coast Times* on January 4, 1884. "Their suffering would have been much abated had the Government despatched a steamer promptly for their relief. A more discreditable piece of red-tapeism, than the delay of the Government in sending help to the shipwrecked crew of the *Sarah W. Hunt*, has never been heard of in this Colony or perhaps out of it," he exclaimed. "It is very lucky that six men out of twelve were saved, and the Government may thank their stars that they were rescued alive."

Miner was not spared criticism—"The captain of *Sarah W. Hunt* has also perhaps learned a lesson from this mishap as to the advisability of jumping to conclusions," the editor of the *Otago Daily Times* wrote, while the editor of the *Timaru Herald* reflected that, "we do not for a moment intend to exonerate the captain of the *Sarah W. Hunt*—

> *His conduct throughout appears to have been simply disgraceful, and it is to be hoped that some steps may be taken to make him answer for it. If the accounts given by the crew are correct—and there is no reason to doubt their correctness—the captain did a thing which any seaman ought to be forever ashamed of. He helped himself to stores from the depôt which has been provided by the Government for the use of castaways, and was with difficulty prevailed on to return them. A more discreditable or unseamanlike deed we never heard of.*
>
> *Then, he abandoned his crew to their fate quite unnecessarily; and, as it now turns out, his unworthy haste in getting away with his vessel, was the direct cause of much of the misery they endured. If he had remained where he was a day or two longer, the mate's boat would have rejoined the schooner. As it was, the poor wretches returned to the bay,*

after infinite labor and hardships too dreadful to think of, only to find the schooner gone.

But the worst part of the captain's behavior, and the part that seems most incapable of explanation, was his cold-blooded indifference about his men after his arrival at Lyttelton. Having secured his own safety and that of his property, he never troubled his head any more about his men. He neither endeavored to rescue them himself nor sought the assistance of the Government. On the contrary, he rather discouraged the proposal to send relief to them; and when the Stella was starting he managed to be out of the way, and stayed behind comfortably at Lyttelton. There is something very suspicious about the whole of the captain's behavior; something which requires to be cleared up, and which, we hope, will be cleared up when he is confronted with the men whom he so shamefully deserted. But putting the most favorable interpretation upon it, he cannot acquit himself of the charge of culpable neglect of what any truehearted sailor would have deemed his highest and most urgent duty.

Though he must have been uncomfortably aware of the criticism, Captain Miner made no mention of either that or the miraculous rescue in his logbook. The entire entry for 28 December 1883—the day after the news of the arrival of the *Stella* with the six men on board was published in the Christchurch *Star*—runs, "Pleasant weather, saw steward on shore gave him in charge for absenting without leave. At court at 2 PM, steward was discharged. Engaged Mr. Warren as watchman."

Undoubtedly, Miner was annoyed that the steward had been discharged without punishment, particularly as he was made to pay court costs—according to the papers, "The

Bench dismissed the case with costs, as Duncan's articles of shipment were not dated." However, the omission of any mention of the rescue seems deliberate, particularly as his subsequent logbook entries remain silent on the subject.

On January 4, 1884, the *Stella* arrived in Lyttelton, and on the following day Captain Grey delivered the whaleboat he had collected at Campbell Island. Though it is easy to imagine the pointed comments that were passed when the two shipmasters met, there is no record of that, either. The entire entry in Miner's logbook for 5 January runs, "Pleasant weather. Steward on shore. Received Boat from Steamer *Stella*."

However, though he must have been preoccupied by the antics of his steward, that was not Miner's reason for making no mention of the rescue in his logbook. Instead, it was simple caution. According to maritime law, he would have to hand in his logbook to the Customs House when he got to his home port, so condemning himself within its pages was not a good option.

He did write a letter to his wife — which she sent to the papers. On February 29, *The New York Times* noted that "Mrs. Minor, wife of Capt. Sanford Minor, of the schooner *Sarah W. Hunt*, owned in Hartford, Conn." had received a letter from her husband giving "the particulars of the loss of seven of her crew —

> *She left New-Bedford on July 10 for a two years' cruise. On Nov. 27, near Campbell Island, Perseverance Harbor, two boats with six men each left the vessel to search for seals in shore. They took no provisions, intending to return in a few hours. The Captain and steward remained on board the vessel. Heavy squalls sets in, and the boats could not be found, and after three days' unsuccessful search the captain*

and steward manned the schooner and succeeded in working her into Littleton, New-Zealand, arriving Dec. 18, having sailed 630 miles through severe gales.

The Governor of New-Zealand sent out a steamer in search of the missing boat's crews and found one. These six men are now in the hospital. The others are probably drowned or have died from starvation. On the outward passage J. C. Jaeger, seaman, fell from aloft and was drowned.

That was bad enough for Miner, but worse was in store.

The reports written by Captains Greig and Grey had reached the Marine Department, and, because of the forthright nature of their criticisms of Captain Miner's actions, an immediate start was made on registering an official complaint in Washington.

"Sir," the Secretary of the Marine Department, William Seed, wrote to the "United States Consular Agent" at Christchurch, in a letter that was dated 3 January, 1884:

I have been directed by the Minister having charge of this Department to transmit for your information the enclosed copies of documents descriptive of the circumstances in which the crew of one of the boats of the United States Schooner "Sarah W. Hunt" were found at Campbell Island by the Government Schooner "Kekeno" and afterwards brought away and landed at Dunedin by the Lighthouse Steamer "Stella," which vessel had been specially dispatched by the Government to search for the Schooner's missing boats.

Copies of the depositions of the Master and Steward of the "Sarah W. Hunt" made before the Collector of Customs at Lyttelton, after their arrival at that Port on the 8th ultimo, are also enclosed.

It would appear from the particulars given in these documents that the Master left the Island somewhat precipitately after the disappearance of the two boats, for it will be seen that if he had remained for only a few days longer, one of them would have joined him, and he would then have been able to have taken his vessel in search of the other boat. He, however, sailed away from the Island early on the morning of the third day following the one on which the boats left the vessel.

The crew of the rescued boat succeeded in reaching North East Harbour on the 1st December and on the 4th December they arrived at Perseverance Harbour the place where they had left the vessel only a week previously, and were dismayed to find that she had sailed. If it had not been for the food the men were able to procure at one of the provision depôts maintained on the Island by this Department for the sustenance of castaway seamen, and for the timely aid produced by the Master of the "Kekeno," they would probably have perished.

I have the honour to be
Sir,
Your obedient Servant
William Seed, Secretary, Department of Marine

Joseph Frederick Ward, being just a stand-in, informed Mr. Seed by telegraph that the right person to contact was Mr. Gilderoy W. Griffin, United States Consul in Auckland, creating a hiatus in the process. This provided a chance for officialdom to abandon the idea of registering a complaint, something that certainly was considered, as the government (and undoubtedly William Rolleston himself) would have liked nothing better than to see public interest in the *Sarah W. Hunt* affair die a natural death.

The attacks in the newspapers, however, continued unabated, with the editor of the Nelson *Colonist* publishing his own condemnation on Friday, 4 January. "The conduct of the members of the Christchurch Chamber of Commerce in spontaneously guaranteeing over £600, if needed, for the purpose of searching for the missing crew is a fine example of public generosity and humanity," he declaimed; "which contrasts favorably with Mr. Rolleston's dilatory and grudging spirit." As the editor went on to muse, the "story of the *Sarah W. Hunt's* rescued men and the sufferings" should be printed and placed in every depot, as an inspiration to others. "The chief lesson derived from the incident is the necessity for prompt action where human life is in jeopardy, and we trust we shall never again hear of hesitation on the part of the authorities should a similar emergency arise."

For William Rolleston, this continued barrage of criticism was cruelly ironic, as he was known for his support of the underdog. He had devoted his political career to looking after the interests of common men, arguing for their equal rights to land and the chance of making a good living, if not a fortune. Against the lobbying of the land-barons, he had argued for the rights of men with small capital to become landowners. That he, with his humanitarian ideals, should be accused of callousness was galling enough, but it was also a political blow, one that he knew his enemies would seize. And so another attempt was made to register an official complaint with the State Department in Washington.

This time, William Seed was instructed to communicate with Consul Griffin in Auckland. This second letter was composed on January 5, 1884, addressed to "W. Griffin esq., United States Consul, Auckland" and made an attack on quite a different front—that of sealing in New Zealand territory, and out of season. "The object" of the *Sarah W. Hunt*'s "mission to the Island named was to hunt for and capture seals, which pursuit, at the present time, is contrary to law, as will be seen by the enclosed copy of an Order in Council dated the 18th October 1881," he lectured. "Printed notices containing the purport of this Order are posted conspicuously on the Island."

And, as the seamen had testified to seeing them, the master of the *Sarah W. Hunt* must have seen them, too—"yet in defiance thereof he sent his boats in search of seals with the manifest object of killing and taking as many as could be caught." As Seed went on to point out, after describing the limits of New Zealand territory in pedantic detail, "it is not lawful at any time for persons other than British subjects to hunt for and take seals within the territorial boundaries of this Colony." Maybe, he conceded, this was not generally known in the United States. Accordingly, Mr. Seed had been asked to request Mr. Griffin "to communicate the fact to the proper authorities in that country."

This caught Consul Griffin in a state of ignorance, one that he was not accustomed to at all. Though the rescue of the *Sarah W. Hunt* boat's crew had been reported in the Auckland papers, he had heard nothing from the consular agent in Dunedin, Henry Driver, who should have interviewed the castaways and forwarded an official report. Griffin had not even known that the Canterbury sub-consul, C. B. Taylor, had left Christchurch to return to the States, or that Mr. Ward was filling in at the Christchurch office while Mr. Taylor was away.

It was obviously high time he took charge of the situation. After writing a letter to Seed acknowledging receipt of his letter and expressing thanks for the "timely aid extended to the seamen" Griffin wired both Henry Driver in Dunedin, and Joseph Ward in Christchurch, tersely reminding them of their consular duties.

Born and raised in Louisville, Kentucky, Gilderoy Wells Griffin was a career diplomat, yet very artistic. It was an impression he reinforced with a carefully groomed appearance, which included a glossy Dickens-style beard and moustache, with clean-shaven cheeks.

In 1861, aged just twenty-one, and newly graduated from Louisville University, Griffin had been admitted to the bar, but this, apparently, did not suit him, because in 1871, after a spell as the associate editor of the *Louisville Commercial and Industrial Gazette*, he started work for the State Department. His first posting was to the consulate at Copenhagen, where he performed well until 1875, when his career was marred by scandal. His first wife, Alice (who described herself as a "poetess"), inherited a large legacy and ran off, taking their five-year-old daughter, Virgilena, with her, because she did not feel like sharing the money.

A year later, after marrying his second wife, Myra, Griffin moved to Apia, Samoa, where he was outstandingly successful, negotiating a treaty of friendship and commerce with the chiefs, and raising the U. S. flag at the king's house. If it had not been for German intervention, he would have overseen the ceding of the island nation to America; as it was, one port in Tutuila became United States territory, and an important coaling station on the steamship route.

Then, in 1879, he was promoted to the New Zealand mission, and arrived on July 3, on the steamer *City of New York*. Tragedy intervened—within months of taking up his post, on January 6, 1880, Myra suddenly and unexpectedly died, at the age of just twenty-nine. "The deceased arrived in this city with her husband only a few months ago, and by her amiable disposition had won the esteem of many friends, who will be sorry to learn of this sad event," noted *The New Zealand Herald*, which went on to remark that the flags of all the other consulates in the town were flown half-mast as a gesture of respect.

Despite this personal catastrophe (and the hurried trip back to Kentucky that followed), Gilderoy Griffin soon proved himself to be a competent consular officer, one who kept a firm hand at the helm. He had much on his side, including a methodical mind, and a clear vision of his job. "The principal duties of this Consulate consist in attending to ships business such as discharging and shipping seamen, settling disputes between masters and crews" and in examining and certifying "invoices, landing certificates, &c." he summarized later, adding, "Another important duty is that of preparing reports upon the commercial relations of the United States and New Zealand."

He was particularly gifted at this last, as writing reports was a task he enjoyed. It was typical of him that even when he was in Kentucky getting his domestic affairs in order after Myra's demise, he still managed to produce a 2,000-word summary called *The Goldfields of New Zealand*. Like all his reports, this was printed in Washington, and distributed worldwide, something that greatly impressed New Zealand newspaper editors, especially when it became evident that Consul Griffin was using his reports to lobby for preferential trade between New Zealand and his own country. They asked for, and got, permission to reprint his statistic-studded studies, and they became a frequent feature in the papers.

Griffin did not limit himself to official reports. Back in 1869, he had published a biographical sketch of George

Dennison Prentice (the co-founder of the *Louisville Journal*) and had followed this up with *Studies in Literature*. Then came a biography of Colonel Charles Stewart Todd (with whom he had worked on the Louisville *Gazette*), and a book about Denmark called *Danish Days*. Once settled in New Zealand, he contributed essays about the country to a science magazine.

As the editor of the *Auckland Star* enthused on 21 May 1881, the American consul, "whose reputation is already well-established among the literati of America" had been penning "sketches of New Zealand" which were published in that august journal, *Scientific American*; he was certain that everyone would agree that this was wonderful publicity and no small honor to the country. The editor of the *New Zealand Herald* was equally admiring, becoming Griffin's loyal fan to the extent of reporting his every movement and speech. In the issue for May 21, 1881, he enthused, "For many years the Government of the United States was very unfortunate in the choice of Consular representatives at this port, and no doubt the interests of the States suffered in consequence" but, with the arrival of "Mr. G. W. Griffin, the present Consul, a change took place."

Mr. Griffin's only criticism of his post—or so he had confided to the writer—was that it was so hard to find American whisky in New Zealand; but undoubtedly, as the editor joked, the "celebrated whiskys" produced by his home state of Kentucky would soon be readily available here, as evidence of the consul's indefatigable endeavors.

So, for Gilderoy Wells Griffin, life in New Zealand had become a placid routine of writing reports and accepting social invitations, occasionally punctuated by pleasant public appearances. On December 7, the same day that Captain Miner arrived at Lyttelton and the strange saga of the *Sarah W. Hunt* began to unfold, Consul Griffin was "warmly applauded" as a guest of honor at a banquet celebrating a new stamping battery in the gold-mining town of Te Aroha, where he delivered a toast dedicated to the captains of industry.

But now, with the arrival of Mr. Seed's letter, that comfortable routine was to be drastically disturbed.

11: *The Castaways Retrieved*

> *They are reported to be an altogether better sort of young fellows, and state that previously to shipping on the schooner they had no nautical experience whatever*
> — Manawatu Times, *January 8, 1884*

Joseph Ward received the terse telegram from Griffin on January 8, 1884, the same day that Griffin wrote to both the State Department in Washington, and William Seed, the Secretary of Marine. Evidently stricken that the chief consul had never heard of him before, he immediately wired an explanation—that he, Joseph Frederick Ward, had taken over as Consular Agent while Mr. Charles Benjamin Taylor was obliged to be absent from New Zealand, and that he, Mr. Ward, being "a leading merchant of Christchurch," was eminently eligible for the post.

Then Ward hurried to Lyttelton in an urgent quest for Captain Sanford Miner. According to the previous day's edition of *The Star*, five of the seamen were well enough to be discharged from Dunedin hospital. Once they were returned to the forecastle of the *Sarah W. Hunt*, the schooner was likely to up anchor and away, and the consular agent knew now that it was imperative that the castaways should give formal evidence before leaving New Zealand.

After finding him, and checking with him that he had not heard from the consular agent in Dunedin, either, Ward instructed Miner to go there right away, and retrieve his men. Then, if Driver had failed to take their depositions, which looked likely, Captain Miner would have to bring them to Ward, so he could hear their testimonies, and a full report to Mr. Griffin could be written.

Miner, however, was less than cooperative. Not only was he very reluctant to leave his schooner, but he objected to the cost of the fare.

As he did not know what the procedure should be, Ward requisitioned consular funds to cover his passage, and firmly saw the shipmaster off on the steamer *Manapouri*. "I left Lyttelton on the 8th of January," Miner testified later. He arrived at Dunedin on the morning of January 10, and immediately set out on his own quest, which was to find Henry Driver.

When Sanford Miner located Driver's office that morning, it was to face an unexpectedly formidable challenge. The American representative in Dunedin was a handsome man with a broad forehead, dark-brown beard, fine eyes, and a brightly direct, aggressive stare—a stare that reflected his personality. Henry Driver, once dubbed "a swaggering unprincipled Yankee" by his Melbourne bank manager, was known throughout town as a charismatic and opportunistic entrepreneur.

Henry Driver had been first brought to the attention of the State Department in 1862, when the current consul in New Zealand, George Leavenworth, forwarded a petition that had been signed by nineteen Melbourne merchants, which recommended Driver for a consular post in Dunedin.

"The recent flow of Emigrants into the Otago settlement N. Z. has caused a number of American Ships to find their way to the Port of Dunedin," the testimonial began, then went on to state that the appointment of Henry Driver as consular agent there "would give much satisfaction to numerous personal and mercantile friends in Victoria" — a sentiment that the U.S. consul in Melbourne, James Maguire, declared he was "happy to endorse."

What Leavenworth and the Secretary of State thought of the idea is unknown, but they were probably puzzled, as Maguire had no legal standing in New Zealand. George Leavenworth forwarded the petition without comment, and when Washington did not respond the matter should have been dropped. Henry Driver, a confirmed adventurer, was never deterred by official silence, however.

Born in Delaware in 1831, as a young man he had travelled to the Victoria goldfields to speculate in sheep and the importation of Yankee trade goods. In 1861 he had followed the Otago gold rush to Dunedin, where he set up as a horse-trader. Then he went on to play a prominent part in local politics, winning a seat on the Otago Provincial Council and becoming a Member of Parliament — which should have automatically disqualified him for any U.S. consular post, but somehow did not.

This was because Henry Driver was closely linked with the powerful New York shipbuilder, William H. Webb, who was expanding into steamers, and eyeing the prospects of the Pacific. With the end of the Civil War, a battle had commenced between American interests and British maritime merchants for domination of the Pacific Ocean, and the various mail routes were an important part of this. Webb proposed a line of mail steamers — in which, of course, he would have a huge financial interest, as well as being their builder — running between Australia, New Zealand, Honolulu, and California, and connecting with the newly constructed transcontinental railroad at San

Francisco. While the State Department looked upon the idea with favor, Congress had failed to vote the subsidy that was needed to get the line started, so when Driver volunteered to lobby the New Zealand government to make up the shortfall, Webb backed him to the hilt.

Because of his powerful patron, Driver did not scruple to call himself "the only representative of the United States in New Zealand," after George Leavenworth left his post in 1864. The next appointee, William Wright, took office in 1867, but still Driver continued to head his correspondence "Consulate of the United States of America at Dunedin, N.Z." and still he insisted on filing reports directly to the State Department, instead of routing them through the consul's office, as was proper.

The situation was further complicated by Daniel McIntyre, the consular agent in Wellington at the time, who also tried to claim that he was the official consul. The appointee who succeeded Wright, James George White, battled both with vigor, leading to a war of words that, as the State Department commented, "did nothing to enhance the prestige of the United States in New Zealand," but managed to deter McIntyre, who gave up and took the job of Marine Assessor in Lyttelton. Henry Driver, however, argued on, confident of the support of William H. Webb.

In June 1874, the State Department's opposition wilted. White was fired (at least partly because Webb had written to the Secretary of State, accusing White of incompetence), and Henry Driver was appointed to the position of consul, with an annual salary of $1500. There was a proviso — that he would move to Auckland, the official site of the consulate. This last was ignored, Driver claiming that he could manage American shipping affairs from a distance, with the help of the local telegraph line (which his own firm had built, after he had lobbied for it in parliament and given the contract to himself). His contract with the State Department also forbid him from conducting private trade, but a letter to Webb fixed that, too. Within six months Driver's powerful sponsor had procured an official exemption—Webb's last favor, before he sold his steamers to the Pacific Mail Steam Ship Line, of which Henry Driver promptly became the local agent—but a very profitable one for his protégé.

It was the refusal to move to Auckland that spelled the end of his tenure as United States Consul. A message from the State Department, dated May 19, 1876, instructed Driver to leave Dunedin and head north, a direction which they sternly expected to "be complied with without further correspondence with the Department." But still Driver prevaricated, playing for time by putting off an answer until August, when he wrote that the instructions "have been in my possession for so short a time that it is impossible for me to advise a compliance therewith."

Meantime, however, the State Department lost patience, and a letter demanding his resignation arrived. Driver sent in his resignation at once, "to deal with as you think proper," at the same time suggesting that New Zealand should be divided into two parts, so that they could have one consul in Auckland, and another (himself) in Dunedin, "this important part of the colony." Washington, in reply, merely asked him to think about a successor.

And so, when the *Sarah W. Hunt* affair evolved, Driver was just the consular agent in Dunedin. And, like McIntyre in Lyttelton, he was pompous enough to resent his down-grading in status.

It is not surprising, then, that Captain Miner found Henry Driver as offhand as McIntyre had been when he had first landed in Lyttelton. The man from Delaware had not even bothered to reply to Consul Griffin's telegram, and neither had he interviewed the seamen.

With Miner, Driver finally went to the hospital, to find Hertwig, Tierney, Henderson, Whittle, and Huber almost fully recovered, though Crawford was still seriously ill, with fears that his arm would have to be amputated. The five ordinary seamen had been pronounced cured of "frostbite, privation" and were ready to be discharged into the consular agent's care.

Driver, however, flatly refused to accept them. Neither would he take down their depositions. This was because, as Captain Miner glumly stated, "the crew positively refused to rejoin the ship." Bolstered by the public support they had received over the past couple of weeks, the sailors defied both the law and the formidable consular agent, and staunchly declined to go back on board the *Sarah W. Hunt*.

According to an item in the Dunedin *Herald*, published that same day, January 10, the five readily agreed to be interviewed by a reporter, and waxed eloquent when asked for their reasons for mutiny. It was not just the fact that Captain Miner had abandoned them that rankled, they said, but his treatment of them, too. Explained Emil Huber, "The captain was all right for a couple of days just after we left New Bedford, and then commenced to swear and be pretty rough. One of my mates here was knocked down by him with a pair of sea boots, and could not take his place in the watch for a couple of days."

Another impassioned complaint was the scantiness of the food, Huber saying, "For the first couple of months we had enough to eat, and then our rations were shorter and shorter." His companions backed him up, declaring that "during the greater part of the time they were on the ship they were almost starved."

Some of Thomas Whittle's worst memories, he said, were of Macquarie Island, where "they lost an anchor and were kept there for ten days, pulling in the boats for eighteen hours a day when attempts were being made to recover it. "He corroborated Huber's statement as to the shortness of their supply of food," the *Herald* added.

Whittle went so far as to swear to the interviewer that the only way Captain Miner could get him back on board the *Sarah W. Hunt* was in shackles. He would rather serve a term of imprisonment than sail on that schooner, he forcefully declared. As the journalist commented, "The men all seem to have a dread of being taken back to the schooner, which is now lying at Lyttelton." And Mr. Crawford, the erstwhile second mate, was at one with his men on the issue—"So dissatisfied is he with the treatment he received that he says that he would not willingly rejoin the vessel for a thousand dollars."

For the men, though the publicity was satisfying, a major problem loomed. However reluctant they might be to clap eyes on the *Sarah W. Hunt* again, they had to get to Lyttelton to retrieve their clothes and other possessions. But, after being discharged from hospital on the following day, January 11, they found that did not have a single coin between them, so had no means of getting to the port. "The captain would pay passage if they would return to the vessel," reported the *West Coast Times*, "but they refused. Having no money, they have applied to the American Consul, Mr. Driver, but he says he can do nothing for them." As far as Henry Driver was concerned, the men were now common deserters, with no claim on consular funds, and he felt no compunction about turning them away from his door.

The press and the public were appalled. The men had been through hell, and deserved a great deal better than this! The German community in Dunedin, who had taken the castaways under their wing, sent a telegram to the Colonial Secretary, Thomas Dick, applying for railway passes so they could get to Lyttelton to retrieve their clothes. The telegraphed reply curtly informed them that "the minister regrets that he cannot authorize further expense in respect of the seamen of the *Sarah W. Hunt,* who being American citizens, should apply to the United States Consul."

Mr. Driver remained obdurate, so "several kindly disposed gentlemen took their case in hand, and obtained for them free passage on one of the Union Company's boats, and also provided them with pocket money," reported the Christchurch *Star*. The five men were "loud in their praise of the generous action taken here, and the determined way in which their cause was taken up when all hope seemed lost. They also desire it to be known that their passage from Dunedin to Christchurch was secured through the liberality of a private gentleman (a German) and his friends, in the southern town. They are beholden for it neither to the American Consul here, nor to our own Government."

"As I am timid or confident enough to consider myself the German referred to, I beg to state that, upon my representation, the Union Steamship Company gave the five men their trip per Wanaka to Lyttelton free of all cost, and not myself," wrote a gentleman who called himself "Palmam Qui Meruit Ferat" to the *Otago Daily Times,* adding dryly, "I may mention that a week after the above free passes were granted to a team of cricketers."

So Whittle, Tierney, Huber, Henderson, and Hertwig made their own way Lyttelton on board the steamship *Wanaka* — "by the same steamer as myself, their passages being given them by the owners of the steamer," testified Miner later, without going into details about what must have been an interesting passage. After reporting their arrival on 16 January, the *Star* added, "The mate who was in charge of the boat is still laid up in Dunedin Hospital. The men even yet show signs of the suffering and hardship they underwent, and are still sore-footed."

The conscientious sub-consul, Joseph Frederick Ward, met the *Wanaka*, took the men in charge, and organized board and lodging in Christchurch, paying for this out of funds that Gilderoy Griffin had authorized. The next step was to hold a formal inquiry into the men's public allegations, so a report could be sent to Washington — or so Griffin instructed Ward. Because of Henry Driver's failure to stop the men from giving interviews, enough damage had been done already, and the chief aim now was to keep them from talking to any more reporters. Accordingly, the consular agent was to make absolutely certain that the press was not invited.

Significantly, however, the three German-speaking seamen — Alexander Henderson, Wilhelm Hertwig, and Emil Huber — were adopted by the German citizens of Christchurch with the same enthusiasm and patriotic sympathy that their compatriots had demonstrated in Dunedin. And on Monday, January 20 — the evening before the inquiry — the German club "Concordia" invited the trio to be their guests at the fortnightly gathering of the club at the Wellington Hotel.

"The routine business having been disposed of, some visitors, including three of the rescued sailors of the *Sarah W. Hunt,* were received and entertained in the hospitable German style, and those presented spent a very pleasant evening," recorded the *Star.* And there they met the German ambassador, the eminent Julius von Haast — a fine scientist, but a man with so little political acumen that William Rolleston called him an "idiot."

And the good doctor was to play a well-meant, but very ill-judged, part in the legal drama to come.

12: *The Consular Inquiry*

An enquiry was held this afternoon by the acting American consul into the charges brought by the rescued crew of the Sarah W. Hunt against Captain Miner
— Evening Post, *Wellington January 22, 1884*

"Christchurch, N. Z.. Jan 21st 1884," wrote Mr. Ward (or his clerk) at the start of the inquiry:

> *"Depositions taken before*
> *"J. F. Ward*
> *"Acting Consular Agent, U. S. A.*
> *"Christchurch, N. Zealand."*

Martin Tierney took the stand first. He was a slight man, five feet, five inches tall, black-haired, with brown eyes. Though just twenty-two years old, he was confident and self-assured enough to act as the leading spokesman for the crew.

"My name is Martin Tierney," he said, then launched into the story of his recruitment:

"I was engaged by Mr. Poyle (I think) in New York about 9th July for a sailing voyage for nine months," he said, adding that the ship was not named. "No wages were mentioned—he told me it was a kind of fishing voyage."

The other men had been recruited that day, too, so they had gone in a group to New Bedford in the steamer *Old Colony*, arriving on the morning of 10 July 1883—"had breakfast & boarded vessel."

Evidently in reply to a question from the consular agent, Tierney stressed, "I am an American of no particular calling, I was never at sea before. I shipped as a landsman or green hand." Asked about the shipping process, he said, "We signed articles in the Cabin in the presence of the Captain & a man who represented himself as a Custom House Officer, he had no uniform on, but Custom House officers usually wear uniforms in the States."

Perhaps because of this, when the so-called officer asked him to sign as an able seaman, Tierney had "objected & shipped only as greenhand." Asked if anyone had forced him to sign, he admitted, "I signed willingly there being no compulsion used to join."

Abruptly the topic changed to the allegations that had been made in the press about the captain's treatment of the men: "I was witness to some brutality on the part of the Captain," he said—"to Tommy Ennis by striking him on the back with a rope's end. He was coiling a rope at the after hatch. I was at the wheel—

> *On October 3rd or 4th a seaman by name Julius Jaeger fell overboard from the mast head, I was below at breakfast at the time, an alarm was given & I rushed on deck with rest of the watch. The Captain at the time was not on deck, the chief mate, the officer of the watch was also not on deck, he was in the forecastle below, the steward gave orders to cut the lashings, by this time the Captain arrived on deck with the officer of the watch. The man was in sight. The steward came out of the galley with a big knife & commenced cutting the*

lashing himself, assisted by another man. The boat was launched & three or four men manned it. I was not one of the boat's crew. After the boat had searched for ten minutes the Captain ordered the boat in, he having hove to after the boat was launched. The vessel I think must have been traveling four or five knots an hour with a moderate sea. I did not see anything of the man after the boat was launched & the schooner hove to. I could not state positively how long it took to launch the boat.

"The Captain although he threatened, never actually used any brutality towards me," Tierney went on, adding feelingly, "I never had half enough to eat while I was on board."

The evidence shifted to events at Macquarie Island, "where the ship lost an anchor & we were searching in the two whale boats for eighteen hours a day for ten days & never found it. We proceeded then to Campbell's Island & anchored in Perseverance Harbour. Landed & got water next day & remained there about two or three weeks."

Then came the day when all hands were called on deck and ordered to man the boats and search for seals. Again, Tierney testified that they had knives and clubs in the boats, and that their orders were to kill any seals they found. "No provisions were in the boats except about one pound & a half of hard bread for the six men in our boat, also one gallon of water. It was our intention to get back that same evening.

After being out about one and a half hours, a land breeze sprung up and increased into a gale and prevented us either pulling or sailing. The boats were not fit for a sail having no centre board nor keel. We were down out of sight of land.

*This was on a Tuesday. We did not sight land for one day &
sighted the Chief Mate's boat on the Wednesday morning.
We tried to hold communication with them but it was
blowing so hard we lost sight of them in about an hour & a
half & never saw them again. We pulled hard till
Saturday — a fair breeze sprang up & carried us towards
land. Altho' we could not see land we had an idea of its
position from the sun's direction. We sighted land during
the morning and landed on Campbell's Island in the evening
about seven o'clock. During the time we were out my feet
were very sore & I suffered intensely from hunger & thirst.
On the Saturday morning we succeeded in catching a few
gills of rain water in our oil coats.*

*On landing we got water & but discovered we were not
in the right harbour & tried the same night & got into
another harbour but found this was wrong. As we were then
so exhausted we landed the boat & I carried William Huber
as he was not able to walk. We rested ourselves for about two
hours, it being about midnight. It was very cold. We
launched the boat again and pulled into another harbour
about five miles along shore & got in there about 4 o'clock on
Sunday morning. We had not then obtained anything to eat.
The wind changed & kept us there till Tuesday morning —
We found two mussels each only. The wind moderated at
about six o'clock — snowing at the time — we pulled down the
same direction we had come from about four miles & found
Perseverance Harbour. We must have passed it in the
darkness. This was four o'clock in the afternoon. We found
the schooner had left & thought that the other boat's crew
had gone in before us & all had gone in search for us. As
they did not return after waiting three days we then gave up
all hopes of being saved.*

But salvation did arrive: "After being on the island about eleven days the N. Z. Govt. Schooner "*Kekeno*" called & rescued us. Our feet were very swollen. He provided us with provisions sails & clothing. He waited four or five days for a fair wind with the intention of taking us to the Bluff NZ but the govt. steamer "*Stella*" arrived & took us all aboard & landed us at Port Chalmers New Zealand."

This should have been the end of Tierney's testimony, but Ward was not satisfied. Evidently because some of the descriptions of ill-treatment had applied to men who, being dead, could not corroborate his statements, he wanted to check for inconsistencies.

Yes, he was in the whaleboat when the captain struck Alexander Henderson, Tierney stated in reply to Ward's question; the incident had happened while they were searching for the lost anchor at Macquarie.

"The reason the Captain struck him was I thought for placing a rope in a wrong position, he struck him with his fist. I also saw the Captain strike the same man on the nose with a piece of iron whilst on the schooner about three weeks before our arrival at Macquarie's Island. I did not know what provocation the Captain had for doing this. I also saw the Captain kick & strike Joseph Arthur one of the boat's crew that went in search for Jaeger when he fell overboard. This occurred after hoisting the boat in. This was for not hauling on the tackle quick enough when getting the boat in."

With that, Ward had finally finished. Tierney signed the testimony on the last page, and initialed the previous five. Then Captain Miner, who had been making notes, asked for a cross examination, which Ward allowed.

He said to Tierney, "You shipped in my presence?"
"Yes."

"Who told you the man was a Custom House officer?"

"The man himself told me so."

"What sail was the ship under when the man fell overboard?"

"I do not recollect."

"Was the schooner hove to after the boat was put out?"

Martin Tierney nodded, saying, "The schooner was hove to after the boat was launched."

Captain Miner sat down, and the next seaman was called.

Alexander Henderson was thirty years of age, and five feet, three inches tall, with brown skin, dark brown hair, and dark eyes. He began, "My name is Alexander Henderson; I am a German by birth." He had lived in America for about ten years, he said, and was "a brass finisher by trade. I've also sailed as a fireman on board steamers trading between Antwerp and New Jersey," he went on, but had never worked under sail.

He had gone to Pearl's office looking "for a berth as fireman," and Pearl had told him "he had no vacancies for firemen but he had a good chance for sailors.

"I told him I was no sailor," Henderson continued; "but he replied the captain would take greenhands." Like Tierney, Henderson had not been given the name of the vessel, just the information that he would have to go to New Bedford to join her. "I agreed to go with him to New Bedford. We left New York in the steamer and arrived at New Bedford early the following morning, and after breakfast we went together on board the schooner *Sarah W. Hunt*.

"At the time I went on board I had no idea that the vessel was going sealing," he went on, "but before signing the shipping agent told me it was for a sealing voyage to last nine months. I signed articles in the cabin before Captain Miner and another man who stated he was a custom house officer, except that he had no uniform on. I asked why we did not sign at the Custom House & he told me as I before stated he was a Custom House officer & this satisfied me." Accordingly, even though no one had read the articles out to him, Henderson signed the paper. Like some of the others, he wanted to post letters, but was told he was not allowed on shore.

Asked if he could confirm the accusations of brutality, Henderson testified that on the second day out the captain had complained to him that he was not smart enough about his work. Demonstrating an independent spirit, Henderson had reminded Captain Miner that he was a greenhand, so knew nothing about the ropes on a ship.

Then, "four or five weeks after we left New Bedford the Captain ordered me to let go a certain rope & I touched the wrong one—

The Captain took hold of a belaying pin & I ran away — the Captain put the belaying pin back. He then sent me for touching the wrong rope, into the fore gaff top sail to shift it over. I had never done this before, not even been aloft. This took me over an hour and a half. The Captain was shouting, cursing & swearing all this time & calling me a son of a bitch &c.. The second mate then came aloft & assisted me. About three weeks previous to our arrival at Macquarries Island the first mate & some men were out on the jib boom working, the Captain was standing at the foot of the jib boom & I was behind him. The Captain turned round and asked if I was dead. I said "No sir I am not dead." The Captain said,

> *"then I will bury you."* He took an iron ring & struck me on the nose twice & cut open my face as you can now see the scar. The Captain was drunk at the time. He again struck me with his fist at Macquarie's Island whilst we were in the boats searching for an anchor that we had lost there. We were searching for this anchor ten days at eighteen hours a day — from half past two in the morning till 9 o'clock at night.

After briefly describing the ordeal off Campbell Island, Henderson signed his testimony and went back to his seat. Then Emil Huber was called.

The Swiss was twenty-eight, brown-skinned and dark-haired, with brown eyes. He was a little taller than the previous two seamen, being five foot, six inches.

"My name is Emil Huber," he said. "I was born in Berne, Switzerland, and resided in America about six months before sailing. I'm a clerk by profession," he went on, and then said that he had gone to Mr. Pearl because he was looking for work. "He told me he had a vessel for sealing and I agreed to go in her for nine months." Because Huber had never served at sea before, he wanted to serve as steward or cook, but was not given the chance. Accordingly, he consented to ship as a greenhand.

Since he had checked out of the boarding house where he had been living, he had all his clothes with him, he said, but Pearl had told him "I should not require those as everything would be provided on board the vessel. I therefore took them back to the hotel and left them there."

Then, with the others, he had taken the steamboat *Old Colony* to New Bedford. After getting on board the *Sarah W. Hunt,* he was called down in the cabin and told to sign the articles. "Not being able to read English, I asked a German who had just signed what the conditions were, and he told me it was to go sealing for two years. I was surprised at this. I nevertheless signed them. It was done in the presence of Capt. Miner & two other gentlemen whose names I do not know. I should say I signed for a greenhand & not as a sailor before the mast. The Steward cautioned me to sign only as a greenhand —

We soon after this proceeded to sea. On the 3rd October I was in the first mate's watch and came on deck at 8 a.m. The mate ordered me aloft to get the staff down to put on a new vane I having put it up & I told the mate I had a sore foot & he called Julius C. Jaeger & told me to instruct him how to unship it. I did so & Julius went aloft. I then went under the port boat & soon heard a rattling in the rigging & a fall in the water & the man at the wheel sang out "A man overboard."

I looked over the side & saw the man sinking at the stern of the schooner. I did not see him rise again. At the same I heard the steward call to the man at the wheel to put the helm hard down. I jumped into the boat with three other men & the chief mate making five men in all. After searching for about ten minutes the Capt. called us back. I do not think by staying out longer we could have recovered the man alive. It was about fifteen minutes from the time I heard the fall till the boat was launched. Louis Scharffenorth was at the wheel but he was lost in the 1st mate's boat. When the alarm was given the Captain rushed up on deck undressed & put his pants on afterwards. I am of opinion the man must have injured himself when falling through the rigging. When we returned the schooner was hove to.

Again, Ward asked about the claims of brutality, and Emil Huber described the captain kicking Joe Arthur before launching into a grievance of his own. "The day previous to the man being lost overboard I was on the main boom outside the stern of the vessel assisting to furl the mainsail when the Captain struck me twice on the face, he standing in the stern boat at the time. I don't know for what reason he did it." He had also been struck during the search for the lost anchor at Macquarie, he said.

Huber then described the arrival at Campbell Island, and the discovery of the cache at the bottom of the flagstaff. After recounting the discovery of the stores in the castaway hut, and the return of the goods that had been taken out of the strong-box, he turned to the events of their ordeal, and for the first time the story of Crawford's plunge into the water was told. "The sea was getting rougher every minute & the second mate got knocked overboard but held on to the boat & three of us pulled him in with great difficulty," he related. "When we got him in we gave him the bow oar to try & warm himself, while I took the steering oar."

Otherwise, his account was the same as those already heard, right up to the arrival at the head of Perseverance Harbour to find that the *Sarah W. Hunt* was gone. "We carried Hertwig and Henderson up to the hut, got something to eat, put some grass on the floor & changed our clothes for what we got out of the chest," he concluded. "We remained here ten or eleven days when the N.Z. govt. schooner *Kekeno* put in, and gave us all we required."

And, with that, Emil Huber silenced.

Just before signing, however, he said he wished to make an amendment to part of his testimony — "there were only four of us in the boat viz: — Streichert (1st Mate) Jim Judson,

Joe Arthur, & myself who were launched to pick up Jaeger when he fell overboard."

Wilhelm Hertwig was twenty-two, the same age as Martin Tierney, and as dark in hair and complexion, but three inches taller. "I'm a German by birth, & resided about one year and a half in America before I joined the *Sarah W. Hunt*," he began, adding, "I was a barman, & was never at sea as a sailor before joining the vessel. I read in a German newspaper that some young men were wanted to join whaling & sealing vessels. I went to Pearl's office 186 West Street New York and asked about it & he told me it was a voyage for nine months sealing."

He repeated what the other men had said about going to New Bedford by steamer, and then went on, "After going on board the *Sarah W Hunt* we were ordered in the cabin & I there signed articles in the presence of the Captain Miner & two other gentlemen one of whom represented himself to be a Custom House officer. Before signing I knew it was for sealing voyage of two years duration and my share would amount to 1/180 lay."

Then, after stressing that he shipped as a greenhand, Hertwig candidly confessed, "I did not give satisfaction." Asked to elaborate, he said, "Two or three days after sailing I was ordered to furl the topsail & I was kept there an hour till the second mate came up & showed me how to do it."

Having heard the other men describe the ordeal in the whaleboat at length, Hertwig was economical with his words: "When I left in the 2nd mate boat we hoisted sail & strong breeze sprung up & drove us out to sea & we did not succeed in getting back again until 1st Dec & only succeeded in reaching Perseverance Harbour on Tuesday Dec 4th. We then landed and took advantage of the shelter & store provided there by the New Zealand Government. After remaining here ten days the *Kekeno* arrived & rendered us every assistance. The steamer *Stella* took us on to Port Chalmers, N. Zealand.

"The Captain never struck me nor ever used any brutal conduct towards me," he concluded, evidently in reply to yet another question. Then he signed the testimony, and Ward stood him down.

"My name is Thomas Whittle," the fifth seaman testified. The drover was just five foot, three inches, a huskily built, muscular man of twenty-five, his fair skin reddened with exposure. He was brown-haired and brown-eyed.

"My name is Thomas Whittle," he began. "I am an American teamster by occupation. I was in the City of New York one Saturday 7ᵗʰ July and noticed an advertisement in a newspaper 'The New York Sun'—'Wanted twelve greenhands to go on a voyage' apply at Pearl's &c. I went to this Shipping office & the agent told me to come round on Monday morning. I did so & called again at 2 o'clock in the afternoon & he took me to New Bedford & after having breakfasted we went on board the schooner. Went down the cabin & signed as a greenhand—in the presence of the Captain & another named Brightman & a cooper. I was particular that greenhand should be put opposite my name. We to each have the 1/180 lay. I wanted to go on shore but the mate said we had to leave in a few minutes. I was in the galley for two months & then was taken out by the mate to be sent aloft that evening—this was the first time I was aloft."

Ward asked, "Did you witness any brutality?"

"Some two or three weeks after we sailed I saw the Captain strike Thomas Ennis with a rope's end over the eyes

& raised a lump. The Captain was drunk at the time & gave as his reason for striking Ennis that he was coiling the rope the wrong way. I also saw the Captain strike Henderson with an iron ring or bolt right across the nose. He was standing at the bow. The Captain was under the influence of drink at the time."

Whittle's accounting of the ordeal in the boat was even briefer than Hertwig's. "We left the *Sarah W Hunt* on the 27th Nov. taking with us clubs, knifes & steel with instructions to go round the bays & look for seals," he merely said, adding, "We were blown off the land and did not regain it till Dec. 1st & reached Perseverance Harbour Dec. 4th & found the schooner had left. We remained ashore about ten days when the *Kekeno* came into Harbour & gave us all the assistance we required."

Asked again about brutality, he simply complained, "I did not get enough to eat while on board." When Ward persisted, he admitted, "The Captain never struck me."

So why had he left the job of cook? "I could not agree with the steward & this is why I left the galley."

Then it was Captain Miner's turn.

The Elephant Voyage

s.s *Wanaka*

13: The Captain's Defense

George Duncan, charged with committing a breach of the peace, pleaded not guilty, and as the charge required two Justices of the Peace to decide, he was remanded until Tuesday. His Worship the Mayor was on the bench
— Weekly Press, *Christchurch, January 19, 1884*

Captain Miner was having a very bad week.

On January 16, he had arrived back in Lyttelton to find that his ex-steward had been charged with a breach of the peace two days earlier. "His Worship the Mayor," who was on the bench, had found George Duncan guilty, but as he was a first offender he had fined him just five shillings, "or twenty-four hours' imprisonment." Unfortunately, one of his drinking cronies had paid the fine, because Duncan was on the loose when Captain Miner stepped off the *Wanaka*.

The following day, Miner was in deep conversation with John Hill (a Lyttelton engineer and also the proprietor of the Albion Hotel), outside Garforth and Lee's, the big butcher's shop on Norwich Quay, when Duncan lurched up to him, chanting, "*We* are the people! We *are* the people! We are the *people!*"

Miner and Hill moved inside the store, but Duncan followed them, shouting insults and obscenities.

The butcher on duty, John Garforth, tried to remove the offender, but without success. The police were called, and Captain Miner laid charges.

Miner, faced with prosecuting a civil case, was forced to find a lawyer, so had engaged Henry Nalder, a prominent (and undoubtedly expensive) Lyttelton solicitor who featured prominently in legal actions that featured seafarers and shipping lines. The case was due to be heard next day, January 22, and Miner should have been preparing for this. Instead, however, he had been compelled to listen to an exceedingly unpleasant litany from the men he had abandoned at Campbell Island. And, where he had been ready to counter a claim that he had given up the hunt for the missing boats too early, instead he was being accused of drunken brutality. It is likely that he felt both incredulous and insulted.

It would have been impossible for him not to relive the frustration of having to turn clumsy, ignorant, often uncooperative greenhands—men who had never served under sail before—into reasonably competent sailors. As a task, it was both daunting and critical. The safety of the ship and the lives of those on board depended on every man knowing what rope to haul and where to stand in an emergency, and so it was absolutely crucial to cram that knowledge into even the thickest head—and the heads of some of these slanderous greenhands had been very thick indeed.

Any whaling captain would have understood and sympathized with his problem, and would have been quick with his fists in the same situation, too. One desperate captain tied notes to various important bits of rigging to try to teach his "dummies" the names and functions of the ropes; another drew a map of the compass and stopped the worst dunderheads from having time off (their "watch below") until they could demonstrate they had learned and understood directions, and therefore were capable of such basic tasks as keeping lookout and steering. Others were exasperated by men who hid themselves in crooks and crannies of the ship when ordered to learn how to climb aloft. "They are afraid they shall fall," a first mate noted, then went on to comment wryly that the greenhands would be the last ones to fall, because they held so tightly to the rigging that they "squeezed the tar out of the ropes."

Slapping and tongue-lashing were the mildest of punishments for obduracy and ignorance. Many captains and mates resorted to shackles, gagging with wooden clubs wedged between the offenders' jaws, and flogging—for though flogging had been outlawed in 1850, a ship was a microcosm on an empty ocean, and on board the captain was king. It was even known for sadistic masters to beat their men to death. By the rough standards of whalers and sealers, Sanford Miner was a moderate skipper—but these mutinous greenhands and Acting Consular Agent Ward were not likely to be easily persuaded of that.

So Miner made up his mind that prevarication was his best defense.

He began very formally, with the words, "I, Sanford Stoddard Miner master of the schooner *Sarah W. Hunt* of Middletown Connecticut, do hereby depose and make oath that the owners of the vessel are John S. Gray of Hartford, Charles H. Smith, Samuel L. Way, J.C. Hill and C Welles also all of Hartford and that the said owners purchased the vessel in July 1882 for the express purpose of sealing."

Then he described the fitting-out process, which had begun in May 1883. When the schooner was about ready, he said, the ship's agent made arrangements with a shipping agent in New York named Pearl to get a crew of thirteen hands. "I do not know what instructions the ship's agent gave to the shipping master but I told him they were to be young able-bodied men and especially a good steward."

After the men arrived the steward was the first to come into the cabin, he said. Miner then went on to describe the difficulties with Duncan—his complaint that the galley was too small, and his demand for a larger share of the voyage than was usually given to stewards. "After this conversation I left the cabin and went on shore to see to some stores which had not arrived. The steward requested to know from the Agent what stores the vessel was provided with and I left the vessel whilst he was being shown the store list. When I arrived on board with the stores I found the Agent has signed all the crew on the articles in my absence, and was making out duplicate articles and copies of Crew List ready for clearing the ship at the Custom House."

As this was at such variance with the boys' claim that they had been signed on by a man who called himself a Customs Officer, Ward asked Miner to elaborate. "When the crew arrived on board, the following people were in the cabin of the ship—the shipping master, Mr. Pearl, Mr. L. Brightman, shipowner of New Bedford, Mr. E. P. Miner (the ship's agent) of Hartford."

Captain Miner then added, "Mr. Thomas Luce was on board the ship, but I cannot say whether he was in the cabin or not."

This was prevarication with a vengeance.

Ebenezer Miner, Captain Miner's brother, was secretary of the Lawnmower company of Hartford, Connecticut, while Leander Brightman was a storekeeper and draper.

"Thomas Luce" (real name unknown) was a native of the Azores, named after his first captain, who after a couple of voyages had settled in New Bedford to establish his own coopering business. He had done very well, becoming the owner and part-owner of a number of ships, including the *Sarah W. Hunt*—but he, like Pearl, like Brightman, and like Ebenezer Miner, was never a Customs House officer. The ignorant young men who had trustingly signed the articles had most certainly been duped.

Joseph Ward, however, was not to know that, and so he did not question Miner further. Instead, he allowed the captain to go on to state that the papers that Ebenezer Miner, as ship's agent, had witnessed, were taken to the Collector of Customs, who "examined the copies with the original and gave me the usual stamped certificate together with my clearance."

Miner countered other allegations. "The only spirituous or intoxicating liquors among the ships or my private stores was a couple of gallons of sweet wine of Barossa," he declared.

Then he attended to the problem of discipline, saying, "The men generally behaved very well in my presence. The Steward was continually growling and cursing at the men and I heard from the officers that he had several fights with them.

"On one occasion Thomas Ennis disobeyed my order and as I had frequently told him and shown him how to do the same thing I struck him with a rope's end," he admitted, but, having successfully insinuated that the steward was responsible for a lot of the roughing up of the boys, he had no hesitation in throwing at least part of the blame for the loss of Julius Jaeger on George Duncan, too. "We had no life buoy on board but I mentioned to the steward at the time that he ought to have thrown overboard a hatch or any other article that would float so as to assist the man to float before the ship got so far off or at any rate it would mark where he fell over."

And, contrary to what the boys had claimed, the lowered boat "was away from the ship in charge of the mate about half an hour, during which time I was directing him from the stern boat the direction in which to search," and, furthermore, "I never hailed the boat to return to the ship, he returned of his own accord evidently thinking further search useless."

The stern boat, as the name implies, was usually hung over the stern of the schooner, so would have made an excellent vantage point. Yet, if it was slung there, why was it not lowered to rescue Jaeger? Miner had already said that both boats were "bottom up on deck" — which was why the attempted rescue of Julius Jaeger had taken so long to get underway.

Ward did not seem to notice this strange contradiction in the evidence, however, because the cross-examination returned to the topic of brutality. "I have no recollection of striking the seaman Arthur when he came out of the boat as stated by the seamen," claimed the captain. And, as for the time the second mate dislocated his shoulder, he said he had done his best to "pull it back again" until Crawford had begged him to stop. "I took his watch for fourteen days," he said, to give the shoulder time to recover.

It was about this same time that "Alexander Henderson was insolent to me and I struck him in the face," Captain Miner went on; "but I had nothing in my hand at the time, if he was struck on the face by any iron at all, it was caused by the shaking of the sail. I was there working myself, the mark on his face was there when he joined the vessel." Henderson had been impertinent again when they were at Macquarie searching for the lost anchor: "when ordered to pay out the sweeping chain and not doing as I told him I struck him," Miner allowed, but no details were given this time.

The arrival at Perseverance Harbour was then briefly described, along with the discovery of the strong-box and the signboard, but with no mention of the message posted on the latter. "Whilst on shore I found a bottle near the flagstaff containing some papers which being damp I took on board so as to dry and read them which I did with the assistance of the Steward. It contained reports of the H.M.S. *Blanche*, *Cossack*, and the American whaling barque *Tamerlane* of New Bedford which vessel was whaling there in 1875. I took a copy of the *Tamerlane*'s report as near as I could decipher it."

Miner then testified that he had ordered the first mate to return the goods to the strong-box, and that he had checked with him that the stores in the castaway hut had not been touched. After that, came the story of the twenty-seventh.

"All hands were called about 5 a.m., and after breakfast were ordered to man the boats, the mate having expressed himself anxious to take a cruise about the Island," he said. While the boats were furnished with sealing clubs, only the mates had knives—"The crew were not furnished with knives. I left it to the mates' discretion to provide all necessary provisions for their boats, they having free access to everything. They had orders from me to take a look about the Island as far as they thought it was safe to go and look for seal rookeries not to trouble any of them at all but simply to report to me on their return."

Having shifted much of the blame for the disastrous excursion onto the mates, Miner then proceeded to describe the weather squalling up and the non-return of the boats:

"Consulted with the Steward and concluded that the boats had been blown off the land. Made preparations to get under weigh and go off shore in search of them. Got under weigh, when outside steered South East until about seven miles off the land when the wind left us and we were becalmed. Consulted again with Steward, he thinking the men were dead and as we were not manned to search far off shore for them induced me to give up my original intention of going off shore in search of the men."

Having neatly implicated George Duncan in the fatal decision to leave Campbell Island, Miner then gave details of the passage to New Zealand, going on to describe the trouble he had reporting his arrival: "Could not ascertain who the United States Consul was in Lyttelton but was recommended by the pilot to see Capt. D. McIntyre formerly Consular Agent at Wellington NZ—

> *Received a telegram about noon from the Acting Consular Agent stating he would be in Lyttelton in the afternoon. I entered the vessel at the Customs and at the request of the Collector I attended at the Custom House Christchurch with the steward next morning at ten o'clock, an enquiry held before him. I also attended a meeting at the Chamber of Commerce on the 13th and volunteered my services and the use of my vessel to go in search of the missing boats but as the New Zealand Government decided upon sending their steamer Stella my offer was not accepted.*

He then denied that he had made no attempt to join the *Stella*.

After that, Miner moved on to his own grievance—that the rescued men had mutinied, refusing a direct order to return to the schooner. "Not having heard from the Consul at Dunedin was advised to go there and see the men, and bring them to Lyttelton to rejoin the vessel, the Acting Consular Agent having provided me with funds to do so. I left Lyttelton on the 8th of January and on my arrival the crew positively refused to rejoin the ship, they did this again in the Consul's office. And as a consequence and by my Consul's advice I refused to put my owners to further expense by bringing them to Lyttelton. They however came to Lyttelton by the same steamer as myself their passage being given them by the owners of the steamer. On their arrival at Lyttelton they were taken charge of by the Consul."

That said, Miner returned to his preoccupation with the insolent behavior of George Duncan. "The Steward, George Duncan, has been away from the ship off and on but refusing duty since December the twelfth, being absent without leave." Miner had done everything in his power, he said — "I reported him to the Consul, he was taken charge of by police" — but had been unable to make the man see where his proper duty lay.

On the night of December 26, "he deserted, taking all his effects with him." The magistrate, however, had refused to have him arrested for desertion, and since then "I have been frequently insulted, threatened and annoyed by him in the street both at Christchurch and Lyttelton, he being nearly always under the influence of drink."

As for the boys' charge of being half-starved, that could be laid at the steward's door, too: "I never had a single complaint from the men that they had not enough to eat," he declared. "The Steward had full charge of the provisions with instructions to give them sufficient without wasting." At one time, the captain said, he had weighed out the bread himself, to make sure they had enough. "There was a cask of bread in the hold, during the whole voyage, which the crew had free access to."

That should have been the last of his testimony. Miner, however, was determined to give vent to yet another grievance: "I wish to state that Michael Crawford was not competent for the duties of second mate," he uncharitably said; "and had it not been for his age I certainly should have reduced his rank and put him in the forecastle."

That said, he sighed with a flourish, "Sanford S. Miner."

Mr. Ward scribbled a note that the testimony had been "sworn before me Joseph Frederick Ward Acting Consular Agent of the United States of America," dated and signed it, and the inquiry came to a close.

14: The Castaways' Revenge

*But there are two or three things about that thrilling story
of desperate danger and timely deliverance that have
never, as yet, at least to our knowledge, been made public*
— The Lyttelton Times, *January 25, 1884*

The last cross-examination was followed by what must
have been a long and awkward silence.

All six men watched Mr. Ward expectantly, awaiting his
judicial decision, but when someone finally asked whether
he found Captain Miner guilty of the charges or not, the
acting consular agent was forced to tell them that he did not
have the power to adjudicate. All he could do, he said, was
send transcripts of the testimonies to Consul Griffin, who
would be the one to advise the State Department whether he
thought the seamen's case against the captain was proved.
Furthermore, the information would not be complete until
the testimony of Michael Crawford, still in the Dunedin
Hospital, had been received.

In the meantime, Ward did have some news for them,
having received telegraphed instructions from the consulate
in Auckland. It was recognized that the six seamen were a
special case, on account of the ordeal they had endured,

and, because of that, Consul Griffin had ordered that they should be formally discharged.

Accordingly, they were no longer considered deserters or mutineers, and Captain Miner had no legal right to demand that they return to the schooner. The captain of the *Sarah W. Hunt* would have to find a whole new crew, and the six men he had left to struggle for their own survival were now free to return to the United States.

There was more. As indigent American seamen, they would be sent to Auckland on the first Union Steam Ship Company ship, and would sail from there to America on the earliest San Francisco steamer. Their fares would be paid by the consular agent, after he had settled their boarding house bill in Christchurch. And, as for Captain Miner, he was to hand over three months' extra wages for each of the discharged men, on behalf of the owners (at the usual rate of $12 per month), as stipulated by American maritime law.

This pleased absolutely none of Ward's listeners.

Captain Miner would have been shocked and dismayed. With eighteen months' wages in total to find—and $216 was a large sum, particularly considering that the voyage had made no money whatsoever — it meant a big charge on the ship's account, an amount that the investors in the voyage would certainly question. On top of that, he would have to pay a fee to Joseph Ward's firm, Kinsey, Ward and Co., to find him a new crew.

His five ex-seamen were, if possible, even more aggrieved than their captain. Martin Tierney and Wilhelm Hertwig, in particular, felt that their accusations of fraud and ill-treatment had fallen on deaf ears. So, when they were accosted by journalists as they left Mr. Ward's office, they disobeyed the strict instructions given by the consular agent, and described their grudges against the captain at length, and in detail.

Noted the *Otago Witness*, "though the inquiry was not open to Press reporters, a long article appears in one of the papers today." Judging by the contents, as the story went on, Captain Miner, who had been present throughout the inquiry, "must have heard some remarkably unpleasant things of himself. If the statements made by two of the sailors are true, he must be a perfect brute."

"The schooner still lies in Lyttelton," the item continued. "His crew have one and all refused to go back with him, and his steward and he are constantly at loggerheads. They fell out to such purpose the other day that the matter came before the Magistrate's Court, and the steward was fined."

"Not one of the men is really a seaman," the article went on, reverting to the sailors' grievances; "they all shipped as 'greenhands'; their papers were falsified — they say, after leaving — were undated, and not worth the paper they are written on. At present they are all looking for work in or near Christchurch, and are simply living on what the consul doles out to them from the three months wages that are due. Captain Miner's side of the story has not yet appeared," the editor tactfully concluded.

The story referred to appeared in not one, but both local dailies — *The Lyttelton Times* and *The Star* — on Friday, 25 January, and over the next few days was repeated in newspapers throughout New Zealand. All were identical in content, even to the heading, which read, "The *Sarah W. Hunt*'s Crew. How Sealing Vessels are Recruited." And in all of them the facts became dramatized — the iron ring that Miner may or may not have had in his fist when he hit Henderson became "an iron hook" while the belaying pin episode was turned into chasing one of the crew around the deck with a "red-hot bolt and a hammer."

"Two of the shipwrecked sailors recently belonging to the *Sarah W. Hunt*—Martin Tierney and Wilhelm Hertwig—gave the following account of their troubles to a representative of this paper yesterday," the story began. "In doing so they acted as a kind of deputation from the five survivors who have been giving evidence during the past few days before the Acting United States Consul, as to their treatment on the voyage of the sealing schooner, and the manner in which they shipped on board her.

"In the first place not one of them, so they affirm, can by right be called seamen at all. From various causes which need not be stated they saw fit to 'follow the sea,' and applied to a shipping agent in New York to get them berths of some kind on board a vessel." This man, whose name was Pearl, "told them that he had something that would just suit them—a sealing cruise, which would last for the next nine months. The vessel was not lying in New York harbor, but they had to go down by rail to New Bedford, some 250 miles off, and join her there.

"They arrived early in the morning of July 10, 1883, and after having 'a bit of breakfast,' went off to the schooner. Shortly after they were called down into the cabin and given papers to sign, promising to serve for two years. All declare that, acting on the advice of the steward, a regular old 'shellback' of 28 years' standing, they inserted the words 'greenhand' after their names. Here it may be mentioned, by way of parenthesis, that they are all landsmen, and anxious to work at their different callings, for they have no money of their own. The Consul pays what is needful for their board and lodging out of a certain number of months' wages due to them from the captain, but declines to give them any money for other purposes …

> The papers, as stated above, were signed by the five green hands. The surprise of the quintette when their papers were shown to them at the Consulate, and they found they were each set down as full blown able seamen may be imagined. 'Green hand' appears in every case to have been erased, and the substitution very cleverly made. They appear to have shipped with the understanding that they were to have a certain share in the profits of the voyage. But as the papers are both false and undated, as Hertwig put it, 'If we had come back with 100,000 sealskins we could have claimed nothing – not one cent.' Altogether the business appears to have been managed in a most curious way by the men themselves. The signatures were affixed in the presence of some person whom they suppose to have been the Captain's brother. According to their account, such attestations are usually made before a Custom-house officer in the United States. As such officers are invariably in uniform, and this individual was dressed in plain clothes, they became suspicious, and asked why they had not signed at the Custom-house itself. The man quieted them by saying that he was the representative of the Customs, and it was all right. This statement, they discovered too late, was far more ingenious than ingenuous; he was the man who brought the 'slop chest' – the box with ordinary seamen's clothing for the voyage – aboard.

"To be duped in this way was bad enough" – but when they wanted to post letters home, they were not allowed on shore. Instead, the letters were taken away from them by "the slop-clothes man" with the bland assurance that they would be mailed. Naturally, the men "have slight doubts as to whether their parents, friends and relations ever saw a line of those epistles to this day."

Once the schooner was in the Atlantic, the story went on, "The captain soon began to show his amiable character. Nothing would please him: nothing was done quick enough to suit his ideas. It was in vain that the men told him they were but 'green hands,' and had only shipped as such. He declared they did their work no better than children, and now and then knocked them about and kicked them.

"Unfortunately he did not confine his efforts in this direction to blows inflicted with fists and feet alone. One man he struck in the face with an iron hook, and he bears the marks yet. On another occasion, a bolt had to be run through the main boom. The skipper took offence at some clumsiness and chased one of the crew round the deck with the red-hot bolt and a hammer. Food was miserably insufficient, and Tierney, who tells the tale, describes with gusto how he used to be lowered stealthily down into the provision room by night and purloin 'hard tack' for his messmates, to supply deficiencies in the commissariat."

Down the full length of the page the story went, and up to another column, in which the two-hour hunt for the lost bucket was cruelly contrasted with the "ten minute" search for Jaeger. The steward's attempt to cut the ropes that lashed the boat to the deck was stopped, according to this version, "by the officers and captain, who had jumped on deck with next to no clothes on. The lashings were cast off in the regular way, and it was 25 minutes at least, according to Hertwig and Tierney, before the boat touched water. In the meantime the drowning sailor had been seen astern once, but the schooner was not put about—she was for the bucket. The captain simply 'luffed up' and waited." According to what the two men told the paper, even Streichert, the mate, "said they had not looked long enough for the luckless fellow, but the skipper said it was all the crew's fault that he had not been picked up."

Captain Miner had also failed to minister to the health of his men. After the second mate's arm was put out of joint, the men averred, "The captain swore he was humbugging, and made him work as if nothing were the matter, though he was sometimes in agony and quite unfit for duty. In fact, the deputation say he never would let a man off when he was sick, or give him any medicine beyond a rubbing with St. Jacob's oil, and a scanty one at that. St. Jacob's oil was his panacea." Hertwig had produced a story of his own to corroborate this—when the tips of his fingers were jammed while moving casks, "the steward, with due caution as to the quantity he expended, applied the wondrous St. Jacob's oil, and bandaged the wounded digit with such dainty remedies as tobacco in a kind of sea poultice."

The reporters, not being seafarers, might not have known that this last was not particularly unusual treatment, as well-chewed tobacco had been used as a poultice at sea since time immemorial. They would certainly have been familiar with St. Jacob's Oil, though, and probably used it themselves. Throughout New Zealand, it was touted as "the great German remedy" for rheumatism, sciatica, lumbago, backache, gout, and burns by its maker, Augustus Vogeler of 205 Clay Street, Baltimore, Maryland. Just months previously, it had received a medal at the New Zealand International Exhibition. Dozens of New Zealanders were paid to write testimonials for this miraculous stuff, which appeared in dozens of papers.

A weak extract of aconite root in ether, alcohol, and turpentine, St. Jacob's oil gave the impression of being efficacious because it numbed nerve-endings. Advertised as the "Best Pain Curing and Healing Remedy known to mankind," it cost New Zealanders three shillings a bottle, and was often accompanied by free cards or a calendar.

"This brings us down to the arrival at Macquarie's Island," continued the journalist, and went on to describe the fruitless, arduous hunt for the lost anchor. Then came the retreat to Campbell Island, and the fateful departure from the schooner. "The captain, at the official enquiry here before the Collector of Customs, stated that he told the men not to hunt for seal when they were sent away in the boats. This they contradict, and ask how it was, if this is true, that the clubs, skinning knives, and everything else necessary for destroying the animals, were taken. A reward of a dollar, too, was offered to the first man in the starboard boats who captured a seal.

"It was from Campbell Island, as we also already know, that the two boats were blown out to sea," the next paragraph ran, and a stirring description of the men's ordeal followed. "Weak and spent as the men were by fasting, drought and despair, they rarely made vigorous play with the oars. The sea was savage in its treatment of them, and the poor second mate with his useless arm could do little at the steer oar. At night the boat drifted at the mercy of the waves, and the exhausted men had much ado to bale out the water that threatened to make their every moment their last."

Martin Tierney had told him, the reporter said, that during that "fearful, foodless week" they were never further than sixty miles away from the island—"Time after time as they recovered their lost ground, the squalls and tempest tore them away again, but never to any great distance."

And yet "the captain, who had his vessel sufficiently under command to work her to New Zealand against head winds and in bad weather" had not delayed even twenty-four hours to tack about the mouth of the harbor.

"Had he done so, he could only have failed by a miracle to sight the boat which ultimately regained the island. Having picked up that crew, he would have been full-handed enough to make a thorough search for the other. But, no! away he sailed straight for New Zealand, and the very day which he says he left his anchorage in Perseverance Harbour they were in sight of the island, *and on the same side of it the whole day!*"

At last, having reached the third column and the arrival of the *Kekeno*, the journalist wound up the story. "In conclusion we may say that the men are loud in their praise of the generous action taken here, and the determined way in which their cause was taken up when all hope seemed lost. They also desire it to be known that their passage from Dunedin to Christchurch was secured through the liberality of a private gentleman (a German) and his friends, in the southern town. They are beholden for it neither to the American Consul here, nor to our own Government."

The Elephant Voyage

s.s. *Takapuna*

15: The U. S. Consul

I really do not know a man who has done so much good and efficient work for the Colony of New Zealand, without forgetting his responsibility to his own government, as Consul G. W. Griffin
— Otago Daily Times, *January 19, 1884*

Meanwhile, Gilderoy Wells Griffin had returned to his literary efforts.

His two latest reports on the commerce of New Zealand, *The New Zealand Fisheries* and *The Financial Statistics of New Zealand*, had just appeared in volume number 34 of the Washington-produced periodical *Consular Reports*, and it was a credit to his energy that they were the only treatises in the Australasian section. "In the report on fishes Mr. Griffin not only deals with edible fishes, but includes whales, seals, sharks, sword-fishes, &c.," commented his fan, the editor of the *New Zealand Herald*. The other paper, on financial statistics, "is naturally one dealing to a large extent with figures, and by many may be regarded as somewhat dry reading," he admitted, then added, "But to business men at a distance these papers cannot fail to be of great interest and value."

Now, Consul Griffin was engaged in a particularly gratifying task—the proof-reading of his book, the galleys of which had just arrived from Mr. George Didsbury, the government printer. Commissioned by the New Zealand government, and called *New Zealand: her Commerce and Resources*, it was a 180-page compendium of his reports, embellished with a folded leaf of plates, and a hand-colored map of the country. As a panel of prominent New Zealanders (including James Drummond Macpherson) commented later, in a ceremonial address, "The Parliament of this colony, in printing your valuable papers in a collected form, has marked its high appreciation of the value of your contributions." In addition to the ordinary copies, which would be put in circulation with the usual blue paper covers, the administration was having a number expensively bound, with gilt letters on the cover, and marbled edges to the pages, intended for presentation to such august figures as the President of the United States.

On February 1, this pleasant literary bustle was brought to a sudden halt. An urgent wire from Mr. Ward arrived, carrying the same disturbing news that was being simultaneously telegraphed to the newspapers. "Two sailors of the *Sarah W. Hunt* crew have instituted proceedings against the captain for fraudulent misrepresentation and breach of contract," the *New Zealand Herald* reported. The case was to be brought on 6 February, and held in the Resident Magistrate's Court in Lyttelton.

Up until that moment U.S. Consul Griffin had placidly assumed that the consular agent had followed instructions, and put the five seamen on a steamer for Auckland as soon as their depositions had been taken. According to the schedule posted in the Auckland *Observer* by Griffin's junior, Thomas Gamble—who was the agent for the Pacific Mail Steamship Company as well as vice-consul in Auckland—they could have easily connected with the

Australia, which was supposed to leave for San Francisco in three days' time. Now, it looked as if they would not make even the *Zealandia*, which was due to sail on 4 March. Griffin urgently wired Ward in Christchurch and, when he received the answer, realized that he was on the brink of a diplomatic embarrassment.

The two German seamen, Hertwig and Henderson, had confided in their friends at the Concordia Club . . . and Dr. Julius von Haast, the Imperial German Consul, had listened with sympathy to their tale.

Dr. Julius von Haast, an illustrious geologist who had come to New Zealand in 1858 to investigate the chances for German migrants, had charted the rocks of Canterbury and Nelson; he had given the expert advice that had saved the construction of the railroad tunnel between Lyttelton and Christchurch; he had named the famous Franz Josef glacier after his emperor (a mountain pass was named after Haast himself); and he had founded the Canterbury Museum, which was becoming recognized as one of the top twenty such institutions in the world. As William Rolleston had already noted, however, where legal and political matters were concerned Haast was a well-meaning idiot.

In a rueful description to the State Department, Gilderoy Griffin wrote, "Two of the seamen, W[m.] Hertwig and Alexander Henderson, being German subjects, I regret to say sought advice from D[r.] Julius von Haast, the Imperial German Consul at Christchurch, who under a mistaken knowledge of the law persuaded them to bring suit in the local court at Lyttelton for the purpose of obtaining damages for alleged violation of contract." And, at the same time, with boundless confidence and great generosity of spirit, Haast had "promised to become responsible for all costs incurred in the case."

So the two German seamen blithely searched out a firm of lawyers, Messrs. Garrick, Cowlishaw, and Fisher, who were equally sanguine about their chances. "Dr. von Haast afterward deeply regretted his action and amply apologized for the same to me," wrote Griffin to Washington. But the damage had been done.

"The Resident Magistrate, John Ollivier Esq., before whom the suit was brought," he wrote, "although fully aware that the '*Sarah W. Hunt*' was an American vessel owned by citizens of the United States and sailing under the American flag, did not hesitate to issue a summons in each of the suits brought by the said seamen requiring the Master to appear before him, and to produce the log books, shipping articles and other papers belonging to the vessel."

Ward had sent Griffin a copy of this demand, which was attached to copies of the two summonses with their attached depositions. Drawn up on February 1, 1884, the writ alleged first, that Henderson and Hertwig had been assured by "Pearl of New York" that they would be employed as greenhands; and second, that after arriving on board the schooner the defendants had "fraudulently and falsely" assured the plaintiffs that the *Sarah W. Hunt* "was bound upon a sealing voyage to the Southern seas not exceeding 9 calendar months in duration, that she would carry a proper and sufficient number of able bodied seamen," and that the plaintiffs would "only be required to do a Greenhand's work."

And, thirdly, the plaintiffs claimed "that the Defendants falsely and fraudulently altered the Plaintiffs designation in the said Schooner's articles from 'Greenhand' to that of 'able bodied Seamen.'" Accordingly, Hertwig and Henderson were claiming sixty pounds for fraudulent representation, and forty pounds "for work and labor done and services rendered as a seaman on board the said ship between the 10th day of July 1883 and the 31st day of January 1884," arguing that they had been worked as both greenhands and able seamen, so merited the extra pay.

Luckily, the hearing had been delayed, at the request of the two seamen's lawyers, and now would be held on "the 20th instant," which meant a welcome breathing space. The stay had been granted, Consul Griffin learned, because there was a problem with serving the summons, which was addressed to "the captain and owners of the vessel." Sanford Miner had refused to accept it, insisting that though he was the captain, he was not one of the owners. These, he averred, were John S. Gray, Charles H. Smith, Samuel L. Way, J.C. Hills, and C. Welles—all of Hartford, Connecticut, and therefore well beyond the reach of New Zealand law.

However, as the Christchurch *Weekly Press* reported on February 9 (under the rather weary headline "That Sealing Schooner"), the lawyer who appeared on behalf of the two German seamen, Mr. Meares, had declared to the magistrate that he thought he had found a solution to the problem. Consequently, he "asked the Court for permission to serve the owners of the *Sarah W. Hunt*, by leaving the summons on board." Since the human owners were out of reach, the writ should be served on the schooner itself—by nailing the notice on the stern, perhaps.

This was patently ridiculous. As Griffin knew beyond doubt, and stated firmly later, it was a blatant "violation of the principles of international law." Recently, however, the Resident Magistrate in Lyttelton, John Ollivier, had become impatient with the antics of American seafarers, and rather trigger-happy where that nation was concerned. Just the previous month, he had been exasperated by the first mate of the American ship *Wakefield*, a lout named Morley who had become locally notorious for taking pleasure in beating up anyone who happened to annoy him, both on deck and on shore. As Ollivier was reported saying, he was a fellow with "a very abusive disposition."

When hauled up in court by one of his unfortunate victims, Morley took over the floor to cross-examine him in a "dictatorial and domineering manner," much to the irritation of the Bench, who "reminded him that he was not on board ship," according to the *Weekly Press*. The defendant was found guilty, fined £5 and full costs (a total of £9), plus a surety of twenty pounds to keep peace in port, and a message was sent to the captain of the ship, curtly informing him "that while his ship was in the port he would be held accountable to English, not American law."

So, when Mr. Meares suggested this novel solution to the summons-serving difficulty in the case of the *Sarah W. Hunt*, the Bench, in its wisdom, decided that serving a schooner with a writ was just as good as serving it on the owners of said vessel. As *The Star* noted, "An order was made at Mr. Meare's request for the service of summons on the owners, to be left with the nightwatchman on board the vessel, or any person appearing to be in charge of the vessel, the owners being non-resident in the Colony."

"The Bench granted the application, and fixed the day of hearing for the 20th instant," reported the *Press*.

"Upon learning these facts I at once repaired to Wellington, the Capital of New Zealand," wrote Gilderoy Griffin to the State Department. He left Auckland on February 14, sailing on the crack coastal steamer *Takapuna*, which was helped along by a stiff northerly gale, giving the passengers a very rough night.

The ship docked in Wellington's Port Nicholson at 2:40 p.m., and the instant the gangplank hit the wharf, Griffin hurried ashore. Gripping his hat to keep it secure on his head, he hailed one of the hansom cabs waiting in line on the pier. The steamboat was due to sail at four, so time was very tight for his meeting with the Attorney-General and Minister of Justice at the Houses of Parliament.

Luckily, the gentleman was ready and waiting in his office, Griffin having wired ahead. This was the Hon. Edward Tennyson Conolly, a 62-year-old politician with spectacular side-whiskers and a liberal bent. Griffin quickly described the situation, then pointed out to him, "that if the case should be allowed to proceed it would be in violation of the principles of international law," as "the United States had amply provided for the settlement of all such cases by its Consular Officers resident in New Zealand."

This could have led to some unpleasantness, the Honorable Mr. Justice Conolly being famously impatient with pomposity. Instead, he was polite and attentive, and the meeting ended on an amicable note. "The Attorney General fully acknowledged our jurisdiction in such matters, and promised to communicate at once with the Resident Magistrate at Lyttelton, making known to him my objections to allowing the trial to proceed," the consul wrote to Washington later.

"After leaving the Attorney General I sailed for Lyttelton," Griffin continued. The *Takapuna* cast off her lines on schedule, and after another rough night was off the southern port when the next day dawned. The sun rose as she came past the mole, outlining the Canterbury hills and turning them pink at the start of a beautiful day.

The steamer moored at Gladstone Pier promptly at six, and though it was Saturday, Griffin met Ward at his office on Norwich Quay — "where," he wrote, "I learned that the Captain of the *Sarah W. Hunt* had employed Messrs. Nalder & Martin, barristers & solicitors of Christchurch to defend him in the said suit."

He must have expressed some surprise when Joseph Ward told him this. As Griffin was unaware of the court case Sanford Miner had already brought against George Duncan, this would have been the first he had heard of the captain engaging a lawyer — and he would have found it annoying, too, as Miner should have conferred with the United States consulate before making such an important decision.

Even more dismaying was the news that the hearing was still scheduled for this coming Wednesday, 20 February, as Mr. Justice Conolly had failed to honor his promise. The Minister of Justice had inquired further into the case, apparently, and had decided that in the cause of justice (not to mention political expediency) the charges against Miner should be heard. Not only was the public howling for Captain Miner's blood, but Conolly had a history of being on the side of the underdog — in this case, six underdogs, the men who had not just been abandoned by their captain in their hour of great need, but claimed they had been cheated and ill-treated by him, too.

"It is well enough to mention here," Griffin wrote to the State Department, "that much indignation was felt against the Captain, on account of the wide circulation given by the press and people of New Zealand to the many stories of his strange conduct at sea, of his having practiced great cruelty to his men, who it was said had not been regularly shipped but were greenhands trapped aboard the vessel through fraud."

As he went on to say, the sailors' accusations of his "great cruelty" had been inflated to the point that the public was perfectly convinced "that under threat of the knife and the revolver" the men had been "compelled to go aloft and perform all the duties of able seamen; that one of them had been actually murdered in this way; and that the second mate was obliged to work with a broken arm and wounded chest." Officialdom was equally hostile — "in addition to all these accusations it was well known that the Captain had been violating a New Zealand law in catching seals at the wrong season of the year."

Oddly, the only crime that could be proved beyond question — that Captain Miner had given up the missing boats too easily — went almost unmentioned. Griffin did note that Captain Greig of the schooner *Kekeno* and Captain Grey of the steamer *Stella* had criticized Miner openly — "that the officers of the relief Schooner which rescued the castaways at Campbell's Island had reflected severely upon him for sailing away within five or six days from the Island without making a sufficient search for the missing men" — but it was seemingly just an afterthought.

Compared to all this bad news, it was a minor irritation to learn that George Duncan was up to mischief again. Captain Miner's case against his ex-steward for insulting behavior, which had been heard on 22 January, had turned into a farce, with Duncan conducting his own defense.

"Insulting language: — Miner v. Duncan, Mr. Nalder for complainant," headlined the Christchurch *Star.*

"Captain Miner, of the *Sarah W. Hunt*, stated that on Jan. 17, when complainant was standing in front of Messrs. Garforth and Lee's premises, defendant came up to him and used the language complained of." John Hill, proprietor of the Albion Hotel, corroborated that this happened while he and Miner were talking in front of the butcher's store—but when the butcher himself stepped up into the witness box, to testify that Duncan had followed Miner into the shop and insulted him there, Duncan also stepped up, to cross-examine him.

"Did you hear me call the captain a son of a bitch?" he demanded. Garforth was forced to admit that no, he had not heard those actual words. Duncan then, according to the paper, "made a rambling statement against the captain." The Bench adjudged him guilty, nevertheless, fining him forty shillings and costs, "or in default of payment fourteen day's imprisonment," but again the fine was paid on his behalf, so the rascal yet again escaped jail.

Despite this lesson in futility, Miner had brought yet another case against him, one that had been heard by Magistrate Ollivier in the Lyttelton court on 30 January.

"LARCENY," headlined the *Lyttelton Times*. "George Duncan was charged with stealing a flag, valued at £1, from the schooner *Sarah W. Hunt*." Captain Miner, in the witness box, had testified that he had missed the flag "about Christmas time." And lo, looking about, he had noticed the Stars and Stripes flying from the Lyttelton Hotel, where it had floated to the breeze throughout the holidays.

"I thought it looked like my flag," said Miner.

Tackling the publican, he had the flag taken down so he could examine it, "and recognized it by some grease marks on it." The publican, Solomon J. Frost, was summoned, and admitted that it was, indeed, the schooner's flag. "I got it from accused, who was steward at the time."

It was common enough practice, he protested—"We have borrowed flags on other occasions from coasters." He thought it was just a minor matter, and Mr. Ollivier, who agreed, dismissed the case.

Regrettably, being let off so easily had emboldened the ex-steward. Having heard about the three months' worth of wages that was being pried out of Captain Miner, George Duncan now publicly asserted that he, too, was a deserter from the ship, "and wished to be put on the same footing as the rescued men." Mr. Ward told his superior about the times he and Captain Miner had appealed to the local authorities to have the man put aboard the schooner — "but" wrote Griffin; "they declined to do so, probably on account of the stories in circulation about the Master." Yet this was in defiance of the fact that an Act of Parliament had been passed some years ago, "giving the local authorities full power to aid foreign Consuls in all such cases."

Luckily, however, Duncan solved the problem the very next day, by getting himself arrested for drunken and disorderly behavior. This time, no one came forward to pay his fine, and the magistrate was not amused. The Justice of the Peace presiding, the Hon. Harry Allwright, had him thrown into jail for 96 hours, effectively removing him from the scene to come.

Gilderoy Griffin must have boarded the Lyttelton train in a preoccupied frame of mind, which could only have been intensified by the fumes and smoky lamp-lit shadows as the engine dragged the carriages upward through the tunnel to Christchurch. *The Star* noted his arrival in its edition for February 16, remarking that he had made his appearance in the city that morning, "and is staying at the Christchurch Club. He will remain in Christchurch till after the conclusion of the case in connection with the *Sarah W. Hunt*, which will be heard on Wednesday next, and then proceed to Dunedin," the writer added.

The beautiful Italianate building of the Christchurch Club was the grandest place in town to stay. Banquets were often staged there, and foreign potentates, politicians, and wealthy landowners were the usual guests, so it was fitting accommodation for the official representative of the United States. Griffin could not spare the time for admiring his surroundings, however. Once settled in his high-ceilinged, wood-paneled, second-story room with its lovely arched windows, he put his mind to the problem of how he could get the hearing canceled.

Obviously, despite the expense, and the uncertainty of getting a refund from the State Department, he needed to consult a lawyer. The next day, Monday, he hired "Mr. George Harper, a leading barrister and solicitor of this city," and together they composed a letter to Mr. Ollivier, "respectfully but earnestly" protesting against the trial being allowed to proceed.

It would have been a long process, involving a very careful selection of words: John Ollivier, as George Harper would have warned Griffin, was a formidable opponent. A 72-year-old retired parliamentarian who was famous for his erudition and his oratory, Ollivier was also known as "the Kingmaker," because of his political influence.

"Sir," it began. "I have the honor to inform you that I am the United States Consul residing at Auckland with jurisdiction throughout the Colony."

Then, after stating the circumstances of the case that seamen "Alexander Henderson and William Hartwig" were bringing in the Lyttelton magistrates' court, "against the Captain and owners of the schooner '*Sarah Hunt*'," this being "for damages arising out of an alleged fraud," Griffin "respectfully" called Mr. Ollivier's attention "to certain regulations issued by the President of the United States of America for the guidance of Consular Officers abroad."

In this book of regulations, he went on, "amongst other things it is prescribed that Consuls shall have exclusive charge over vessels belonging to their nation, and shall alone take cognizance of differences and disputes which may arise between the Captain and officers and crew either at sea or in port, particularly in reference to the adjustment of wages in the execution of contracts. And further that the local authorities shall not interfere in these differences." Therefore, as the plaintiffs were American seamen and the defendant was the captain of an American vessel, the case should be heard "in the Courts of the United States" and "according to the law of the United States" — if it was heard at all.

"For these reasons I feel it my duty as Consul to protest," he concluded; "which I do most respectfully against the said Alexander Henderson and William Hartwig being allowed to prosecute the above mentioned action in the said Court."

Then after Griffin had signed it, "I have the honor to be, Sir, Your most obedient servant, Gilderoy Wells Griffin, United States Consul for Auckland, New Zealand and the dependencies thereof" the letter was sent by messenger to Magistrate Ollivier's house.

He waited in vain for a response. Night passed, and the next day dawned. Then it was February 20, the scheduled day of the hearing, and still Consul Griffin had received no reply.

The Elephant Voyage

s.s. *Manapouri*

16: *The Court Case*

Mr. J. B. Fisher appeared as counsel for the plaintiffs; Mr. H. N. Nalder and Mr. J. C. Martin for the master and owners, and Mr. George Harper for the American Chief Consul at Auckland, the Hon. G. W. Griffin
– The Press, *Christchurch, February 21, 1884.*

The court must have seemed as packed with lawyers as it was with the public.

"The Bench was occupied by John Ollivier, Esq. R.M., and Messrs. Guinness and Allwright, Justices of the Peace," noted the reporter for the *Lyttelton Times*. In the forward part of the body of the court, lawyers solemnly arranged papers and legal tomes on their desks. Outside, it was a mild day with slightly overcast blue skies and gentle breezes, but inside it was uncomfortably warm.

Wilhelm Hertwig's case was called first.

Consul Griffin's lawyer, George Harper, immediately stood up, waving a copy of Griffin's unanswered letter to Mr. Ollivier. This action should not be heard at all, he remonstrated; he wished to call the attention of the Court "to a protest which had been lodged on behalf of the American Consul, who respectfully submitted that the Court had no jurisdiction after being requested by him not to act." He, Mr. Harper, had advised on the wording of the letter, he said, and if their Worships thought it necessary, he was prepared to substantiate the points Mr. Griffin had made by citing precedents. He had a copy of Wheaton's massive treatise on international law with him, and would be very happy to quote relevant passages to anyone who might want to debate the rights and powers of the United States consular service to adjudicate in the differences and disputes of American seamen on American vessels, whether in port or at sea.

The instant he had run to a stop, the seamen's representative, Mr. James Bickerton Fisher, jumped up in dismay — "while begging his learned friend's pardon," he wished to object to both Mr. Harper's presence and his sudden and unexpected argument. It would have been only fair to all the other parties if they had been given notice that a protest had been lodged, he complained. As it was, he felt "quite unprepared to meet the array of talent" that had arrived to argue the case.

There was no need for any warning to be given, Harper countered. The Consular officer was "supreme in this matter, and had a perfect right to protest without any notice." And Mr. Fisher was quite mistaken if he thought that he, Mr. Harper, had come to argue the case. "He (Mr. Harper) was not appearing on either side, but wished merely to show that the Consular officer, if he chose to exercise his power of putting a stop to the hearing of the case, had that power."

Magistrate Ollivier (undoubtedly recollecting the reasons he had chosen not to answer that letter of protest) briskly countered this argument. While he admitted that there were cases—"and this might be one of them"—in which the court had no jurisdiction, that "was for their Worships to say," and not the U.S. consul.

"If Mr. Harper proposed to draw his attention to any particular cases he would be happy to hear them," Mr. Ollivier went on, but he felt he should warn Mr. Griffin's counsel that "he agreed with the principle set out in Addison on Contracts, that the contract must be such as to be valid in both countries, the country in which it was made, and the country in which its breach was being tried."

Mr. Harper was not here to argue this, he said: "His learned friends, Messrs Nalder and Martin, would take that up." He was present purely on behalf of the American Consul, who had been appointed in America. "There was no treaty between the United States and this country, there had never been any necessity for one, and, therefore, Mr. Griffin was in the position of Consular officer in a foreign country, and was subject to the regulations laid down by those appointing him" — which were the regulations of the United States.

Mr. Ollivier again begged to differ, observing dryly that he was convinced that "the Consul assumed a higher position than that." He had read Consul Griffin's protest, he said, and wanted to draw Mr. Harper's attention to the second paragraph — the one that ran, "I would respectfully call your attention to certain regulations issued by the President of the United States of America for the guidance of Consular Officers abroad," and which went on to claim "that Consuls shall have exclusive charge over vessels belonging to their nation and shall alone take cognizance of differences and disputes which may arise between the Captain and officers and crew either at sea or in port, particularly in reference to the adjustment of wages in the execution of contracts," and directed, further, that "local authorities shall not interfere."

If this had just been a matter of wages, it would have been a different matter, the Magistrate said, but the two seamen had a different problem, one of being shipped fraudulently. This required a swift remedy, "and that remedy could only be obtained by these men by coming to Court." Accordingly, therefore, His Worship could not and would not let Consul Griffin put a halt to the hearing.

Mr. Harper admitted that indeed "it would be a grave matter to determine whether or not the Court could be asked to set aside the contract," but went on to deny that this was any part of his case. What he argued, he said, was that Mr. Griffin, being the accredited United States Consul, had full power to act and adjudicate. As the *Lyttelton Times* dutifully reported, "He was in a position to discharge the seamen in case of complaint, and to award them any compensation he might think fit." And with that, apparently without pause to take breath, the lawyer cited precedent, just as promised, describing in detail "two cases which had come before the Court of Admiralty" in London, "and which were not questions of wages solely."

His Worship, not at all fazed, counteracted this learned argument by quoting from James Kent's four-volume *Commentaries on American Law*. And Mr. Harper, equally undaunted, counter-quoted from Henry Wheaton's *Elements of International Law*.

And so the learned argument went on.

The lawyers might have been enjoying themselves, but the crowd was growing restive—almost as restive as Mr. Fisher, who jumped up and objected again. It was "manifestly unfair," he protested, "that the plaintiffs should be met with an array of talent like that, without notice."

Before this day, he complained, it would have been hard to conceive that "his learned friend, Mr. Harper, could be capable of acting so unfairly." Right up until the moment the hearing had opened, he had had no idea that the U.S. Consul was playing any part at all. He had come "prepared to meet only the owners and the captain," and so it had put him at a most disagreeable disadvantage.

Mr. Ollivier found this easy to dismiss, reminding Mr. Fisher that there had been previous cases heard by the court in which captains and consuls played a part. "Mr. Ward had thought proper, in so important a case, to communicate with his chief officer," he said, and so Mr. Griffin was here. That was the fact of the matter, and Mr. Fisher just had to accept it.

He did accept that Consul Griffin was simply doing his duty, Mr. Fisher complained, but he really should have been given notice of the protest, so he could have had a chance to prepare for it. Then he sulkily sat down.

The representative of the two seamen having been quelled, Mr. Harper changed tack slightly, adopting a more conciliatory tone. Consul Griffin, he told His Worship, had intervened only because he was looking after the best interests of fellow citizens of the United States. None of them had starved, or gone without medical care or lodging. "He had provided for the seamen's wants, and had the means of shipping them back to their own country." And when the consul had used the word "protest," he had only meant to establish his position.

Placated, Mr. Ollivier agreed that the protest had indeed been most courteous, at which Mr. Harper went on with his learned argument, just as if Mr. Fisher's interruption had never happened.

Mr. Consul Griffin had referred to consular regulations, he said—and these, as laid down in Wheaton, pages 219 and 220, confirmed his sole power to adjudicate over such matters. There were many instances where the consul's right to intervene had been recognized, he declared. And, to back this up, he cited cases "of the *Timor* 9 *Law Times* N. S. 2977, of the *Herzgoven Marie* 5 *Law Times* N. S. 88, of the *Agincourt Law Journal* Reports, Admiralty 37," before moving on to William Hall's *Treatise on International Law*.

"That," he said, finishing up at last, "was the position his client took up with regard to the right of intervention." In Mr. Griffin's view, it was an American matter, solely— and it was a testament to this that ever since the matter had been brought to his notice, the U.S. consul had paid for the men's maintenance.

Someone in the gallery roared, "He has not!"

"Who is that delinquent?" Mr. Ollivier demanded. When no one answered, he warned the crowd not to interrupt the proceedings again. One more outburst like that, and the offender would not just be ordered out of court, but committed for trial as well.

Silence restored, Mr. Harper said he had come to the end of his argument, and "would now leave the matter in their Worships' hands."

Their Worships were not long in making up their minds—"notwithstanding all that had been said by Mr. Harper," Mr. Ollivier pronounced, the Bench was of the opinion that the hearing should proceed.

Accordingly, Mr. Nalder was called.

Captain Miner's lawyer at once declared that he was here only under protest, "on behalf of the master and owners of the schooner." And, while he did not wish to go into the erudite kind of exposition on international law that his learned friend Mr. Harper had demonstrated, he could quote cases like "Reuter, 1, Dodson 23, and of the *Nina* 3, *Maritime Law*, cases 10" (the latter of which dealt with the prickly matter of wages), and he could expound on the law of flags, too, if necessary. "He would also submit," he said, "in the authority of Johnston v. Machielson, 3, Campbell 44, that though the plaintiffs were suing on a tort founded on a contract, that fact did not alter the position of the parties."

And because of the position of the parties, he said, speaking plainly at last, the court had no jurisdiction in this matter. And, even if it did, it would be advisable not to exercise it.

"And what grounds do you have for that statement?" His Worship inquired in frosty tones.

"The summons, your honour. The summons was taken out against the master and owners without the parties being named, as required by the Resident Magistrates Act."

As Miner's lawyer went on to elaborate, "Neither the captain nor the owners were corporations, and therefore should be sued in their proper names." Additionally, as the unnamed owners were in America, Mr. Nalder submitted that the Court had no power to summons them.

And, to back this up he cited "Howarth v. McBeth, *Macassey's Reports* 653." Furthermore, he said, "The Court, or rather his Worship, as Justice of the Peace, had made an order that was *ultra vires*." In short, his Worship had decided that the summons might be served by leaving it on the schooner, though there was "no power in the Act authorizing such service." Instead, according to section 33, the summons had to be left "at his last or usual place of abode" — which was obviously impossible, as the owners were in the United States.

"But what about section 292 of the Merchant Shipping Act?" asked Mr. Ollivier.

"The Act restricts its operation to British ships, your Honour."

But surely, Mr. Ollivier said, Mr. Nalder was aware that everyone involved in this case had agreed that "the service of the summons should be taken for what it was worth."

He had not agreed, Mr. Nalder emphatically denied. He had tried to raise an objection to the proposal that the summons to the unnamed "Captain and Owners of the schooner *Sarah W. Hunt*" could be served on the vessel itself, but his objection had been barred by Mr. Meares.

Again the harried seamen's representative interjected. The Merchant Shipping Act provided for the serving of a summons "on board any ship to which the master belonged, on a person appearing to be in charge of such a ship," Mr. Fisher argued — "in his experience of 15 years at the bar, in all actions against owners and captains the service had been made in this way." It was merely a matter of procedure. "Where the parties could not get the names they could not be compelled to furnish them."

For once, Mr. Ollivier agreed with Mr. Fisher. Mr. Nalder was determined to destroy this important case on the basis of "a mere quibble or unimportant formality," he complained — at which Captain Miner's lawyer stood up to protest energetically that he was *not* just quibbling. Instead, he was raising *important* points of law. "The names of the defendants must be given," he repeated — the names of *all* the defendants, yet the summons had simply been addressed to "the Captain and owners."

But that was enough, Mr. Fisher objected — the "captain was *dominus navis*" — the supreme power and representative of the owners on board. To legalize the matter, all that was needed was for Mr. Ollivier, as the Resident Magistrate who had issued the summons, to insert the captain's full name.

His Worship said that of course he could do that. He would insert the captain's full name. What was it?

A pause. "I don't know," said Mr. Fisher.

Mr. Nalder protested incredulously at this, asking if it was not playing games with the Court to say that the name of the master, who had been living in Lyttelton for three months, was unknown — as for himself, he "would say at once that his name was Miner."

Mr. Fisher admitted that he understood that the captain's name was Stephen Miner.

A voice from the gallery called out, "Sanford Stephen Miner."

There was another pause while His Worship amended the summons by inserting the (erroneous) name of the captain, and Mr. Nalder asked how the plaint stood now.

"William Hertwig versus Sanford Stephen Miner, master, and the owners, and so forth," said Mr. Ollivier.

"But the names of the owners must be set out," insisted Mr. Nalder. Then he pointedly added that "this was by no means a quibble," and quoted from the judgment of his Honour Mr. Justice Johnston, in Latter v. Brogden.

"Then strike out the owners," Mr. Fisher suggested.

Mr. Nalder objected to this too, saying that the Court "could not strike out parties to a suit." It could make amendments "as would secure justice being done between the parties, but could not alter the parties." And, to back this up, he asked whether he could trouble the Court by reading the judgment of Mr. Justice Chapman, given in Howarth's case, as reported by Macassey.

Mr. Ollivier assented, and the packed gallery listened numbly as Mr. Nalder quoted at length. Mr. Fisher, however, was still unconvinced; he argued again that the words "and Owners" could be struck out from the summons. And that, he said, "would bind the ship" to the outcome of the case.

"But that would cause a war with America!" exclaimed Mr. Harper, and had a good laugh at the very idea of the New Zealand justice system confiscating an American ship because of a legal action against its master and owners.

And, with that, the lawyers silenced.

The magistrates conferred, while everyone waited. Then Mr. Ollivier banged his gavel and announced "that the Bench had determined that they would nonsuit the plaintiff, on the ground that the plaint was informal."

Mr. Fisher, puzzled and plaintive, asked in what way was the plaint informal.

"Because the names of the owners were not given," said His Worship.

"The actions brought by two of the seamen of the *Sarah W. Hunt* against the master and owners were brought before the Lyttelton Resident Magistrate's Court this morning," reported *The Star* that night. "In the first the plaintiffs were non-suited, as the owners are non-resident in the Colony. The second was withdrawn."

Against all expectations, the case had been won by Captain Miner's lawyer.

17: The Verdict

United States law recognizes men of all nationalities as American seamen, and entitled to protection as such, if lost, when shipped on board American vessels
– Lyttelton Times, *21 February 1884*

"A very foolish summons by the seamen of the *Sarah W. Hunt* against the master and owners of the vessel was dismissed yesterday by the Bench of Magistrates at Lyttelton, after much useless talking and waste of time," wrote the editor of *The Star* next day. "If there is any point in international law more clearly defined and decided than another, it is that the Consular authorities of a foreign power are the sole judges of any dispute between the masters and crews of any vessel sailing under their flag."

And had the magistrate been "so ill-advised as to give judgment against the American vessel, and enforce it, there might have been serious complications with the United States Government, which would have been only too delighted to stir up a little mild amusement of this sort." However, "as they say in Parliament, the question passed in the negative," he concluded; "which was a very good thing. The crew of the *Sarah W. Hunt* may depend upon getting justice from the United States Consul, who is the proper authority to apply to."

Hertwig, Henderson, and their three shipmates did not agree with this at all, being angry and confused. Instead of talking their future over with them, however, Consul Griffin put the spare time to good use by doing some research into the New Zealand dairy industry. The court case had finished by noon, so he drove off with the Secretary of the Agricultural and Pastoral Association to inspect the model dairy at the Agricultural School at Lincoln. "Mr. Griffin, who left Christchurch for Dunedin this morning," reported the Christchurch *Star* the day after the hearing, "is preparing a series of papers upon New Zealand matters, in order to give the American Government full information upon them. Among the subjects he is reporting upon is that of cheese and butter making. Mr. Griffin expressed much pleasure at what he saw at the model farm."

Indeed, Gilderoy Griffin was so pleased with what he saw — plus, of course, the outcome of the trial — that he took time to send a telegram to Auckland. "Our readers will remember that Mr. Consul Griffin last week proceeded to Lyttelton for the purpose of taking steps to put the affairs connected with the American sealer *Sarah Hunt* into a ship-shape position," noted the *New Zealand Herald* the next day. "A private telegram which was received from him in Auckland yesterday stated that all the difficulties connected with the matter had been satisfactorily arranged, and that he had visited the Agricultural College at Lincoln, where the strictest courtesy was shown to him. It is Mr. Griffin's intention to visit Dunedin before his return to Auckland."

The next day, Thursday, February 21, Griffin boarded the s.s. *Taiaroa*, which left at 6 p.m., and arrived at Port Chalmers the following day, in the early afternoon. After traveling the short distance to Dunedin by rail, he walked to Henry Driver's office at 9 Bond Street, in the business part of town, and was glad to find that the consular agent was expecting his visit.

Back in November 1881, Consul Griffin had taken a tour of the South Island, and Henry Driver had treated him like a royal guest, escorting him about the southern lakes; back then, the handsome, energetic entrepreneur had impressed Griffin so much that he had written about him in glowing terms to the State Department. Driver's "fine abilities, superior mental accomplishments and great wealth have made him quite a power in the land," he marveled. Since then, however, he had been greatly disillusioned, to the extent that it was a distinct relief to find that the consular agent had actually got around to taking down Crawford's testimony.

On January 29, nearly a month ago, the papers had reported that "Michael Crawford, the second mate of the American sealing schooner *Sarah W. Hunt*, is still an inmate of the Dunedin Hospital," going on to say: "It will be remembered that he had his shoulder badly injured on the vessel. The direct result of his sufferings when he was left on Campbell Island with his comrades is the loss of a big toe and one of his fingers." Even that public mention had failed to remind Henry Driver to follow Griffin's instructions to visit the seaman and take down his evidence. Instead, the consular agent had put it off until 12 February — and had probably only done it because of the wire he had received from Griffin, informing him that he would be coming on to Dunedin after the trial in Lyttelton was over.

Driver did have the excuse that he had a great deal on his mind. The contract between the Pacific Mail Steam Ship Company and the governments of New Zealand and New South Wales was in danger. While the agreement, which had been renewed in November 1883, was supposed to be binding for two years, agents of the New Zealand Shipping Company were lobbying hard for the mail to be carried by a direct steam service from London, and lately, Driver had heard whispers that they were about to combine with yet another rival company, Shaw Savill, to secure a parliamentary vote in their favor. According to the small print, if the United States refused to pay one-third of the total subsidy the contract could be terminated this coming November, on just three months' notice; Congress, so far, had failed to vote for the subsidy, and if the situation stayed that way, the British companies intended to take advantage of this loophole.

Because of his ambition to further commerce between the United States and the colony, Consul Griffin would have felt some concern when he was told this inside gossip. He would also have been alarmed to learn that in the latest round of trade talks the U.S. government had refused to reduce tariffs on wool. Driver, who was a wool exporter as well as an old parliamentarian, understood exactly how political winds could blow. As both men would have agreed, it was an ominous sign of the mood in Washington.

But the pressing matter was to get the report on the *Sarah W. Hunt* case written and sent to Washington, so Gilderoy Griffin wasted little time before heading to the hospital.

As he described to the State Department, he was pleased to find Crawford "progressing rapidly toward recovery," and to hear from the medical staff that he would be able to proceed to America in the course of a few weeks. "His arm and hand were severely injured and at one time amputation was thought to be necessary but through the skill of the surgeons at the Hospital they were saved with the exception of one of the fingers," he wrote.

Then Griffin went over Crawford's statement with him, referring to the transcription that Driver (or his clerk) had made, and asking for confirmation or elaboration of certain details. The second mate had begun his testimony by confirming to Henry Driver, "I, Michael Crawford, seaman, now in the Hospital Dunedin New Zealand suffering from injuries sustained on board the Schooner '*Sarah W. Hunt*' and from exposure in an open boat off Campbell Island do hereby depose and make oath that I am a native of Ireland sixty-four years of age. I shipped as Second Mate on the schooner '*Sarah W. Hunt*' (whereof S.S. Miner is Master) in July last at New Bedford Massachusetts United States of America for a sealing voyage to last two years. I was not aware of the locality of the sealing ground."

This was the first contradiction of what his erstwhile shipmates had stated, because the other men had insisted that they had been told by Pearl that the voyage would last just nine months. Crawford also called into question their claim of having been shipped fraudulently, stating, "The crew came on board at New Bedford of their own accord and were all sober. They were nearly all greenhands and foreigners mostly Germans. The crew were fully cognizant of the objects and duration of the voyage and frequently spoke among themselves on the subject."

He did back up what the others had said about the loss of Julius Jaeger. "Not more than a quarter of an hour had been taken up in looking for the man before the boat was recalled by the Captain," he said, and added, "I do not think the search was continued long enough." He also confirmed what had been said about his own injury—"The Captain would not recognize that I had hurt my arm and was unable to work and after lying up for a few days I was obliged to do my duty on board the '*Sarah W. Hunt*' as usual." As

Griffin noted later, in a letter to the State Department, the story about the second mate being obliged to work with a broken arm and wounded chest "had some foundation in fact."

Crawford's next contradiction of what the others had claimed came in his recounting of what Captain Miner had said as they left the schooner: "Our orders were to remain in company and if seals were seen in any numbers to return to the schooner and report. If a few seals only were met with we were to do our best to capture them.

"This was on a Tuesday in December I cannot recollect the day of the month," he went on:

> *We saw no seals and had not been away from the vessel more than two hours before we were blown away to sea. I tried to communicate with the mate to ascertain what he considered it best to do for the safety of the boats but could not get him to reply. The sea was very rough and the wind high and we had great difficulty in keeping the boat from filling. On Wednesday morning about four o'clock as nearly as I could judge we were within sight of the other boat, we lost sight of her about two hours afterwards and did not again see her. On Wednesday & three succeeding days we made repeated efforts to regain land & it was not until Sunday when the wind and sea had moderated that we effected a landing on the Island. The next day Monday it blew hard and we were afraid to venture out for fear of being again blown off land but on Tuesday morning the weather having moderated we sailed out of the bay round to the harbour in which we left the 'Sarah W. Hunt' at anchor and found she was not there.*

This was the first time Consul Griffin had heard the horrifying story firsthand, from one of the survivors. It would have eloquently provided any confirmation needed that his early decision to officially discharge the men from the crew of the schooner, "on account of their hardships and sufferings in the open boat and at Campbell's Island" was the right one.

As far as Captain Miner's treatment of his crew was concerned, however, Crawford was inclined to avoid the issue. "I have no complaints to make against the Captain," he said. "The Cabin table was well supplied and I had plenty to eat." However, as he emphatically went on to say, "If I were in a fit state to go to sea, I would not willingly rejoin the '*Sarah W. Hunt.*' I do not think the voyage will be profitable," he explained, thus betraying the experience of many years on whalers, where the men's pay depended on the profitability of the voyage; "and I do not like the conduct of the Captain when at sea."

Strangely, Crawford was not asked to elaborate on this, because he could have described more than mere bad temper — lapses of seamanship, or poor decisions made, perhaps. Instead, however, the topic returned to the seamen's grumbles about food. "Several complaints were made to me by the crew of insufficient food and I do not think the men in the forecastle had enough to eat," Crawford agreed, but, like Miner, he blamed the steward — "The Steward dealt out the provisions and I consider it more his fault than the Captain's that the men were short of food.

"I have seen the Captain strike members of the crew more than once," he finally admitted. He had paid little attention at the time, most probably because it was an everyday part of his long whaling experience. Though evidently asked for names and instances, he hedged: "I do not recollect how often or who were the men assaulted."

By contrast, Crawford was openly bitter about what he considered to be Miner's most reprehensible crime — that he had had so little hesitation in abandoning his men to a very cruel fate. "I do not think the Captain was justified in leaving Campbell Island as soon as he did," he said. "The harbour in which we left the '*Sarah W. Hunt*' at anchor was perfectly safe." Not only was it an inhumane decision, but it was tantamount to robbery. "All my clothes and Bank Book were on board the '*Sarah W. Hunt.*' I heard from the mate that some of the crew owned a few dollars and a watch or two."

In reply to a final question, Michael Crawford denied doing any sealing. "The mate shot a seal which sank," he said; but "we did not recover it." And, with that, he had appended his very shaky signature, and Henry Driver, after scribbling, "Subscribed and sworn to before me Henry Driver consular Agent of the United States this 12th day of February 1884" had signed the document, too.

And so the last testimony joined the written evidence of Captain Miner and the other castaways. Griffin's file on the *Sarah W. Hunt* case was at last complete.

There was no grand tour of the southern lakes this time. Even if Gilderoy Griffin had felt like being lavishly hosted by the unreliable Henry Driver, the weather prevented it, being appalling, with gales and thick rain.

There was a great deal of office work to do, as well as much to discuss about the consequences if Congress failed to vote for that crucial support for the Pacific mail run. As the reporter for the *Lyttelton Times* had correctly reported, Griffin had promised all the castaways, the foreign-born as well as the Americans, "they were entitled to be sent home," and would be put on board the next "Pacific mail steamer unless they should elect to go elsewhere."

They had all chosen to go to the States. Accordingly, over that busy weekend, Henry Driver booked steerage passages for the five men on the San Francisco-bound Pacific Mail Steam Shipping line steamer *Zealandia,* which was due to depart from Auckland on 4 March. Not only was this very convenient, as it would get the boys speedily away from New Zealand journalists, but putting them on board a Pacific Mail steamship was much easier on consulate finances.

As Gilderoy Griffin had found in the past, getting reimbursement from the State Department was slow and unreliable; his drafts were occasionally dishonored, which was embarrassing, and his accounts were often questioned, which was exasperating. So, it was an excellent idea to save money wherever possible, and because both Henry Driver and Griffin's deputy in Auckland, Thomas Gamble, were agents, the consulate enjoyed a favorable arrangement with the Pacific Mail Steam Ship Line. If the castaways sailed on the *Zealandia*, the fare would be just $50 per head, while if Griffin was forced to put them on a British ship, it would be at least twice that amount.

But, to put them onto the *Zealandia*, he had to get them to Auckland — which meant they had to be booked onto the Union Steam Ship Company's crack steamer *Wairarapa*, which was due to arrive at Port Chalmers from Melbourne on Tuesday, 26 February. After leaving the south, she would call at Lyttelton on the way to Auckland, where she should arrive in good time to meet the Pacific Mail ship.

Telegrams flew forth between Griffin in Dunedin and Ward in Christchurch, directing Ward to arrange passages for the five castaways on the *Wairarapa*. And, to make sure that they left New Zealand, Consul Griffin would travel on the *Wairarapa* too, and personally see the seamen on board the *Zealandia*.

There was a hitch, however.

The *Wairarapa* steamed into Port Chalmers with her port quarter badly dented, and her poop deck awry, creating a storm of gossip.

Apparently she had left Melbourne with all her lights blazing, belting along at top speed. Steamship captains were a flamboyant lot, and Captain Chatfield was no exception. However, he was not just "show-boating" for the edification of watchers on shore.

According to what a passenger related to the press, the local steamship *Adelaide* was coming close behind, traveling at such a headlong speed that "flames fully six feet high" billowed from her smoke-stack. Chatfield hung back so that the *Adelaide* could catch up, and then the two steamers pelted down the harbor past Williamstown, "coaling up at a great rate" — as the passenger phrased it.

In a word, they were racing.

"It was fully known on board that a race was intended," he said. Everyone on their ship was most animated, with lots of "holloaing and making all sorts of noises," while bets were being placed. Then the race came to a sudden end, as the captain of the *Adelaide* altered course, steering straight at the port quarter of the *Wairarapa*.

Apparently, he meant "to jockey the *Wairarapa* out of her running" by forcing her toward the starboard side of the channel, but unfortunately there was a miscalculation, and the *Adelaide* ran right into the rear end of the New Zealand steamship, "making a most dreadful noise as she blew off her superfluous steam."

The crash was terrific. For a moment or two the steamers were so closely locked together that one athletic (or terrified) passenger jumped from one ship to the other. Then a sudden fog had come down. Losing sight of each other, the two steamers had come to a stop, and had sent boats across the water, asking if everything was all right.

Neither ship, as it turned out, was badly damaged. Though her beauty was marred, the *Wairarapa* was still just as seaworthy, as her speedy passage from Melbourne to New Zealand had demonstrated. The problem, for Consul Griffin, was that she was to be delayed in Port Chalmers while an inquiry was held in the Dunedin Custom House.

It must have been a comfort to reflect that because the *Wairarapa* had the local mail contract—which meant she collected all the colonial mail for onward shipment—the *Zealandia* would have to wait for her, to take on the postal bags. The timing of getting the five castaways from one ship to the other was going to be very tight, however.

The *Wairarapa* was due to arrive in Auckland on the very same day that the *Zealandia*, by the terms of her own contract, was bound to depart.

The Elephant Voyage

ss. *Wairarapa*

18: Departures

Here was a crew in distress. They had a grievance against their skipper, which they made a reason for refusing to go back to his ship. Their story was not a pleasant story by any means. It was enquired into carefully by a representative of their Government, with the result that, instead of being regarded as deserters, or poor wretches for whom there was no remedy, they were at once taken care of and despatched to their homes in the distant Union. This is behaviour in every way worthy of a great country
— The Lyttelton Times, *editorial, March 3, 1884*

On Thursday, 28 February, Gilderoy Griffin caught the 2:30 p.m. train to Port Chalmers, where the *Wairarapa* was ready for boarding at last.

The inquiry, which had finally been wound up earlier that same day, had ended inconclusively, as not a single one of the passengers from Melbourne had been willing to testify against such a popular skipper as Captain Chatfield. And anyway, as the *Otago Daily Times* gaily remarked, there was nothing in the law about steamboat racing, and so the board could do nothing about it.

After going up the gangway, Mr. Griffin was ushered through an entryway in a central deckhouse to a grand spiral staircase, which was carved out of teak. This led to an enormous dining saloon that was paneled with many exotic woods, and hung with fancy mirrors. Four rows of dining tables were surrounded by 120 revolving chairs, while at either end doors led to the first class cabins.

Above, reached by another curving stairway, was a music room that furnished with a piano, and paneled in polished sycamore. Forward of this was a smoking room, with chairs upholstered in American buffalo hide. It was in this last room, most probably, that Consul Griffin set out his writing desk, and arranged all the papers relating to the *Sarah W. Hunt,* putting the testimonies he had obtained from Joseph Ward and Henry Driver into their proper order, ready to be forwarded to the State Department. Having read these carefully, and jotted down some notes, he was set to write his reports to Washington, which he intended to do the next day.

Next morning, no sooner was the steamer safely moored alongside Lyttelton wharf, than Consul Griffin was down the gangway, on board the train, and on his way into Christchurch. When he arrived at Ward's office, it was to find that he had the castaways with him, and all the arrangements to get the boys to Auckland and onward had been made. As usual, the conscientious Joseph Ward had followed instructions.

Also as usual, George Duncan posed a problem. According to the Consular Regulations, he was entitled to relief even when adjudged a deserter — support that in cases of distress included being sent home. He had, however, done some temporary work on another vessel during the two months in Lyttelton, which made his case ineligible. Consul Griffin decided that it would need a special dispensation to include him with the others, a favor he did not feel inclined to grant. Therefore, he decreed, the ex-steward of the *Sarah W. Hunt* was to be left in Lyttelton, to find a States-bound captain who was willing to let him work his way home.

After Joseph Ward had left the office with the boys, on the way to putting them on board the *Wairarapa,* Griffin appropriated Ward's clerk, and a piece of official stationery was headed, "United States Consular Agency, Christchurch, New Zealand" with the date, "Feby. 29th, 1884." That done, he dictated a letter to John Davis, the Assistant Secretary of State in Washington, describing the testimonials he had assembled by referring to the notes he had made.

"After a careful perusal of these depositions, together with other facts elicited at the investigation by the Consular Agent and also from my own examination of the Master and crew during my visit to Christchurch," he intoned, "it does not appear to me that the charges made by the men against the Master have been sustained." For a start, as Griffin went on to point out, Crawford's deposition "acquits the Master of any intentional wrong to him." Additionally, the second mate had stated he had no complaint to make, and that the cabin table was well supplied. "Nor," Griffin continued, "is there any evidence to establish the charges of fraud in the shipment of the men. The shipping articles are such as are usually furnished to whaling vessels and the copy held by the Master was duly authenticated by the Collector of Customs at New Bedford."

However, as he reiterated, because "of their hardships and sufferings in the open boats and at Campbell Island," he had directed that the men should be discharged from the vessel, "and three months' extra wages collected in the case of each of them and disposed of as prescribed by the Consular Regulations."

The castaways were about to be "sent to Auckland via the Union Steam Ship Co. and from there to the United States," and Crawford, the second officer, would follow as soon as he was fit enough to sail. And, in the meantime, Michael Crawford's medical costs were being paid out of consular funds.

"P. S.," he added. "Up to the moment of closing the mail I regret to say that I am still without news of the boat which contained the First Officer, Charles Striebert, and the following seamen, Louis Scharffenorth, James Judson, Alymer Samis, Thomas Ennis and J. M. Arthur.

"G. W. G."

When this was signed, packed up with the testimonials, and the envelope sealed, another sheet of paper was headed up. This time, Griffin dictated a detailed report of all that had happened since he "arrived in this City on the 16th inst. for the purpose of endeavouring to settle some of the vexed questions growing out of the case of the American Sealing Schooner '*Sarah W. Hunt*' of New Bedford, Mass. of which S. S. Miner is master."

The background of the unfortunate court case two of the seamen had brought against Miner was described, along with the circumstances of his protest to Magistrate Ollivier. As Griffin went on to relate, the case was non-suited on a technicality, but, as his lawyer, Mr. Harper, had informed him, "the case apart from this objection would not have continued very long as the evidence would disclose the fact that the contract was made in the United States and that my protest would ultimately prevail."

After he had signed this, and attached the two original summonses, along with a copy of his protest (also penned by the clerk), and the page from the *Lyttelton Times* that gave a detailed account of the trial, this was sealed up, too.

Then Consul Griffin pocketed the two packages, and headed back to the railway station, to catch the train to Lyttelton and return to his cabin on the *Wairarapa*.

The journey north was not without excitement.

At six the next morning, March 1, the *Wairarapa* berthed in Wellington — and the instant she was moored George Duncan bolted down the gangway, pursued by the ship's officers. People threading through the heavy traffic on the cluttered wharf were treated to the sight of a hot chase as the ex-steward fled from one teetering pile of freight goods to another.

After a great deal of shouting he was finally captured, and frog-marched to the nearest police station, where he was handed in as a stowaway. The day was Saturday, but the magistrate's court was in session, and so Duncan was promptly charged "with having travelled from Lyttelton to Wellington by the s.s. *Wairarapa* without paying his fare."

Defiant as ever, Duncan pleaded, "Not guilty."

Chief Detective Browne stepped up to conduct the case for the prosecution. First to be called was "Henry Taylor, purser of the vessel, who gave evidence that he found the accused in the steerage last night, and asked him for his ticket. The prisoner replied that he had not one," so the purser told him to hand over one pound, ten shillings. "Duncan replied that he had no money, and said he considered he was entitled to a passage to Auckland."

Duncan then took the stand to deliver one of his rambling statements in his own defense, claiming that "at the suggestion of a gentleman in Lyttelton" he had gone on board to get the signatures of his late shipmates appended to a document, on which he had drawn up with a list of charges against Captain Miner. While he was doing this, to his surprise and dismay, he said, "the steamer moved off," which meant that "he was reluctantly compelled to come on to Wellington."

But he should have been on board legally, or so he reckoned—when the consular agent had paid for his shipmates to sail to Auckland, he, George Duncan, had been left behind in Lyttelton, "simply because he had preferred some charges against the captain of the schooner." He had come on board "to try and see the American Consul," he said, "as he had serious charges to prefer against the captain of the *Sarah Hunt.*"

After Duncan had finally been persuaded to quit the witness box, the arresting officer, Constable Cullinane, took the stand to describe the comic circumstances of Duncan's capture—"that when he arrested the accused this morning he was running up the wharf and endeavouring to elude the officers of the vessel." Martin Tierney, who had come on shore with two other members of the late crew of the *Sarah W. Hunt*, spoke up then to give evidence for the defense, but the magistrate, who knew the circumstances of the case as well as anyone else who read the papers, considered their testimony "of no importance whatever."

Duncan was fined five pounds and tossed out into one of Wellington's notorious northerly gales, while his three erstwhile shipmates returned to the steamer *Wairarapa* without him.

The s.s. *Wairarapa* arrived alongside the Queen Street wharf in Auckland at 11:30 a.m. on March 4, to find that the *Zealandia* had been ready and waiting for twelve hours, having docked at 11:30 the previous night. Luckily, she was at the same quay. Consul Griffin collected Whittle, Hertwig, Henderson, Huber, and Tierney, made sure they had their kitbags with the possessions they had collected from the *Sarah W. Hunt*, walked with them down the wharf, and escorted them up the gangplank onto the United States-bound steamer.

It is not known whether the boys were aware that they had been traveling on the same ship as the consul, but the meeting, whether expected or not, was not a happy one. What they did know was that Captain Miner had been ordered to hand over three months' wages for each and every one of them, and they fully expected Mr. Griffin to give them what they considered was their fair due for three months of hard work and bad usage.

He certainly was not going to do that, Consul Griffin frostily informed them. If there had been any money at all, it would have paid for their medical expenses in Dunedin, and their board and lodging in Christchurch. They were to count themselves fortunate that the consulate had provided their fares to San Francisco, instead of leaving them to fend for themselves in New Zealand.

And, with that, the consul put on his hat and disappeared down the wharf, intent on his next task. This same evening he was to be one of the "large and influential company of gentlemen" invited by the directors of the New Zealand Shipping Company to a banquet on board their crack steamer *Ruapehu* (also berthed at Queen Street wharf, which was particularly busy that day), and he had a speech to prepare. It was one that promised to be unusually difficult, the New Zealand Shipping Company being the hot rival of the Pacific Mail Steamship Company. Griffin would be forced to be very diplomatic in his phrasing, taking refuge in vague descriptions of his recent visit south—the large herds of cattle and flocks of sheep, "the multiplying blades of grass and stalks of grain" like "banners of peace in green and gold," which signaled the prosperity that had enabled the people of New Zealand to subscribe "so liberally for the support and perpetuation of the direct steam service with Europe."

So it would not be surprising if he forgot the five disgruntled seamen. They were not to be fobbed off so easily, however. Once they had settled in their berths in the dormitory-like steerage quarters of the mail steamer, the young men set to writing letters to their friends in Christchurch, complaining that they had been denied their rightfully earned compensation, and asking for legal advice. They had to write quickly, as they had to hand them into the postal agency on shore before the *Zealandia* cast off her lines at four that same afternoon, but somehow they managed it, because the letters were delivered within the next three weeks.

"Private letters have been received here from the crew of the American schooner *Sarah W. Hunt*, that sealing vessel about which so much has been published," related the editor of the Christchurch *Press* on 26 March, going on to note that the writers complained that when they arrived at Auckland *en route* for America, they were informed "that of the three months' wages they were alleged to have been promised, one month's pay was to go towards defraying their expenses whilst in the hospital in Dunedin, and the remaining two months' pay to defray the cost of their board and lodging subsequently in the different places at which they were billeted.

"This very proper arrangement," he dryly remarked, "appears to have been regarded by the crew as unexpected and unsatisfactory."

The item, along with the editor's comment, was reprinted in the Auckland *Star* on March 27, drawing an instant response from an unnamed correspondent, who could well have been Consul Griffin himself. As he wrote, "an idea appears to prevail amongst those not acquainted with the laws of the United States that the three months' extra wages collected by the American Consul for every seaman ordered to be discharged by him belong to the seaman." This, however, was not so. "According to section 4,580 of the Revised Statutes of the United States, one month's extra wages is the property of the United States Government, and is credited to the Relief Fund." The rest of the money belonged to the seaman, *but only* if there was not a charge on the consulate. If his board, lodging, and transportation needed to be paid, then the consulate would do it, and any money left over — "*if there be any*" — was given to the seaman.

This, the writer went on, was not the case with the crewmen of the *Sarah W. Hunt*, for the simple reason that the schooner was classed as a whaler, where the seamen were not paid wages, but a share of the profits of the catch. The consul had sent an order to the owners of the vessel "duly signed by the master" claiming the six men's share of the money the voyage had made. Unfortunately, the *Sarah W. Hunt* had made no money whatsoever, and so the total cost of medical care, board, and lodging had been paid out of consular funds.

For Gilderoy Griffin, that drain on consular funds was to prove critical. On the same day that he delivered the boys to the *Zealandia*, he wrote to the State Department with a statement of expenses: "I have the honour to report my return to Auckland from Christchurch this morning after an absence of 19 days on account of business connected with the American schooner *Sarah W. Hunt*," he dictated to his clerk, going on to state that his fares by steam and railway had come to a total of $196. Then he asked for permission to charge the full amount on his next quarterly account.

He certainly deserved it, according to that loyal fan, the editor of the *New Zealand Herald*. On 5 March, when the paper noted that Consul Griffin had returned the day before, the editor commented that he had emerged triumphant from his critical role in the strange saga of the *Sarah W. Hunt* — "This tangled case he succeeded in getting satisfactorily settled, and after that took a run to Dunedin in connection with the duties of his office. He is much pleased with what he saw, and the universal hospitality and kindness which he had extended to him wherever he went. He found that his name was well known throughout the length and breadth of the colony."

More accolades came when his book, *New Zealand: her Commerce and Resources*, was launched in April. A "handsomely bound volume of 180 pages," containing chapters on subjects ranging from woolen manufactures to horse-breeding and systems of credit, plus a "valuable map showing road, railway and steamer routes and distances," it met with good sales and warmly admiring reviews from everyone — everyone, that is, except the reviewer for Wellington's *Evening Post*. He, by contrast, was so furious that Auckland merited more pages than his own city that he recommended that the government should withdraw it, and replace it with one that devoted "a few lines to make clear the fact that Wellington has a harbour."

Well, expostulated the editor of the *Auckland Star*, "for true Wellington bombast," that would be hard to excel. It was an excellent book, the editor of the *New Zealand Herald* declared—not only was it impartial and informative, but it was also "very readable." Wrote a reviewer of the *opus* in the *Taranaki Herald,* "The book contains a vast amount of information respecting New Zealand, and cannot be too widely circulated."

Ominously, however, when Griffin went to the bank that same month with "a draft on the Secretary of State for the relief of the destitute American seamen of the unfortunate American sealing schooner *Sarah W. Hunt*" to the amount of the expenses he had claimed, $196, the bank refused to cash it, on the grounds that the U.S. Treasury had dishonored Griffin's last two drafts, which were for $110 and $149.44 respectively. Two years previously, Griffin had cashed a $200 draft on the State Department, claiming it was compensation for expenses involved "in compiling statistics and other information for my Consular reports" but after a long deliberation in Washington, the Secretary had decided that it had not been warranted. According to the State Department books, therefore, the consul had been overpaid, so this was the State Department's way of getting back the money—plus, presumably, accumulated interest.

Feeling hard-pressed and unappreciated, Consul Griffin decided to look for another job, preferably in a port where many more fee-paying American ships dropped anchor. Therefore, he applied for a sixty-day leave to return to America, "with the hope of obtaining a transfer to a more lucrative post." This was given, and on 27 May he sailed off on a Pacific Mail line steamer, carrying with him a long testimonial that had been ceremoniously handed over by the Auckland Chamber of Commerce three days previously.

The Mayor of Auckland, William Waddel, had opened the proceedings by announcing that "the business men of the city had taken advantage of Mr. Griffin's approaching visit to his native land to recognize in a small way the literary ability of this gentleman" while the testimonial itself applauded, "that patient research, unwearied industry, and acquired knowledge" that Mr. Griffin had displayed "with distinguished ability." Everyone there knew that Gilderoy Griffin had ambitions for a higher rated post, and though they regretted this, they wished him well. "In presenting the testimonial His Worship the Mayor very felicitously expressed the hope that the services of Mr. Griffin would be recognised by the American authorities in giving him deserved promotion," wrote the *New Zealand Herald;* "either in the form of a more important appointment or in conferring on him the status of Consul-General."

They were not the only ones to wish him the best of luck in getting a transfer. Thomas Gamble, the man Gilderoy Griffin left in charge of the office, wrote to Washington the very same day that Griffin sailed. He wished to apply for his job, "should his mission prove successful."

19: *The Political Fall-out*

*Mr. Rolleston will certainly not face the Avon electors
again, and unless he is "kicked upstairs" his grave face
will be lost to politics — which, considering his experience
and honesty, is a pity*
— Otago Daily Times, *March 8, 1884*

The political ramifications of the *Sarah W. Hunt* affair
festered on, particularly in Canterbury. On March 3, the
editor of the *Lyttelton Times* acerbically pointed out that the
most fortunate aspect of the whole sad business was "the
accidental arrival of the Government schooner *Kekeno* at
Perseverance harbour before the provisions in the depot had
given out.

"And that is really not the nicest chapter in our naval
annals," he jibed; "of which the less that is said in future the
better for Mr. Rolleston's reputation as an administrator."

There were, of course, other issues. On March 25, the
small but vociferous North Island paper, *Egmont Courier,*
attacked Rolleston's vision of a lend-lease system, one that
would allow ordinary men to invest in farmland, calling it
"Rolleston's fad." In the South Island, where Rolleston
battled the local land-barons in his fight for economic
fairness for all, the *Ashburton Mail* was particularly bitter.
"Mr. Rolleston at one time stood high in the opinion of the
Canterbury farmer, and deservedly so," wrote the editor.

Since then, though, the costs of freighting grain by rail had gone up, and in his candid opinion, "The *Gazette* which contained the new railway tariff should also have contained a notification that Mr. Rolleston had resigned office."

Besieged by bad press, William Rolleston scheduled a meeting with his constituents on Saturday, 19 April, which promised to be very stormy indeed. If he was looking for auguries, he needed to read no further than a satirical poem, called "Major Atkinson to the Honourable W. Rolleston" which was published in the Christchurch *Star* just two days before the engagement:

> *Wink at me, Rolly, with thine eye (it began)*
> *And I will wink with mine:*
> *Go, tell the good old ancient lie,*
> *That's served full many a time.*

When Rolleston entered the hall, it was to be received with hisses, punctuated by a few loyal cheers.

"Mr. George Harper" (coincidentally, Consul Griffin's lawyer in the *Sarah W. Hunt* case) "was voted to the chair," with a taxing challenge to face. When he asked for a "fair and impartial hearing," the plea went quite unheard, the mood being so hostile. Despite constant heckling, William Rolleston tried to answer questions and explain his position, but inevitably the resolution was made: "That this meeting has no confidence in the Hon. W. Rolleston as the representative of the Avon district in Parliament."

Much loud applause, whistling, and stamping of feet followed. "The motion was carried by acclamation and the meeting broke up," reported *The Star*. But that was not the end of it, by any means. As the editor commented in the same issue, "The further natural sequence is that the 'Want of confidence' declaration must be repeated on the occasion of the Premier's forthcoming speech in Christchurch."

As predicted, the Premier, the Hon. Major Atkinson, who had come to Christchurch in support of his minister, met an equally hostile reception. His meeting was held on Saturday April 26, and long before the start of proceedings "the large auditorium was closely packed," with over 2,500 people present. And the mayor, who was in the chair, had the same trouble securing a fair hearing that George Harper had had the previous week.

The land and tariff grievances were aired, with many comments and interjections, and then one of Atkinson's questioners abruptly demanded, "Can you justify the action of the Government in the *Sarah W. Hunt* case?"

"I do not know the exact particulars," Atkinson evaded, going on to bluster, "I was in Sydney at the time, but as the Head of Government I am prepared to take the fullest responsibility, and I have no doubt that my colleagues did what was right."

A voice from the audience shouted, "They did nothing!"

"Yes, they did," countered Mr. Atkinson lamely. "They sent a steamer."

On June 18, William Rolleston gave way to the unremitting hostility, and retired from the Avon electorate, retreating to the newly formed electorate of Geraldine. The Premier, Harry Atkinson, applied to the Governor for permission to dissolve parliament, and received it, and a general election was held in July 1884. Rolleston won the Geraldine seat, but the government was lost.

As Major Atkinson remarked, they were defeated by a combination of hostile groups with no common policy and no leader they could agree on. They prevailed by harping on a list of issues, and the government's tardiness in the matter of the *Sarah W. Hunt* rescue mission was one of them.

That Miner was still in Lyttelton had probably aggravated the political situation, as he was a constant reminder of the controversy, being featured in the papers as frequently as ever.

"Now that the last has been heard of the *Sarah Hunt's* survivors," the editor of the *Lyttelton Times* meditated on 3 March, at the same time that the five castaways were on their way Auckland, "two things strike one particularly. One is, that the abandonment in his hour of need of a skipper by a crew that was abandoned by him in an hour of much greater need, satisfies to some extent one's sense of poetical justice. The other is, that though there is no authority under the British flag to deal with subjects of the United States in any matters occurring outside British jurisdiction, Uncle Sam takes great care of his children wherever they may be."

The very next day, March 4, the *Lyttelton Times* editor must have felt slightly embarrassed, because the *Star* ran an unexpected message of support for the captain from Connecticut. "A voluntary testimony as to the humane character of Captain Miner was yesterday tendered to a member of the reporting staff of this paper, by a ten years' resident in New Zealand, who in August 1871, was in charge of the medicine chest on board the barque *Milwood*, then on a two years' voyage, under the command of S.S. Miner, from New Bedford to the Polar regions," it began:

> *This gentleman warmly testifies as to the kindly disposition of the master, under whom he sailed, and specially mentions two facts — one, that when a man fell*

from the main yard while furling the mainsail, a boat was manned and lowered within three minutes, and the sailor rescued through the promptitude with which Captain Miner gave his orders; the other, that in the only occasion when he remembers the men to have grumbled, the cause of their discontent was turned into one of satisfaction. The cook had served the men, on their return to the ship from a chase after a whale, with cold potatoes. When they complained, the captain not only soundly reprimanded the cook, but made him always afterwards have hot soup ready for the men on their coming on board under similar circumstances.

This was most mysterious. Unlike British and colonial ships, American vessels did not carry a surgeon, and the man in charge of the medical chest was the captain. So, had Captain Miner written this testimonial himself? It seems possible, particularly as the embarrassing fact that the *Milwood* had been wrecked during that voyage was not mentioned.

The Christchurch correspondent to the *Otago Daily Times* certainly wondered about it. As he pointed out, after the castaways had "sent a deputation to the *Lyttelton Times*, and some very awkward stories as to the treatment they were received were printed in the columns of that journal," Captain Miner had said nothing in his own defense. But, as soon as the seamen were "safely out of the way, a gentleman tenders testimony to the general sweetness of temper and care of his men displayed by Miner on a sealing voyage in Polar Seas as long ago as 1871." It was both odd and a pity that the fellow had not come forward sooner, in time to "forestall nasty insinuations."

There were two obvious conclusions, "either that this last evidence is cooked, or that the mariner's genial heart has grown preternaturally sour during his last 13 years of voyaging where the raging seas do roar and the stormy winds do blow."

There was at least one man in New Zealand who could have given an educated opinion of the unlikely testimonial. However, there is no record of anyone taking that issue of the *Otago Daily Times* to Michael Crawford (still in the Dunedin hospital), and asking what he thought. While he is likely to have found the image of any whaling captain ordering his cook to provide hot soup amusing, he would also have been able to point out that the medicine chest was kept in the captain's cabin, and so another man who could (at a push) describe himself as being in charge of it, was the captain's steward.

The steward on the ill-fated *Milwood* in August 1871 was named Francis Gerard—and in March 1884 a Francis Gerard was an assistant at the Zetland Hotel, 88-92 Cashel Street, Christchurch.

Was he the man who so belatedly stepped up to deliver this strange testament to Captain Miner's well-hidden heart of gold? It is impossible to tell. As it turned out, the story, being so hard to believe, did nothing to retrieve Miner's reputation as a harsh and heartless captain.

On 26 March—two days after Michael Crawford had been discharged from Dunedin Hospital with no fanfare whatsoever—the editor of the *Press* reported, "The schooner *Sarah W. Hunt* is at present lying at her moorings here, and should Captain Miner not find a purchaser for her, as it is said he probably may do, her destination in all likelihood will be San Francisco."

That the schooner was on the market was just part of the gossip that still surrounded the besieged shipmaster.

Selling the *Sarah W. Hunt* could have been an attractive prospect for him, but apparently he did not have the option, because the vessel was never advertised. Instead, Miner — with the help of Mr. Ward's shipping agency, Kinsey & Ward — continued the search for men to help him sail away from the gossip-ridden town of Lyttelton. Just three seamen were needed to sail the *Sarah W. Hunt* to Auckland, where there was a better chance to ship a crew, but even finding that small number seemed unattainable.

On May 6, it looked as if Captain Miner was going to take his schooner away, removing the last reminder of the contentious business. The Christchurch *Star* reported, "The American schooner *Sarah W. Hunt*, after a stay of about five months in the inner harbour, yesterday moved into the stream. Captain Miner, her commander, has engaged a crew, and it is whispered that the schooner is to take her departure for an American port."

But it was just a shift to the outer harbor. The *Sarah W. Hunt* swung at her new moorings for another month, while Joseph Ward struggled to find men who would agree to ship with such a poorly regarded captain. It was not until June 9 that Miner was able to write, "This day shipped three A.B. by the month for Auckland, N.Z. to report on board at 8 a.m. on the 10th of Jun. 1884 — they are August Ritenger, George Wilson and C. Sandberg."

June 10 dawned with no sign of the three men, who had evidently been hearing stories in the Lyttelton taverns. "Went on shore to bring them on board," wrote Miner. "But could not find them." Sub-consul Ward managed to locate them again, so the captain returned to shore next day, and ferried them out to the *Sarah W. Hunt* "after great trouble."

The *Sarah W. Hunt* finally weighed anchor on June 13, the shipping reporter for the Christchurch *Star* musing, "It will be remembered that this vessel arrived in port, after losing her crew, on December 8, 1883 (and has thus been in harbour over six months)." Now, at last, Captain Miner "proceeds to Auckland tonight, the schooner carrying her original stores."

Miner dropped anchor in Auckland at 3:30 p.m. on June 20, furled his sails, briefly noted events of that date in his logbook, and put down his pen. He did not pick it up again until July 2, after the three temporary hands had been replaced. "Fine and clear through the day. The old crew left the vessel and in the p.m. a new crew came on board to go on a sealing voyage. Look-out attended to," he wrote, without mentioning that the new crew had been sent on board in dribs and drabs, as Gamble, like Ward, had had trouble getting the men to turn up for duty.

His mood was more eloquently expressed in a letter he sent on that date to the owners of the schooner, which was published in *The New York Times* on September 21, under the dismal headline "A Very Unfortunate Voyage."

"The most disastrous voyage on record" from New London, it revealed, "is that of the sealing schooner *Sarah W. Hunt*." First, one of the seamen was lost overboard. Then, in "Perseverance Bay" two boats had set off to hunt Campbell Island shores, and had never returned. "Only the Captain and cook were left on the vessel. After waiting several days Capt. Minor gave them up as lost. He and the cook weighed anchor and under short sail made their way to Lyttelton, New-Zealand."

Then the second mate and his crew were rescued, "in a very exhausted condition and were placed in the Dunedin Hospital, New-Zealand, for treatment," the newspaper report continued. "On recovering they protested against continuing the voyage and were discharged by the Consul.

Now a letter has just been received by the owners from Capt. Minor, from Auckland, New-Zealand, informing them that he had secured a second mate and seven seamen and should sail on his voyage the next day toward and about Cape Horn."

The trigger for Miner's gloomy description of "the most disastrous voyage on record" could well have been a small item in the previous night's Auckland *Evening Star*, dated 1 July. "The United States Government has made a prompt and graceful recognition of the services rendered some months ago by the New Zealand Government steamer *Stella* and the schooner *Kekeno*, in rescuing from Campbell Island the castaway seamen of the sealing schooner *Sarah W. Hunt*," it began, going to reveal that the source of the news was Mr. Thomas Gamble—"the American Consul"—who had shared a despatch from the U.S. Secretary of State that strongly commended the "promptitude of the New Zealand authorities and the opportune movement of the *Kekeno* and *Stella*," both of which contributed so much to the rescue of the castaways of Campbell Island.

"In view of the facts the department has directed that a gold watch and chain be awarded to Captain J. B. Greig, of the *Kekeno*, and to Captain W. J. Grey, of the *Stella*, with a suitable inscription commemorative of the event," the notice continued. "These testimonials will be forwarded through the regular diplomatic channel, and will be accompanied by a letter expressing the Department's appreciation of the great kindness shown to these unfortunate seamen."

While all of New Zealand was still marveling over this "handsome recognition from Brother Jonathan" (as one of the papers phrased it), the *Sarah W. Hunt* slipped quietly out of Auckland. "July 4: this day wind SW with hard squalls," wrote Miner in the logbook. "Crew employed in cleaning ship. Lights, Pumps and Lookout attended to. Started on the passage from Auckland to Cape Horn."

He had a crew of ten—B. Anderson (first mate), James Rigg (second mate), a steward by the name of Smith, and seven men described as able seamen. This last listing was as misleading as the shipping of the greenhands had been in New Bedford. Just three days after weighing anchor, Miner found that at least one of them was not a seaman at all. "Seaman B. Ward not able to steer the vessel being a coal trimmer," the logbook laconically recorded.

Despite such difficulties, the schooner made it across the Pacific without incident. In August, the west coast of South America was sighted, and the crew hauled the schooner onto a tropical sandy beach, and heaved her down to scrub her bottom clean of weed and barnacles, while at the same time they fossicked for clams. On September 1, the logbook recorded that they "hove up anchor to sail the vessel through the channel — could not on account of the current setting in too strong to the Westward. Noon tide slackened and proceeded to sea." Then they turned south for the rock-studded southwest coast of Argentina.

The sealing part of the voyage had at last begun.

In August, in New Zealand, the papers were noting the twenty-fifth annual meeting of the Christchurch Chamber of Commerce. The business of the year was reported, with due attention given to the members' successful efforts in the *Sarah W. Hunt* affair, along with the news that Mr. James Drummond Macpherson, the unsung hero of the drama, had resigned as chairman.

The president's gold watches arrived in September, having been forwarded from London to the Governor of New Zealand, Sir William Jervois, along with a covering letter from the American ambassador at the Court of St. James, the famous plenipotentiary, James Russell Lowell.

"I have the honour to transmit herewith two gold watches which have been awarded by the President to Captain W. J. Grey of the New Zealand Government steamer '*Stella*,' and to Captain J. B. Greig, of the New Zealand Government schooner '*Kekeno*,' in recognition of the valuable services rendered by them to the crew of the American schooner '*Sarah W. Hunt*,'" it began, and went on to describe the circumstances.

According to what the State Department had been informed, "on the 27th November last, while the *Sarah W. Hunt* was lying in Perseverance Harbor, Campbell Island, the captain had ordered the two mates, with nine seamen, to cruise outside the harbor in search of seals" and a storm had suddenly blown up, driving them out to sea. One of the boats had managed to get back to the island, "where its occupants were found several days afterwards and rescued—after they had endured great privation and suffering—by the New Zealand Government schooner *Kekeno*, whose captain showed them every care and attention until the arrival of the steamer *Stella*, which had been sent by the authorities to their rescue."

In recognition of this, Ambassador Lowell continued, "I am instructed by the Secretary of State to convey to Her Majesty's Government an expression of the President's high appreciation of the kindness and humanity displayed by the masters and crews of the above vessels, and by the authorities of New Zealand in rescuing and caring for the unfortunate crew of the '*Sarah W. Hunt*.'"

Unrecorded in the papers that lauded this generous American gesture was a sense of discontent. In Canterbury there was a simmering complaint that while Captain Grey and Captain Greig had been recognized for the parts they played in the widely reported drama, the valiant efforts of the Canterbury Chamber of Commerce to get a ship down to Campbell Island on a search and rescue mission had gone unnoticed.

Both the Right Reverend Henry Harper, Bishop of Christchurch and Primate of New Zealand (coincidentally, the father of George Harper, Consul Griffin's lawyer) and Charles Traill, an internationally regarded naturalist who lived on Stewart Island, were greatly concerned about the unfairness of this — so much so that they wrote to Ambassador Lowell, to tell him about the fine people who, "upon hearing of the unhappy case of these men, immediately took measures for chartering a steamer at their own expense to go to Campbell Island on what seemed the very slender chance of rescuing three or four American seamen, and this in the face of the opinion expressed by the captain of the schooner that further search would be useless."

As the Bishop stressed, a timely meeting had been held in the Chamber of Commerce, and "subscriptions to the amount of £630 were promised by merchants of Christchurch and Lyttelton, and resolutions were passed urging prompt action independently of the Government in beginning the search at once"—an effort that ended only when it was learned that the government had finally listened, and dispatched a steamer.

Then, with the letters posted, the two writers waited for justice to be done.

On the far side of the Pacific the crew of the *Sarah W. Hunt* was engaged in the same kind of desultory, time-wasting behavior that had infuriated Captain Miner on Macquarie and Campbell Islands. On September 22, they lost the stock when hauling on an anchor, and the very next day one of the boats almost came to grief on "Dundee Rock." On September 25, Miner gave up, made sail, and tried to get out to look for a more promising beach, but, in an echo of the past, he was set back by a current, while all the time a heavy storm was blowing up.

In New Zealand, on that same day, Captain Grey was being presented with his "valuable gold keyless watch" which, according to the Wellington *Evening Post,* was accompanied by an inscription that read, "Presented by the United States President to Captain W. J. Gray in recognition of his search for, and rescue of the crew of the American brigantine *Sarah Hunt* at the Auckland Islands, December 1883." Captain Grey must have found the misspelling of his name as disconcerting as the mistakes in the name and rig of the schooner and the location where he had found Captain Greig with the missing men. However, it was an undeniably grand occasion.

The Clerk of the Executive read out the despatch from the United States Government that accompanied the watch, "at the conclusion of which his Excellency the Governor handed the watch to Captain Gray, accompanying his action with the remark that it gave him great pleasure to make the presentation on behalf of the American Government."

Captain William Grey responded with becoming modesty, though with a veiled jibe at the tardiness of the government in sending out the *Stella.* "The recipient replied in suitable terms," the *Evening Post* reported, "and expressed regret that he had not been able to rescue the whole of the crew. He thanked his Excellency for the present, but said he had only been carrying out his duty as a seaman in rescuing the castaways. Nothing would have given him greater pleasure than to have brought them all back."

Captain James Greig, who would otherwise have been at Government House with his brother shipmaster, was looking for castaways from the bark *Marie Ange*, which was believed to have been lost in Foveaux Strait, after a medical chest painted with her name had been found on the beach, along with scattered wreckage and a lifeboat.

Accordingly, his presentation had to be delayed until he was back in Invercargill, but on October 9, 1884, his gold watch was finally handed over at a well attended civic ceremony. "The Mayor said he had much pleasure in passing on from the ordinary business of the Council to the presentation to Captain Greig of a magnificent gold watch, on behalf of the American Government," reported the *Southland Times* the next day.

The letter from the American ambassador in London was read out in full, and then the mayor made a speech, to inform the assemblage that "it gave him very great pleasure in making the presentation, and he was sure equal pleasure would be felt by everyone in this part of New Zealand where Captain Greig was so favourably known.

"Gentlemen in the Captain's profession were remarkable for zealous and faithful discharge of duty," he orated, but "more perhaps than in any other, men frequently discharged their duties bravely, conscientiously, but unknown to the world and unhonored." That was not the case with the *Sarah W. Hunt* affair, however, "for the eyes of that great nation, America, had been upon the rescuers, and an earnest of the country's gratitude had been forwarded to them."

Captain Greig "accepted the present with thanks" and said he "was grateful to his Worship for the flattering terms in which he had spoken," but admitted he did not feel as if he had deserved it—"He was sensible of small merit he could claim to in his action in rescuing the Campbell Island castaways" as, after all, he had only found them by accident.

In looking after the poor fellows, he had done what any other man would do, because "had he not done so he would have been in some respects lower than the brute creation."

At the very same moment that the "gentlemen present" had gathered around to shake the hand of the hero, Captain James Greig, Captain Sanford Miner was facing another mutiny.

"A.M. Moderate breeze from N.W. daylight light breeze from N.N.W. with light showers of rain," wrote Anderson, the mate, in "*Sarah W. Hunt* Harbour," close to the southern tip of Argentina;

> *6.30 a.m. boat started for the seal rock. When half way to the rock the crew refused to pull out. When asked why they would not go, the awnser, it is to long a distance & to much sea & we could not get any seal to pay them*
>
> *Capt S S Mainer report*
>
> *10 a.m. Boat returned. The Mate reported that the men refused to go off to the rock. Called all hands asked them why they refused to go to the rock.*
>
> *George Allen acted as spokesman, said the wind was off the land, and too high a sea, and was there yesterday & was not going to run any risk of been caught away from the vessel with both anchors down, and also said the did not car to get any Seal at all. The following men refused, G. Allen, F. Janson, H. Paulsen, F. Hoffman, G. Endfield, B. Ward.*

Captain Miner found it impossible to reason with them, so he "hove up anchor and proceeded to sea." He steered straight for Sandy Point (Punta Arenas, at the western mouth of the Magellan Strait), and dropped anchor in the harbor on 14 October. At seven the following morning he called the crew aft, and gave them an ultimatum—would they go sealing, or would they not?

No, they would not, declared the six men. The decision was put in the log, and witnessed by the first mate, B. Anderson. Then Captain Miner sent for a police boat, and charged the man he considered to be the ringleader, second mate James T. Rigg, with mutiny. And history repeated itself yet again, because James T. Rigg, like the Campbell Island castaways, had a ready letter-writing pen, and a willingness to tell the world his side of the story, via the New Zealand newspapers.

"Our readers will not have forgotten the episode of the *Sarah W. Hunt*," announced the Christchurch *Star* with well-founded confidence on 26 January 1885, going on to reveal that a letter had been received from "Mr. James T. Rigg, second mate of the schooner."

"I shipped on board the *Sarah W. Hunt*, American sealing schooner, on the 1st of July, 1884, bound to the coast of Cape Horn," Rigg had written, by way of introduction, and launched himself into his story:

> The crew refused to go off in the boat to a rock five miles from the main land. The rock is surrounded by reefs and breakers. They had been off the day before and got the boat half filled with water. They said it was not safe to go there as there was too much sea on. The master of the schooner then

got under way to Sandy Point. Arrived at Sandy Point on October 14, 1884. The captain of the port came on board.

The master, S.S. Miner, stated that the crew refused to go to the sealing rock. He then called the crew aft and asked them what they were going to do — if they were going sealing any more or not. They said he brought the vessel there of his own accord. They had not refused to seal when the weather was fine. If anything happened to the boat there was not crew enough to go and look after them; also that there was not sufficient of a crew on board to work the schooner in among shoals and reefs. The crew then pulled the captain, S.S. Miner, ashore [in the boat]. He put them in gaol. They [the Argentinean police] told them that they would get ten years if they did not go back on the schooner.

The men are getting the 140 lay. The owners would have to make a large fortune before their crew get ordinary wages. Captain Miner wants the mate and me to go to Montefiedo to get another crew. He can get plenty of men to go sealing if he pays them as they are paid here. He will do that. He wants men to work for their food. I expect to go to gaol to-morrow because I will not work for my food. I would sooner take ten years in gaol than stay another six months in this vessel.

—I remain, &c., JAMES T. RIGG, second mate of schooner Sarah W. Hunt, Sandy Point.

"That delightful man, the master of the *Sarah Hunt*, has been once more before a strangely disliking public," commented the editor of the *Colonist*. "This time he has applied to some American Law Court to punish sundry of his crew who refused to go off from the ship among the rocky straits and rough seas off no worse a latitude than Cape Horn, on the paltry ground that in case of accident there were not enough men left on the ship to go to their rescue. Evidently untaught by the bitter experience of Campbell Island, an experience paid for by the lives of six brave men and the tears of their widows and orphans, this captain actually tried to put another boat's crew in a similar peril.

"Luckily for themselves, the men had heard of their commander's experience, and refused to run the risk. The only thing to be regretted is that Mr. Miner cannot be treated to a rope. If he lives long enough he will be. Nothing is more certain than that the loss of a boat's crew for want of hands to work the ship in chase, will, in his case, be morally the guilt of wilful murder."

Gilderoy Wells Griffin was not in New Zealand to read this savage prediction. The American consul had arrived back in New Zealand at midnight on September 20, and just weeks later, on November 17, had received a despatch informing him that he was now the American consul in New South Wales, and that he was to take up the post in Australia within the next thirty days. His quest for a better job had been successful.

"This is a substantial promotion, as Mr. Griffin will have jurisdiction at Sydney, Newcastle, and Brisbane, and the fees at these posts will amount to double those which Mr. Griffin has hitherto been receiving," noted his fan, the editor of the *New Zealand Herald*, adding rather plaintively, "While the people of Auckland will be glad to hear of Mr. Griffin's promotion, they will be sorry that he is leaving the place."

On December 10, 1884, a gathering of the town's highest dignitaries assembled to present him with a yet another long and admiring address, "in recognition of his services and the ability with which he had performed the duties in connection with the consulate here," as the *New Zealand Herald* reported.

Again, he was presented with a testimonial, this time signed by the presidents of all the major Chambers of Commerce (with the notable exception of Wellington, which still held a grudge for being overlooked in Griffin's book). In accepting the testimonial, and thanking the Mayor, just as everyone expected, and to general delight, Griffin "cited a number of statistics to show the rapid progress of New Zealand."

On Monday, December 15, when he left for Sydney on the mail steamer *Australia,* a large crowd of friends stood on the wharf to wave goodbye.

Days later, on December 19, American Ambassador James Lowell sat down at his desk in the American Legation in London, and wrote a letter that was intended to set matters straight. Delivered to Earl Granville, the British Foreign Secretary, it was then forwarded to the mayor of Christchurch, arriving in April 1885, and was published in the papers with justification and pride.

Ambassador Lowell referred to his letters of recommendation to "certain British officers" (Captains Grey and Greig) "for their services in rescuing some shipwrecked sailors of the American schooner *Sarah W. Hunt.*" At the time, he had not been in possession of the full facts, he believed, because since then he had received letters from the Bishop of Christchurch and Mr. Charles Traill of Stewart Island, acquainting him with the gallantry of "the people of Lyttelton, New Zealand" and informing him about the meeting in the Chamber of Commerce, "when subscriptions to the amount of £630 were promised by the merchants of Christchurch and Lyttelton." Though the money had not been needed, as the New Zealand government had decided to take the matter in hand, he now saw that it was important that the "humane intention" should be duly acknowledged.

"The above facts having been brought to the knowledge of the President," he wrote, "I am instructed to request Her Majesty's Government, through the proper channel, to convey to the inhabitants of Christchurch and Lyttelton, New Zealand, an expression of his high appreciation of the generous and humane spirit displayed by them in making arrangements with such promptness for sending a steamer to Campbell Island in search of the unfortunate Americans."

The recognition might have come late, but without doubt James D. Macpherson was pleased to read it.

In July 1885, after having been anchored at Punta Arenas, Argentina, since January, Sanford Miner abandoned this "most disastrous voyage on record." He shipped a new crew of eight for the passage home, and headed for New London. "Sept. 14: — Nontulk lite bearing NW 6 miles — run into New London and ankered off Barby warf," wrote his latest first mate, Grayland. "At 10 am. Hove along side and moored with cables fore and aft. This ends the passage. 12:30 health officer came on board. So ends."

The news took just a month to reach Auckland. "The sealing schooner *Sarah W. Hunt*, which was at this port some time ago, and which vessel, it will be remembered, lost a boat's crew while engaged illegally sealing at the Islands in the South, arrived in New London, Mass., on September 15," reported the *New Zealand Herald*. "The vessel was last from Patagonia, and the voyage had not been a successful one."

The *Sarah W. Hunt* had arrived home at last — with no oil or skins to report. In the strange whaling parlance of the time, she was "clean." After three years, much controversy, and going all the way round the world, her holds were as empty as the day she had sailed from New Bedford.

"In narrating their experiences to their friends, the crew of the *Hunt* will probably dilate on the numerous items in their chapter of accidents," the editor of the Christchurch *Press* meditated on 26 March, 1884.

This was the date when it had been expected the *Zealandia* would dock in San Francisco, but, as it happened, the *Zealandia* arrived three days ahead of schedule. The five boys who had survived a remarkable ordeal off Campbell Island walked down the gangplank into a cool, clear day, in the company of a mob of passengers who were probably thankful to be ashore, because the seven-day passage from Honolulu had been very rough, with a heavy beam sea.

And, empty pockets or not, they had disembarked into one of the most exciting cities in the world. The port was crammed with steamers, ships, barks, and schooners, many with their bowsprits extending far into the waterfront streets, all of them loading, or unloading, or getting steam up, or making sail, preparing to weigh anchor for local and exotic ports. This was the city where the streets were paved with gold, according to the legend, and bordered by land where men could go into the hills with a simple grubstake and come out millionaires.

But, even if they emerged from the "diggings" even poorer than when they had set out, they had gained a great store of stories of hardships, disappointments, triumphs, disasters, and amazing things they had seen. In a phrase, they had "seen the elephant."

California was where the phrase that symbolized the great American nineteenth century adventure was spawned.

And this was where the newspaperman was right in his prophesy.

Whether Whittle, Huber, Tierney, Henderson, and Hertwig shipped out as seamen, found work in town, or headed for the hills is unknown. But wherever they went, they certainly would have had tales of "their chapter of accidents" to tell.

In Californian parlance, they most surely had "seen the elephant."

Epilogue

Sir,
I have the honor to inform the Department that the present contract between the Pacific Mail S.S. Company of New York and the Colonies of New South Wales and New Zealand for the conveyance of mails between San Francisco and said Colonies, expires in November next.
—*Thomas Gamble, to Assistant Secretary of State, September 15, 1885*

Pacific Mail Steamship Company gives notice that, dating from October 1ˢᵗ, they will cease to receive on any of its steamers or offices any letters except such as are destined for countries with which the company has contracted to carry outward mails
—New Bedford Whalemen's Shipping List, *29 September, 1885*

The Elephant Voyage

Pacific Mail Steamship *Zealandia*

Commentary

This book is the result of years of research, as I first became fascinated with the strange story of the castaways of the *Sarah W. Hunt* and the controversy that followed their rescue as far back as the year 2000. At the time, I was fortunate enough to have a grant from Creative New Zealand, which enabled me to research the history of sealing in Australia, New Zealand, and the sub-Antarctic islands. Then, in 2001, I had the great good fortune of being the John David Stout Fellow at the Stout Research Centre for New Zealand Studies, at Victoria University, Wellington, where I was welcomed by the Director, Lydia Wevers. This wonderful centre, with its welcoming collegial atmosphere, and its interested and helpful staff, residents, and volunteer librarian, Annette Fairweather, is the ideal environment for writing. Here, I continued my studies into the story of sealing, with particular emphasis on American involvement, which led me to a study of United States consuls in New Zealand and Australia.

Still, the focus was on the abandonment of two boats from the *Sarah W. Hunt* in the gale-wracked seas off Campbell Island, the long, arduous, but successful struggle one boat's crew made to get back to shore, and the political and social controversy that followed their rescue. Then fate intervened. The early part of the story involved an account of the castaway huts on Auckland and Campbell Islands, including the stories of the well-publicized wrecks that led to their establishment. My editor became fascinated with one of these wrecks, that of the sealer *Grafton,* which ran onto a reef on the icy southern coast of remote Auckland Island in January 1864, and persuaded me to write a book about it. And so *Island of the Lost* was conceived.

It is easy to see what drew her to this story. *Island of the Lost* is a remarkable tale, because another ship, *Invercauld* wrecked on the northwest coast of the same island, just five months after the *Grafton* — but, because of the precipitous terrain, there was no contact between the two parties.

The account of what happened to the *Invercauld* survivors is a savage comparison to the experiences of the *Grafton* castaways. One crew coped, because of their resourcefulness, their sense of brotherhood, and their democratic ideals, while the other group descended into chaos and cannibalism; of the 19 men who struggled ashore, only three survived the castaway ordeal. The two stories, told in tandem, are a stirring contrast of human nature at its best, and at its worst. Unsurprisingly, *Island of the Lost* was — and still is — an extremely successful book.

But still I was intrigued by the experiences of the marooned men from the *Sarah W. Hunt*. Like the crew of the *Grafton,* they displayed remarkable endurance in the face of a truly dreadful ordeal, but that is only half of the story, the rest being the social and political events that followed their rescue. Because of the *Grafton* and *Invercauld,* the castaway huts had been established; and because of the huge publicity that followed the rescue of the *Sarah W. Hunt* castaways, search and rescue missions were launched, leading to the humane situation we have today. There were political consequences, too. The *Sarah W. Hunt* controversy was a definite factor in the fall of the current New Zealand government, and certainly contributed to a plunge in the fortunes of one of the country's most competent and well-regarded politicians. This litany of consequences makes the story of the castaways of the *Sarah W. Hunt* a fitting sequel to *Island of the Lost.*

Until recently, however, this story was limited to jottings in notebooks, and a sketched-out draft on my computer. Then, in 2011, I was fortunate enough to get a grant from Copyright Licensing Limited and the New Zealand Society of Authors, which sent me back to that ideal writing environment, the Stout Research Centre. There, I met with the usual warm welcome from Lydia Wevers, Richard Hill, and Louise Grenside, and as I went through my records of United States consuls in New Zealand, I was again fascinated by the strange story of the *Sarah W. Hunt*. This book is the result.

My thanks to all these people, and to the Stout Trust, the Alexander Turnbull Library, the National Library of New Zealand, and the Beaglehole Library, too. I was most fortunate to have the assistance of Gillian Smythe in the search of items in contemporary papers; of Helen O'Dea in pinning down genealogical details; and of John Illingworth in obtaining meteorological records of Campbell Island.

My other debts of gratitude will be acknowledged in the chapter-by-chapter commentary that follows. It should also be noted that while I read newspapers in hard copy and on microfilm early in my research, picking up the story in 2011 was made easy by the "Papers Past" facility on the website of the National Library of New Zealand, where all the newspapers, save the *New Zealand Herald,* the Christchurch *Weekly News,* and the *Lyttelton Times*, are readily available.

Prologue

Any writer who is worth his or her salt, whether writing fiction or non-fiction, thinks deeply about motives—what makes their characters tick, why they decide to behave in a certain manner. So, why did Captain Miner abandon the two boats so early? I found the probable answer within a short biography of Sanford Stafford Miner in Barnard L. Colby's *For Oil and Buggy Whips, Whaling Captains of New London County, Connecticut* (Mystic Seaport Museum, 1990, pages 160-164), which told the story of the tragedy that followed the loss of the *Delia Hodgkins*. The first notice of the tragedy was published as "Tidings of Marine Loss," in the *New York Times,* November 8, 1881. New Zealand reports were read in the *Timaru Herald,* January 4, 1882 and *Wanganui Herald*, December 31, 1881.

Chapter 1: The Seal Rush

In New Bedford, Massachusetts, Judith Navas Lund, editor of the compendious *Whaling Masters and Whaling Voyages Sailing From American Ports: A Compilation of Sources* (New Bedford Whaling Museum *et al,* 2001) was extremely helpful with the crew list of the *Sarah W. Hunt;* I see from our email correspondence that she consulted with Paul Cyr, librarian at the New Bedford Free Public Library, and so I thank him, too. While resident scholar at the Kendall Whaling Museum, at Sharon, Connecticut, Rhys Richards looked up Miner's background for me, helped (as I also see from email records) by Bill Peterson, resident local historian at Mystic, Connecticut; I am very grateful to them both.

The *New York Times* editorial on the coolie trade was published on April 21, 1860. There is no logbook on record for the last voyage of the *Milwood,* but an account of its loss was published in the *New Bedford Whalemen's Shipping List* on September 10, 1872. The log of the 1883 voyage of the *Sarah W. Hunt*, which includes notations for the previous Caribbean ventures, was held by the Kendall Whaling Museum when I first read it, and is now in the Kendall Institute of the New Bedford Whaling Museum. It is on microfilm in the Pacific Manuscripts Bureau holdings (administered from Canberra, Australia), as PMB 841. While I have looked at the original, my reading was mostly of the microfilm, at the Alexander Turnbull Library in Wellington.

Further study into the background of his venture to Macquarie and Campbell Islands involved more reading of sealing logs and journals (much scarcer and less revealing than whaling logbooks, sealers being so secretive), along with four invaluable books:

Briton Cooper Busch, *The War against the Seals: A History of the North American Seal Fishery.* Kingston and Montreal: McGill-Queen's University Press, 1985

James Kirker, *Adventures to China: Americans in the Southern Oceans, 1792-1812.* New York: Oxford University Press, 1970

Rhys Richards, *Sealing in the Southern Oceans 1788-1833.* Wellington, New Zealand: Paremata Press, 2010

Ian Smith, *The New Zealand Sealing Industry.* Wellington, New Zealand: Department of Conservation, 2002

I owe gratitude to Rhys Richards, Ian Smith, Nigel Prickett, and the late Briton C. Busch for their interest and help during these early stages.

Another major source was my own paper on the "father" of sealing in the south, Rhode Islander Samuel Rodman Chace. Called "Of Ships, and Seals, and Savage

Coasts: Samuel Rodman Chace in the Southern Ocean, 1798-1821," it was published in the Stout Research Centre periodical, *Journal of New Zealand Studies,* NS 2-3 (2004). I also must mention Janet West's paper, "Elephant Seal Scrimshaw and Sealing on the 'Islands of Desolation'," which was published in *Polar Record,* v. 22, no. 141 (1985), 701-706, which she very kindly sent me. I am always complimented by the interest and helpfulness of Janet West and Martin Evans, both of Cambridge, England.

The first chapter of Kirker describes the beginnings of the seal rush. Kerguelen "cabbage" was a mega-herb, *Pringlea antiscorbutica.* The stories about captains' wives on Desolation Island come from my own book, *Petticoat Whalers, Whaling Wives at Sea 1820-1920* (Auckland, New Zealand: Collins, 1991, and University Press of New England, 2001), pp. 96-97. Flinders is quoted in J. S. Cumpston, *The Furneaux Group, Bass Strait, First Visitors 1797-1810,* Canberra: Roebuck, 1978, p. 5. The quotation from Cook comes from, *The Journals of Captain James Cook: the voyage of the Resolution and Adventure, 1772–1775,* edited by J. C. Beaglehole. Cambridge: Hakluyt Society, 1961, p. 126.

The diary kept by Captain Donald Sinclair, who was in charge of an elephant gang between December 1877 and January 1878, is held at the Alexander Turnbull Library, MS-papers-1200. Edited by F. I. Norman, and called "A horrible road to travel—the diary of Captain Donald Sinclair at Macquarie Island December 1877-January 1878," it was published by the Tasmanian Historical Research Association in March 1989 (vol. 36, no. 1, pp. 33-49). Also see, Charles H. Stevenson, "Oil from Seals...", *Scientific American* 57 (1904): 23614-15 (quoted in Busch, p. 184).

A detailed description of the "elephanting" trade, penned by an old sealer, can be found in, Briton Cooper Busch (editor), *Master of Desolation, The Reminiscences of Capt. Joseph J. Fuller* (Connecticut: Mystic Seaport Museum, 1980), pages 19-22; 53-56.

Chapter 2: The Crew

Happenings on board the *Sarah W. Hunt* are taken from the log. Also see a paper by Edward Lee Dorset, "Around the World for Seals, the Voyage of the Two-Masted Schooner *Sarah W. Hunt* from New Bedford to Campbell Island, 1883-1884," which was published in *American Neptune* 11 (1951), pp. 115-133. Dorset's transcriptions are often inaccurate, occasionally leading him to wrong conclusions, and he relied on abstracts sent from New Zealand instead of the actual reports, so the paper, while useful, had to be consulted with care.

The advertisement in the New York *Sun* can be read on page 4 of the issue for July 7, 1883. The true name of Max Augenstein (Joseph M. Arthur) was revealed in an item in *The Star* of Christchurch, 28 December 1883, and the details of his parents' arrival in New York from Hungary, along with his occupation as clerk was researched by Helen O'Dea, as was the background for another of the lost men, James Aylmer Samis. The details of the boys who survived marooning are taken from their own testimonies, which were sent by the U. S. Consul in Auckland, New Zealand, to the State Department on February 29, 1884. These despatches to Washington were read in the Alexander Turnbull Library, micro-ms-0934-08. Annie Ricketson's journal was published as *Mrs. Ricketson's Whaling Journal* by the Old Dartmouth Historical Society, Massachusetts, in

1958. The entries mentioning Michael Crawford's illness are on pages 37-38.

Chapter 3: Macquarie Island

The story of the *Concord* is told in the *Oriental Navigator,* 3rd edition, edited by John Purdey (1826), page 88. The loss of Jaeger comes partly from the logbook, but mostly from the men's testimonies, which were collected at a consular inquiry in Lyttelton, on January 21, 1884, and sent to Washington on 29 February. The bucket incident took place on August 28, 1883. The next day several men were hurt when the boom swung over as the schooner gybed (brought her stern around). On September 9 the boats were turned up on deck and lashed. The bucket incident and the loss of Jaeger were also described in detail in the *Lyttelton Times,* January 25, 1884.

Evocative descriptions of Macquarie Island, with much mention of the detritus of elephant sealing, can be seen in "Notes on a Visit to Macquarie Island," which was read before the Otago Institute by A. Hamilton on November 13, 1894, and published in *Transactions and Proceedings of the Royal Society of New Zealand 1868-1961,* vol. 27, 1894, pages 559-579. Here, the cairn of bones is described. For von Bellingshausen's description of the sealers' hut, see, F. Debenham (ed.), *The Voyage of Captain Bellingshausen's to the Antarctic Seas, 1819-1821* (London: Hakluyt Society, 1945), page 367.

Captain Joseph Fuller described the breeding habits of the sea elephant in detail: see *Master of Desolation* (Busch, editor), pages 138-145. A more modern description is in Busch, *War Against the Seals,* pp. 161-164. According to Captain Donald Sinclair (Alexander Turnbull Library, MS-papers-1200) the elephanting season on Macquarie lasted until January. The list of wrecks on Macquarie Island comes from Hamilton's "Notes on a Visit to Macquarie Island," page 561. See J.S. Cumpston, *Macquarie Island* (Melbourne, Australia: Australian Antarctic Division, 1968) for further details. The *Betsey* saga is on pages 33-34. For the story of the fruitless effort to retrieve the lost anchor, see the men's depositions (Despatches, February 29, 1884) and the *Lyttelton Times,* January 25, 1884.

Chapter 4: Campbell Island

For descriptions of Campbell Island and general background, see, I.S. Kerr, *Campbell Island, a History.* (Wellington: A.H. & A.W. Reed: 1976.) A particularly good contemporary description of the island and Perseverance Harbour can be read in the *Southland Times,* 1 April 1868, p. 2, this being a report written by Henry Armstrong, who sailed there on the *Amherst* to help establish the castaway depot. For Hasselburg's death, see, J. Cumpston, *Macquarie Island*, pp. 13-14. For the loss of the brig, see, C.W.N. Ingram, *New Zealand Shipwrecks* (Wellington, New Zealand: A.H. & A.W. Reed, 1977), page 7.

The events described are all taken from the logbook.

Chapters 5 & 6: The Lost Boats; and the Battle for Survival

The descriptions of the ordeal in the boat, and existence in the castaway hut are taken from the men's testimonies, which were collated by Griffin and sent to Washington on February 29, 1884, together with their revelations to the papers, published initially by *The Lyttelton Times,* January 25, 1884 (page 5, columns 3, 4, 5), and copied throughout New Zealand.

The source for events on the schooner was the sheet of paper used as an interim log and written up by the steward,

George Duncan. Luckily, he was very much more eloquent than Streichert. I wish to thank my husband, Ron Druett, and members of the maritime history discussion list, marhst-l (sponsored by the Marine Museum of the Great Lakes at Kingston, and Queen's University, Canada), who deduced from Duncan's entries how Miner managed to adapt the schooner to be sailed by just two men.

Chapter 7: Hailed as Heroes

The arrival of the *Sarah W. Hunt* in New Zealand was described in Duncan's log entries, as well as many newspapers, e.g. Christchurch *Star*, 10 December 1883, p. 1 (arrival of schooner); *Weekly Press* (of Christchurch), December 15, 1883 (Miner's report of loss of boats). For descriptions of Lyttelton and Christchurch, I am grateful to John Illingworth for his interest and help. In the search for the backgrounds of the various New Zealanders who feature in this part of the story, Helen O'Dea was very helpful with her impressive genealogical expertise.

Miner's next movements come from his testimony to Joseph Ward on January 21, 1884. (Despatches, February 29, 1884.) Details of McIntyre's career come from his obituary, *Lyttelton Times*, May 18, 1887. His strange experiences as a consular agent in Wellington are described in, Rhoda Elizabeth Hackler, "Our Men in the Pacific: A Chronicle of United States Consular Officers at Seven Ports in the Pacific Islands and Australasia During the Nineteenth Century" — PhD dissertation, University of Hawaii, (1978), pp. 196-200.

In the surprisingly difficult search for details of James Drummond Macpherson, I am grateful for the detective work of Annette Fairweather, volunteer librarian at the Stout Research Centre. For his background, see, L. G. D. Acland, *The Early Canterbury Runs*. Whitcoulls, 1975 (4ᵗʰ ed.),

p. 259. For details of the Custom House inquiry, all three papers were consulted, but the major source used was the *Lyttelton Times*, December 12, 1883.

Chapter 8: Questions

The call to send out the *Stella* appeared in *The Star*, 10 December 1883, p. 3.

For the history of the steamship *Stella,* see, *Marine Department Centennial History 1866-1966,* by E. R. Martin (Marine Department, Wellington, 1969), pages 72-75. The Premier, Major Harry Atkinson, was Minister of Marine from 10 October 1879 to 20 August 1884. In December 1883 Rolleston was *"locum tenens"*: *Otago Daily Times,* 28 December 1883. For Allwright's telegram and Seed's reply, see, *Daily Telegraph*, 12 December 1883, p. 3.

There are two biographies of William Rolleston: William Downie Stewart, *William Rolleston, A New Zealand Statesman* (Wellington, New Zealand: Whitcombe & Tombs, 1940); and, Rosamond Rolleston, *William & Mary Rolleston, An Informal Biography* (Wellington: A. H. & A. W. Reed, 1971).

R. Rolleston, pp. 41-42, has the interesting note that Rolleston used to swear at his sheep in Greek. Rolleston's career up to this time comes mostly from Stewart, 28-41 (as a prudent, thrifty, cautious superintendant); 74 (MP for Avon); 93 (physical description); 137-138 (in Sir John Hall's ministry); 140-142 (Minister of Lands for Atkinson, backs plan for deferred payment for land, with fixity of tenure).

Rolleston's press release, at the time of his first exchange of telegrams with Macpherson, was published in most papers, including the *New Zealand Herald* (December 13, 1883, p. 5).

Quotations from the Chamber of Commerce meeting, together with those from the telegrams, come from *The Star,* December 13, 1883, p. 3.

François Raynal's story of his castaway experience, *Les naufragés,* was published by Hachette in Paris in 1870, after being serialized in three issues of *Le tour du monde* in July 1869. Illustrated by Alphonse de Neuville, and publicly admired by Jules Verne, it became an immediate bestseller, being translated into Italian, German, and Norwegian as well as English. Thomas Nelson brought out the English version in 1874 as *Wrecked on a Reef,* and it was reprinted at regular intervals right up to the end of the century. In some form or another, it has never been out of print. My story of the huge success of this book, "Shipwrecks and Castaways, the Creation of a Nineteenth Century Bestseller," was published in *Fine Books & Collections* (March-April 2008), pages 48-53.

The rise in the freight rates for grain is discussed in Stewart's biography of Rolleston, page 164.

Miner's failure to board the ferry was reported in *The Star*, Dec. 14, 1883, p. 3. The antics of the steward were all noted by Miner in the logbook.

Chapter 9: Rescue

The story of the flamboyant James Greig, including the background to his appointment as a seals inspector, is told by John McCraw, as *Coastmaster: the Story of Captain James B. Greig* (Hamilton, New Zealand: Silverdale Publications, 1999). The history of the little schooner *Kekeno* is told in *Marine Department Centennial History,* pp. 33-34, 85-86.

Copies of the relevant portion of Greig's logbook, along with Crawford's deposition to him, and Captain Grey's letter, were sent by William Seed to Joseph Ward, with a letter dated 3 January 1884 (see next chapter). Ward (or his clerk) made another copy, which was sent with a transcript of the depositions given by Sanford Miner and George Duncan before the Collector of Customs on 11 December 1883 to Consul Griffin. (All of these are in the same script.) Griffin sent them to the State Department (evidently with his letter dated January 8, but without comment, which hints that he was uncharacteristically flustered), as the collection is now with his despatches in the archives.

The "comic incident" was described within the *Lyttelton Times* story published January 25, 1884.

Chapter 10: Public Outrage

The newspaper editorials criticizing Rolleston and Miner are all as dated in the text, as is the item in the *New York Times*. The small magistrate's court item about Duncan's case being dismissed was found in the *Wanganui Chronicle*, 28 December 1883.

William Seed was Secretary of Marine (directly below the Minister of Marine, so virtually in charge of the department) from October 1880 to 1887, when he retired: *Marine Department Centennial History*, p. 10, 11, draft of the hierarchy insert between pp. 132 and 133. The letter, with the enclosed copies of Greig's log, the depositions, and Grey's letter, is in the US Despatches, having been sent to Washington by Consul Griffin.

For the physical description of Gilderoy Wells Griffin, I am very grateful to Robin Lynn Wallace, Associate Curator, Special Collections, of the Filson Historical Society in Louisville, Kentucky, who provided me with an image of a portrait of Griffin (painted by G. Frankenstein), which is undated, but appears to be of the subject when he was about twenty, so perhaps was made at university. Details of his earlier career come from Hackler, "Our Men in the Pacific ..." pages 201-210. For his time in Samoa, see, *Auckland Star*, April 2, 1877, p. 3; *Report on Samoa and the Pacific Islands to the House of Representatives, New Zealand*, 1894: appendix A 6, "List of Historical Events," p. 9.

When his wife died, a letter was sent to the State Department, January 14, 1880, testifying that "Mr. Griffin is suffering from shock from domestic trouble (the loss of his wife) and requires a change." Despatch to State Department, signed by W. J. Scott, health officer at Onehunga, Auckland.

Just before the events of this story, Griffin's treatise on "The New Zealand Fisheries" had been reprinted in *The Auckland Star* (September 8, 1883), and his adaptation of his report on the commercial potential of the bark of the native *tanekaha* tree had appeared in *The New Zealand Herald* (17 December 1883). Notice of his Band of Hope lectures appeared in the Auckland *Evening Star*, 30 October, 23 November 1883.

Chapter 11: The Castaways Retrieved

Griffin wrote to the State Department appraising them of the change of consular agent that same day, January 8, 1884, after getting Ward's wire. Taylor never returned to New Zealand, resigning on July 21. 1884, in a letter to the State Department written in Boston, so after a short delay Ward was appointed to the position. Despatches, January 8, July 24, October 31, 1884

Henry Driver (1831-93), the "horse-trader" from Delaware, has his own entry in *Southern People: a dictionary of Otago Southland Biography* (Dunedin: Longacre Press, 1998); he also features in volume 4 of the *Cyclopedia of New Zealand*, and in A. H. McLintock's *Encyclopaedia of New Zealand* (Wellington: Government Printer, 1966).

It is the entry in *Southern People* that quotes his Melbourne bank manager; it also tells the story of the telegraph line to Port Chalmers. He was a Dunedin City Councillor 1865-68, a member of the Otago Provincial Council 1866-71, and Member of Parliament 1869-71, 1878-81, and 1881-84. All this (and a period of bankruptcy) should have disqualified him for consulship, but Henry Driver was not a man to let the rules get in his way. His obituary (*Otago Witness,* 26 January 1893, p. 16) describes his links with the Pacific Mail Steam Ship Line.

Hackler, "Our Men in the Pacific ...", describes the fracas over the consulship, pages 195-200. The business can be followed by tracking the despatches: December 5, 1861 (from Maguire); a long summary written in Washington, headed "The Consular Agency at Dunedin, New Zealand," and dated April 4, 1872; and energetic rejoinders from Driver to Washington (all headed "Consulate of the United States"), dated September 2, 1873, August 22, 1876, and August 22, 1877.

Griffin wrote a report on the mail line in January 1883. For a biography of W. H. Webb, see, Edwin L Dunbaugh, with William duBarry Thomas, *William H. Webb, Shipbuilder* (New York: Webb Institute, 1989).

The five seamen left the hospital next day, January 11, 1884. (Dunedin Hospital discharge book, Dunedin Archives.) Michael Crawford was pronounced cured of "Frostbite" and discharged on March 24. The *Herald* item about the men's complaints was repeated in *The Star*, on that same day, 10 January 1884.

Driver's obduracy was reported in the *West Coast Times*, 14 January 1884, p. 2. Dick's reply to the Germans was reported in the Wellington *Evening Post*, 15 January 1884, p. 2. The confusion over who paid the fares was aired in the

Lyttelton Times, 25 January 1884; also *Otago Daily Times*, 26 January 1884. The German hospitality in Christchurch was reported in the *Star*, 22 January 1884; *Weekly Press*, January 26, 1884, p. 19.

The letter where Rolleston called Haast an idiot is quoted on page 62 of R. Rolleston.

Chapter 12: The Consular Inquiry

The transcriptions of the testimonies extracted by Ward were attached by Griffin to a letter to the State Department, dated February 29, 1884. Griffin called Ward "John F. Ward," but his name, according to his own despatches, was "Joseph Frederick Ward."

The men's appearances are taken from the crewlist that was most kindly sent by Judith Lund, who had found the details in the Bethel Seamen's Registers in the New Bedford Free Public Library.

Chapter 13: The Captain's Defense

Duncan's trial for drunkenness was noted in the *Weekly Press*, January 19, 1884, reporting events of Monday 14 January. The *Weekly Press*, January 26, 1844, also reported Duncan's strange behavior outside the butcher's shop.

The comments made by beleaguered captains and mates are in the logs of *Peru*, 29 May, 8 June, 1851 (Nantucket Historical Association, PMB 384); *Florida*, September 20, 24, October 2, 5, 1858 (New Bedford Whaling Museum, PMB 301). The appalling story of one captain who beat his men to death is told my true crime book, *In the Wake of Madness* (North Carolina: Algonquin, 2003).

Chapter 14: The Castaways' Revenge

The *Otago Witness* report appeared 2 February 1884. The *Lyttelton Times* item for 25 January, quoted at length, was repeated without change in many other papers, including the Christchurch *Star* (same date).

Chapter 15: The U.S. Consul

The editor of the Auckland *Evening Star*, March 5, 1884, made the admiring comment about Griffin's reports being the only ones published. The address was reported in *The New Zealand Herald,* May 24, 1884, p. 6. The Auckland *Evening Star,* May 17, 1884, p. 4, revealed that the book would be presented to various august people. The *New Zealand Herald* reported that the case was being brought, February 2, 1884; the same item appeared in papers all about the country.

All the details of the background of the case come from Griffin's two letters to the State Department, dated 29 February 1884. The Morley case was reported in the *Weekly Press*, December 15, 1883.

That the summons had been served on the schooner was reported by *The Star,* February 6, 1884, p. 3.

Griffin's departure from Auckland was noted by the *Evening Star* —"*Takapuna* with Griffin left yesterday": 15 February 1884 issue.

The latest case against Duncan was reported by *The Star*, Monday, February 18, 1884; the earlier case was reported in *The Star*, January 23, 1884, p. 3.

The comment about Ollivier comes from, *The Port Hills of Christchurch,* Gordon Ogilvie (Wellington: A. H. & A. W. Reed, 1978): p. 120.

A copy of the letter ("the protest") to John Ollivier, Esq., dated 19 February 1884, was sent by Griffin to the State Department.

Chapter 16: The Court Case

While the case was reported, either briefly or at length, in papers all over New Zealand, the best account is in the *Lyttelton Times,* Thursday, February 21, 1884, p. 3. This is a long and often verbatim description of the hearing, from which all the quotations are taken.

Chapter 17: The Verdict

New Zealand Herald, February 22, 1884, p. 5, noted Griffin's telegram. *Otago Daily Times,* 23 February 1884: "arrived, *Taiaroa* ..."; passenger list includes "Mr. Consul Griffin." Crawford's testimony was packaged with the others, and sent to the State Department with a covering letter on 29 February 1884.

The interesting information about the cost of the fares to San Francisco was revealed in a letter from Griffin to the State Department, dated July 28, 1884, protesting because the Department had refused to sign an agreement with W. H. Soul, Secretary of the PMSS line, which would have continued to fix the sum of $50 per man for transport from Auckland to San Francisco. It was impossible, he averred, to put destitute American sailors on British vessels for less than $100 per man.

The collision between the *Wairarapa* and the *Adelaide* was widely reported in both Australia and New Zealand, while the passenger's anonymous and lively account was published in the *Otago Daily Times,* 28 February 1884, p. 3.

That paper also published a detailed report of the inquiry in that paper, and that for 29 February (page 2).

Chapter 18: Departures

Griffin certainly sailed to Auckland on the s.s. *Wairarapa,* because the papers noted his arrival; he also wrote to the State Department, stating that he arrived back in Auckland on 4 March. However, his name is in none of the *Wairarapa* passenger lists. This is most probably because he traveled as a guest of the shipping company.

The luxurious appointments of the *Wairarapa* were described in detail in an account headlined "The New Steamship Wairarapa," published in the Wellington *Evening Post* on 16 September 1882, page 3.

Duncan's final escapade (because he never appeared in the papers again, presumably having found a berth to take him out of New Zealand), was reported by *The Star,* 1 March 1884, p. 2; *Evening Post,* 1 March 1884; and was noted throughout the country.

Griffin's toast at the banquet on the *Ruapehu* was reported by the Auckland *Star,* 5 March 1884, p. 2.

The *Press* commentary about the seamen's letters was republished in the Auckland *Evening Star* on March 27, 1884. The rejoinder was published in the same Auckland paper, 28 March 1884, p. 2.

The Auckland *Evening Star* expostulated about the bad review from Wellington on 6 June 1884, p. 2.

The trouble with getting expenses refunded can be tracked through the despatches—April 16, 1884, from Griffin to William Laurance, Comptroller of the Treasury, and April 17, 1884, from Griffin to John Davis, Assistant Secretary of State. Griffin sent another account on 24 June, for expenses occurred in "the case of the *Sarah W. Hunt*, with my certificate in lieu of vouchers which it was impracticable to procure," but instead of the money he received a form, dated September 25, reminding him that "No allowance is made for traveling expenses," and that office expenses totalling more than $200 had to come out of his $1000 annual salary. (Note: Henry Driver, when "U.S. Consul," received a salary of $1500.)

Both the *New Zealand Herald, Auckland Star,* 23 May 1884, reported the farewell to Griffin. Gamble promptly asked for his job: Despatches, Gamble to Secretary of State, May 24, 1884.

Chapter 19: The Political Fall-out

The contentious political meetings were reported in the Christchurch *Star,* 21 April 1884 (two items, p. 3, and an editorial, p. 2), and 28 April 1884 ("The Premier at Christchurch"), p. 3. Also see the *Taranaki Herald,* 3 March 1884 ("Rolleston's fad"), and *Akaroa Mail* , 25 March 1884 (freight rates). Rolleston's retirement from the Avon seat was published 18 June 1884, and his announcement that he was standing for Geraldine, 19 June 1884, both in the Christchurch *Star.* Atkinson is quoted in Stewart, p. 164 (page 165 is also relevant). I am grateful to Brian Easton, Brad Patterson, and Edmund Bohan for their thoughts and comments.

The ruminations about the plausibility of the testimonial to Captain Miner were in a column headed, "Canterbury Gossip," dated March 5, and published in the *Otago Daily Times* 8 March 1884. I thank Helen O'Dea for the detective work that tracked down Francis Gerard.

The meeting of the Christchurch Chamber of Commerce was noted in the *Otago Daily Times,* 30 August 1884, p. 2.

For the watches, see, Despatch no. 22 from Lord Derby to the Governor of New Zealand, dated 6 June 1884, enclosing the letter quoted from J.R. Lowell, dated, 19 May 1884. Appendix to the Journals of the House of Representatives, 1885 session 1, A-02. The presentation to Grey was reported in detail by the *Evening Post,* 25 September 1884. Papers throughout New Zealand noted the presentation much more briefly; all of them repeated that the reward was for the rescue of the crew of the "brigantine Sarah Hunt at Auckland Islands," but most corrected the spelling of Grey's name.

For more about the gold watches, read, McGraw, *Coastmaster,* pp. 143-150. Greig sold the watch to his son, which McGraw found odd; it could have been that he did not feel as if he deserved to carry it, as he had found the castaways by accident, and had just behaved humanely.

The *Colonist'*s comment about "that delightful man" was published in the issue for 4 February 1885.

The *New Zealand Herald* regretted the departure of Griffin on November 17, 1884. *Thames Star,* 11 December 1884, "The Wellington Chamber of Commerce has declined to comply with the request of the Auckland Chamber, to join in a valedictory address to U.S. Consul Griffin."

Ambassador Lowell's letter was reported in the *Southland Times,* 4 April 1885.

Events on the *Sarah W. Hunt* are taken from the logbook.

Index

Rolleston, William, M.P.,
  131, 146, 183
appearance and
  background, 92-93
political fall-out, 229-31
search and rescue mission,
  91-92, 93-94, 97, 100-02,
  124-25

Rose, Alexander (collector
  of customs), 87, 89, 93
Ruapehu, steamer, 223

Samis, Alymer, *see* Harris,
  Elmer
San Francisco, 6, 8, 139,
  172, 183, 213, 234, 249, 251
Sandberg, C. (seaman), 235
Sanford, Stoddard, 5
Sapphire, British navy ship,
  108
Sarah Pile, sealing
  brigantine, 106
Sarah W. Hunt, schooner, 8,
  20, 21, 22, 23, 25, 26, 29,
  32, 33, 37, 39, 40, 41, 42,
  45, 47, 48, 49, 50, 59, 62,
  64, 68, 76, 78, 81, 82, 83,
  88, 90, 91, 93, 95, 96, 102,
  121, 124, 129, 130, 131,
  132, 137, 141, 147, 151,
  152, 154, 157, 163, 165,
  167, 176, 178, 184, 185,
  186, 188, 189, 190, 191,
  202, 204, 205, 207, 208,
  210, 212, 218, 220, 224,

225, 226, 227, 229, 230,
231, 232, 234, 235, 236,
237, 238, 239, 240, 242,
243, 244, 245, 247, 248
Sarah W. Hunt crew
ordeal after abandonment,
  72, 74, 75, 79, 80, 90, 92,
  93, 111, 113, 122, 123, 150,
  151, 189, 241
reasons for sailing, 20, 29,
  30, 249
reasons for survival, 72, 73,
  77, 79
refusal to rejoin schooner,
  169, 191, 211, 218
shipped, 25, 27, 28, 29, 30,
  31, 113, 128, 148, 151, 152,
  153, 154, 155, 157, 158,
  162, 164, 165, 173, 174,
  184, 185, 188, 198, 209,
  219, 238
Scharffenorth, Louis, 27,
  34, 155, 220
Scientific American, 135
sealers, 10, 11, 13, 16, 24,
  38, 62, 107, 167
life-style, 34, 37,
flouting law, 108, 132, 189,
  248
history, 12, 13, 39, 62
Sealing, 9, 10, 11, 13, 14, 15,
  33, 41, 107, 109, 110, 163
Seals Fisheries Protection
  Act, 106
Seed, William, 92, 119, 129,
  130, 132, 133, 136, 137

Old Salt Press is an independent press catering to those who love books about ships and the sea. We are an association of writers working together to produce the very best of nautical and maritime fiction and non-fiction. We invite you to join us as we go down to the sea in books.

Joan Druett is a maritime historian and an expert on whaling history and women at sea, and the author of the bestseller *Island of the Lost*. She lives in New Zealand with her husband, the internationally acclaimed maritime artist, Ron Druett. Her website is *http://joan.druett.gen.nz*

5992534R00160

Made in the USA
San Bernardino, CA
28 November 2013